Samuel Pepys Esq.ʳ *Secretary to the* Admiralty.

From an Original by Sir Godfrey Kneller.

CONFLICTS WITH OBLIVION

BY

WILBUR CORTEZ ABBOTT

FRANCIS LEE HIGGINSON PROFESSOR OF HISTORY IN
HARVARD UNIVERSITY

CAMBRIDGE · MASSACHUSETTS

HARVARD UNIVERSITY PRESS

1935

Second edition, November, 1935

PRINTED AT THE HARVARD UNIVERSITY PRESS
CAMBRIDGE, MASS., U.S.A.

To

M. S. A.

PREFACE

SOME of these studies in reputation have seen the light of print before, though in rather different form. Of these the essays on COLONEL SCOTT and COLONEL BLOOD, published separately, are now out of print, and the continuing demand for them has seemed to make it desirable to include revisions of them here, rather than reprinting them independently.

The author takes this opportunity to thank those under whose auspices the material already published has appeared for their permission to use it here; and to express his gratitude for the kindly interest of his correspondents, many of them otherwise unknown to him, who have furnished him with information and suggestions for these essays.

PREFACE TO THE SECOND (REVISED) EDITION

The publication of another series of essays — *Adventures in Reputation* — provides an opportunity, if not an excuse, to republish this volume, now some years out of print. This, in turn, enables the author to make a few minor corrections and additions to bring certain of these essays in line with more recent developments in their respective fields, but otherwise to present them as first printed.

CONTENTS

PROËM

Our joy is like a narrow raft
  Afloat upon the hungry sea,
Hereon is but a little space,
  And all men, eager for a place,
Do thrust each other in the sea —
  And each man, eager for a place
Doth thrust his brother in the sea.
  And so our joy is wan with fears,
  And so the sea is salt with tears.
Ah, well is thee, thou art asleep.

Our life is like a curious play,
  Where each man hideth from himself.
'Let us be open as the day,'
  One mask doth to the other say,
When he would deeper hide himself —
  'Let us be open as the day,'
That he may better hide himself.
  And so the world goes round and round,
  Until our life with rest is crowned.
Ah, well is thee, thou art asleep.

OLD SONG.

INTRODUCTION

INTRODUCTION

THE essays in this volume are not, as their separate titles might suggest, merely a series of disconnected and unrelated studies of the actions and character of a group of individuals who meet here for the first time by virtue of an author's personal caprice. They are, rather, as their collective title indicates, bound together by a common thread. Each in its way is an illustration of the vicissitudes of fame, a story of the struggle to achieve reputation, and the adventures of those reputations once they were achieved. They are, in effect, not so much biographical essays in the ordinary sense as they are studies in the universal conflict with oblivion.

In that conflict most of us have an interest. Among the springs of human action — food, fortune, power, pleasure, love, hate, self-sacrifice — the desire for fame, or even mere remembrance, holds high place. From the rudest initials carved on a tree or scrawled on a wall by a casual wayfarer, to the most magnificent of monuments; from the worst of books to the most eminent of benefactions, it is not absent. What scribbler does not dream that some line from his pen may live when he is gone; what judge but hopes that some decision may find permanent place in the great fabric of the law; what wit does not aspire to achieve immortality in an epigram? Next to establishing for himself a place in the world, comes the desire of nearly every man to be remembered when he has departed from it.

"I have," says a modern of some consequence in the world of letters, "by dint of much effort achieved a pleasant little reputation of which I am very fond. I nurse it carefully; I do not overtax its strength; hoping it may

last out my time, for I find it an agreeable companion."
It is a whimsical fancy of more than passing interest;
since it raises the whole question of the theme of this
volume. How is reputation achieved? and, above all, how
is it maintained? For he speaks truth lightly. A reputation is a delicate plant of a peculiar character. It may
die with its owner. It may be buried with him; yet it may
revive after a generation or a century, perhaps in such
guise as he would scarcely recognize. It may endure,
altering through the years, as taste, or knowledge, or
opinion changes. For reputations have no permanence.
"The substance dies, the shadow doth remain," and like
a shadow alters with the altering light of years.

What happens to the memory of a great man when he
dies? The answer seems simplicity itself — first panegyrics of his friends and followers, the dispraise of the
enemies he made; then the slow, final judgment of history. There is a feeling common among men that, this
achieved, that is the end of it; that, once set among the
immortals, his place is as secure and as unchanging as
that of Jupiter or Hercules. Yet it requires no long reflection to perceive that this is far from true. Hardly less
than his career itself, his fame is modified by time and
circumstance. The fortunes of the nation, party, cause,
with which he was identified in life may alter with the
years, and his fame with them. The shifting balance of
opinion or events, the increase or decline of knowledge
and experience, shed new light on his times, or darken
them. Some accidental circumstance may serve to elevate or depress his reputation, the genius or stupidity of
a biographer, the industry or prejudice of an obscure
scholar, may make or mar it for centuries. In this view,
when great men leave the stage their chief adventure has
but just begun.

This is more true of men of action. An author's words
remain — preserved, forgotten, revived, re-edited, they

are essentially the same. Succeeding generations may neglect them, but the printed page can hardly suffer the same fate as the less tangible memories of past actions, motives, character, which are seen for the most part through the medium of other minds, and taken on the word of other men for what they were and meant. So men write *apologiae*.

Few of us have posterity always before our eyes. We go our ways, for the most part, careless of what oncoming generations may think of us, or whether they will think of us at all, contented — or discontented — with whatever consideration we can wrest from our own time. Yet to seek the bubble reputation at the cannon's mouth, to pluck the flower of honor from the heart of the nettle danger, this last infirmity of noble minds has its humbler counterpart in the lives of most of us; and soon or late the desire to make ourselves remembered manifests itself.

Yet who knows how, or why, or for what, a man shall be remembered? He takes a great part in the world's affairs, and men recall that he once wrote a play. He may, like Sandwich or Nesselrode, be a king's minister, and have his name preserved in a species of refreshment. He may be a great commander with a royal name, and acquire a laboratory immortality in Prince Rupert's drops. Like Madame de Pompadour, a king's mistress may be recalled by hairdressers who never heard of her. Like Cæsar, he may achieve remembrance far beyond the view of history in a false etymology of surgery. Like a great character in Scottish history he may have two conflicting immortalities, recalled by one faction as "bluidy Claver'se," and by another as "bonny Dundee." Or, like many a man who little dreamed of fame, his name may be a household word, such as that of Macadam, who devised our roads, or that of Stillson, who devised a wrench. A multitude have achieved immortality in the vocabulary of science or horticulture. "Who hath

fame? He who died a' Wednesday." In truth, he has as
good a chance at immortality as the next.

For Oblivion is a capricious spirit. "Some deserve
fame and have it," observes Milton, "some have it, not
deserving; others, though deserving, yet totally miss it
or have it not equal to their deserts." Death we know;
it is inevitable and inexorable; it has no favorites; for
"The wings of men's lives are plumed with death."
"Whom none could advise, thou hast persuaded; what
none hath dared, thou hast done; whom all the world
hath flattered, thou only hast cast out of the world and
despised." Death is no respecter of persons. Nor, in a
far different sense, is Oblivion. For she "blindly scat-
tereth her poppy, and deals with the memory of men
without distinction to the merit of perpetuity. In vain
we compute our felicities by the advantage of our good
names, since bad have equal duration; and Thersites is
like to live as long as Agamemnon. Who knows whether
the best of men is known, or whether there be not more
remarkable persons forgot than any that stand remembered in the known account of time? Without the favour
of the everlasting register, the first man had been as unknown as the last. . . . Oblivion is not to be hired. The
greater part must be content to be as though they had not
been, to be found in the Register of God, not in the record
of man. . . . There is nothing strictly immortal but
immortality."

Thus old Sir Thomas Browne. And to this Milton adds
his testimony of the Fathers of the Church, who, if anyone, it might seem, should be exempt from this caprice of
fortune. "Whatsoever time, or the heedless hand of
blind chance, hath drawn from old to this present in
her huge drag-net, whether Fish, or Seaweed, Shells, or
Shrubs, unpickt, unchosen, these are the Fathers."

Here, then, you have this little company, culled, like
the Fathers, by the chance which is so great a part in our

salvaging of the past; yet each, in his way, a representative of some phase of man's conflict with oblivion. To this their earthly activities are but incidental. They may serve to illustrate not merely the process by which a reputation is achieved, but how it managed to maintain itself against its ancient enemy.

"Time hath its revolutions," runs the somber eloquence of old Chief Justice Crewe. "There must be a period and an end to all temporal things — *finis rerum* — an end of names and dignities, and whatsoever is terrene; and why not of De Vere? For where is Bohun? Where is Mowbray? Where is Mortimer? Nay, which is more, and most of all, where is Plantagenet? They are in the urns and sepulchres of mortality." Yet in his very elegy, in the epitaph of their fallen grandeur, if nowhere else, their names reverberate; and in so far, more fortunate than their fellows, they have won their contest with oblivion.

Nay, more; for even to countless names now mingled with the dust remains that still more glorious immortality which forms the theme of the greatest of all orations. "So they gave their bodies to the commonwealth, and received, each for his own memory, praise that will never die; and with it the grandest of all sepulchres, not that in which their mortal bones are laid, but a home in the minds of men, where their glory remains fresh to stir to speech or action as occasion comes. For the whole earth is the sepulchre of famous men; and their story is not graven only on stone over their native earth, but lives on far away, without visible symbol, woven into the stuff of other men's lives." And this, which might well have served for the epitaph of the Unknown Soldier, must do for most of us.

THE SERIOUS PEPYS

THE SERIOUS PEPYS

WHOEVER," says Montaigne, "will justly consider and with due proportion, of what kind of men and of what sort of actions the glory sustains itself in the records of history, will find that there are very few actions and very few persons of our times who can there pretend any right." "Of so many thousands of valiant men who have died within these fifteen hundred years in France with their swords in their hands," he goes on, "not a hundred have come to our knowledge. The memory not of the commanders only, but of battles and victories is buried and gone; the fortunes of above half the world for want of a record stir not from their place and vanish without duration; . . . it must be some very eminent greatness or some consequence of great importance that fortune has added to it that signalizes" an action to make it and the actor remembered.

There is, in effect, no recipe for immortality, even for the greatest; and if fame's vagaries thus affect captains and kings, what chance have men in lesser stations? If conquerors are so frequently forgotten, what of the men of peace, which has its oblivion far more profound than war! Above all, perhaps, what hope has one who devotes himself not to the destruction or manipulation of his fellow men but to their service, in particular as that bulwark of organized society, an honest and able civil serv-

ant? Little enough, indeed. The worst of demagogues,
the most incompetent of commanders, the harshest of
tyrants, the most depraved of rakes, has far better chance
for an undying, if an undesirable, fame, under present historical conditions, than even the best of these "sons of
Martha." Save when preserved by other means, some
share in politics, some gift to literature, their fame is
mingled with the air. Only among the unwritten traditions of their service and its unread documents their reputations lie, safe from the praise or blame of those they
served. Of this great class, paradoxical as it may seem,
there is no better representative than the well-known
subject of this essay.

On the twenty-sixth of May, 1703, while England
girded herself for that far-spreading conflict which in a
twelvemonth was to bring to her Gibraltar and the great
Marlborough's "famous victory" of Blenheim, there died
at Clapham, near London, one Samuel Pepys, sometime
a notable figure in the world he left. Member of Parliament, Treasurer of Tangier, Surveyor-General of the
Victualling Office, Clerk of the Acts, and Secretary to the
Admiralty, he had played no trifling part in the eventful
years of the last Stuart kings. Aside from his official life,
Pepys had been scarcely less well known in widely different fields. He was Master of Trinity House and of the
Clothworkers' Company, Governor of Christ's Hospital,
twice President of the Royal Society. A patron and critic
of the arts, music, the drama, literature; an indefatigable
collector of manuscripts and books, broadsides, ballads,
music-scores, and curios, he had been no less at home in
gatherings of scientists and virtuosos, in Covent Garden
and in Drury Lane, or the booksellers' shops about old St.
Paul's, than in the Navy Office and dockyards. He had
arranged, even composed, some music, and he was no
mean amateur performer on certainly one instrument.
He had contributed to the Royal Society; not a few books

had been dedicated to him; and he himself had published at least one. His portrait had been painted three times by Kneller, once by Lely, and again by artists of less note. Among his friends were statesmen and scientists, authors, officials, musicians, royalties; Hans Sloane, Christopher Wren, Isaac Newton, John Evelyn, John Dryden, and that "admirable Lord High Admiral but less than admirable king," James the Second, now long an exile at the court of France. Surely, if a man's achievements are to count for anything, here was a candidate for at least a moderate immortality.

"In the judgment I make of another man's life," says the old French moralist-philosopher, "I always observe how he carried himself at his death; — this is the day that must be the judge of all the foregoing years." This supreme test the Secretary met bravely. "Last night," wrote the nonjuring clergyman, George Hickes, who was with him at the end, "I did the last offices for Samuel Pepys. . . . The greatness of his behaviour in his long and sharp tryall before his death was in every respect answerable to his great life, and in accordance with his motto, *Mens cujusque is est quisque,*" — as a man's mind is, so is he. "This day," wrote old John Evelyn, "died Mr. Sam. Pepys, a very worthy, industrious, and curious person, none in England exceeding him in knowledge of the Navy, in which he had passed thro' all the most considerable offices . . . all which he performed with great integrity. . . . He was universally beloved, hospitable, generous, learned in many things, skilled in music, a very greate cherisher of learned men of whom he had the conversation; . . . for neere 40 yeares . . . my particular friend." Such was the esteem of his contemporaries for one who had been called successively the right hand, the Nestor, and the father of the English navy; reckoned the ablest civil servant of his time, a shrewd, strict, serious man of business, a faithful friend, a generous patron, an accomplished gentleman, and an honest man. May none of us have a worse epitaph!

His will bore out the character of his life and death. The wide distribution of mourning and rings, according to the custom of the time, witnessed his many and eminent friendships; his numerous bequests to his acquaintances and servants further testified to an agreeable side of his nature. The bestowal of his fortune on his nephew, and the devising of his library to Magdalene College, Cambridge, after that nephew's death; the gift of his ship-models to his partner and friend, William Hewer, with recommendation " to consider how these, also together with his own, may be preserved for publick benefit," gave evidence of a strong family, college, and public spirit — which, again, often contributes somewhat to posthumous reputation.

This, for the son of a tailor, who owed small thanks to birth or fortune, some to circumstance, most to himself, for all the blessings he enjoyed in life, and in such unusual and such long unsuspected degree passed on to posterity, was no small achievement as a bid for fame. To his success his schooling at Huntingdon and St. Paul's, then at Magdalene College, contributed somewhat; but the determining factor in his career had been his connection with his father's cousin and his own patron, Sir Edward Montagu, the friend and relative and follower of Cromwell. When, after a brief excursion in diplomacy, the youthful Pepys entered the service of this capable commander, whom the Protector had summoned from his place in the New Model to a seat in the Council of State with charge of naval operations against Spain, Dunkirk, and the Northern powers; and, in particular, when, after a period of retirement, the Convention Parliament commissioned Montagu to bring back the exiled Charles to England and the throne, the fortune of his secretary, Pepys, was settled with his own. Clerk of the Acts and of the Admiralty Board; then, by successive stages of advance, wresting increasing reputation and authority from the catastrophes of fire, plague, and war, Pepys had outgrown the need of a patron long before he became Secretary to the Admiralty. Through twenty busy years, save for the interruption of the Popish Plot, the history of naval administration more and more became the story of his life, as he refashioned his office on the lines it held for more than a century. Not without color and incident, verging more than once on tragedy as he became involved in the vicissitudes of politics, but in the main absorbed in the reform and conduct of naval affairs, until the Revolution drove him and his master, James the Second, from their posts, his life was one in which increasing purpose ran with vigor and success. Such was the Pepys of the seventeenth century, the greatest secretary of what is, in one view, England's greatest service; thus he lived and died.

Thus was he not remembered! It is, indeed, amazing to find how soon he was forgotten and how completely. A dozen years after his death, his name found place in *The Continuation of Mr. Collier's Supplement to his Great Dictionary*; a dozen more, and Burnet noted his connection with the Popish Plot; while, thanks chiefly to the fact that Kneller had painted and White had engraved his portrait, Granger gave him a page in his extraordinary *Biographical History of England*. Another fifty years, and Hume observed that naval tradition still recalled Pepys' administration as "a model of order and economy." The rest was all but silence. Among the innumerable "characters" which entertained the readers of the *Annual Register*, his found no place; the long files of the *Gentleman's Magazine*, save for a brief note on his library, knew him not; in its three editions in the eighteenth century not even the *Encyclopædia Britannica* recorded his name.

Members or visitors of Magdalene College still observed, as now, the building which contained his books.

Some found their way inside; at least two recorded something of the treasures they discovered there; and part of the material for Percy's *Reliques of Ancient English Poetry* was drawn from that source. Frequenters of St. Olave's Church may have taken notice of the Secretary's tomb; members of corporations or societies to which he once belonged might now and then recall him by his gifts; lovers of art noted his portraits as examples of the painter's skill. Family pride, the industry of genealogist or antiquarian, might have found in parish registers the entry of his birth, marriage, and death; or in the college books, besides the record of his entrance and exit, that he was once reproved for being drunk. An occasional reader may have looked in his *Memoirs of the Royal Navy*, a scholar or an archivist here and there have noted the unread masses of his memoranda in the Public Records Office or the libraries. This was the sum of Pepys' impression on the world a hundred years after he left it — a handful of mementos and a fast-fading memory.

Of these, only his papers and his books still stood between him and oblivion. The books, indeed, had been not seldom used; the papers were still all but unexplored. Sometime during that eighteenth century, which concerned itself so mightily with very many things much less worth while, a now unknown enthusiast began a catalogue of the Pepysian collections in the Magdalene library. He was soon, far too soon, discouraged. There lay "a vast collection from our antient records . . . relating to our naval affairs, and those of other countries. Books of musick, mathematicks and several other subjects all excellent in their kind." Among them were two hundred and fifty volumes, chiefly of naval manuscripts, gathered, doubtless, as a basis for a projected history. There lay the Lethington Collection of Scottish poetry; masses of tracts and pamphlets; with the largest body of broadside ballads in existence. Above all, in the mind of at least one bibliophile, was what "he hath collected with respect to the City of London, for the illustration of that famous city," besides "a vast collection of heads both domestic and foreign, beyond expression, copy-books of all the masters of Europe," and "a large book of title-pages, frontispieces . . . not to be paralleled," the whole crowned with an "admirable catalogue." Besides these, fifty volumes more of Pepys' manuscripts had found their way into the hands of the great collector, Rawlinson, and so to the Bodleian Library at Oxford. Besides these, still, his documents in public and in private hands, had they been even catalogued in print, would have reared a monument whose very size might have compelled attention and revised the eighteenth century's knowledge of the past and of Pepys.

But the exploiting of this material was reserved for later generations, when its fulfilment became a romance of literature and scholarship alike. It is a well-known story how, among the masses of historical material which found their way to print in the first quarter of the nineteenth century, the *Diary* of John Evelyn, with its mention of the Secretary, inspired the Master of Magdalene College to put in Lord Grenville's hands six volumes of cipher manuscript from Pepys' collections which had long puzzled curious visitors; how that accomplished nobleman, having transcribed some pages, found them of such interest that an undergraduate, John Smith, was entrusted with the completion of the work; and how, after three years of labor on his part, there presently appeared, under Lord Braybrooke's editorship, the *Memoirs of Samuel Pepys, Esq., F.R.S., Secretary to the Admiralty . . . comprising his Diary from 1659 to 1669 . . . with a selection from his private Correspondence.*

It is, perhaps, scarcely so well appreciated how, with that event, ensued a revolution in posthumous fame unparalleled in literary history. From the obscurity of a

century emerged no mere man of affairs but a Personality. What a lifetime of great endeavor could not do, a
book accomplished almost in a day. By the transcriber's
magic the forgotten Secretary to the Admiralty was transformed into a Prince of Diarists and set among the immortals. So complete was the triumph over oblivion that,
within twenty years, even Macaulay, who had drawn
largely on the Secretary's books for his *History*, allowed
himself to write of "Samuel Pepys whose library and
diary have kept his name fresh to our time." So vivid
was the book that even the great historian seems to have
felt, like many since, that its author had always been well
known.

It is not surprising that he was misled, nor that the first
transcriber often spent fourteen hours a day upon his task,
when one considers how amazingly alive the book is still,
how every hour promises a fresh surprise. Read but the
opening lines with their directness, reminiscent of Defoe,
and you feel the charm impelling you to go on:

Blessed be God, at the end of last year I was in very good health.
. . . I lived in Axe Yard, having my wife and servant Jane and no
more in family than us three. . . . The condition of the State was
thus, . . . the Rump after being disturbed by my Lord Lambert
was lately returned to sit again. The officers of the Army all forced
to yield. Lawson lies still in the river and Monk with his army in
Scotland. . . . The new Common Council of the City do speak very
high. . . . My own private condition very handsome and esteemed
rich, but indeed very poor, besides my goods of my house and my
office. . . . This morning . . . I rose, put on my suit with great
skirts, . . . went to Mr. Gunning's Chapel at Exeter House. . . .
Dined at home . . . where my wife dressed the remains of a turkey,
. . . supt at my father's where in came Mrs. The. Turner and Madam
Morrice. . . . In the morning . . . old East brought me a dozen
bottles of sack. . . . I went . . . to speak with Mr. Calthropp
about the £60 due my Lord . . . [and] heard that Lambert was
coming up to London.

There you have, in little, Pepys and his Diary; his house,
his clothes, his wife, his food, his health, his office, his ac-

quaintances, his amusements, his relatives, his gossip of affairs. You have, indeed, much more: at once an incredibly lifelike picture of the times, and a true romance, surpassing all fiction, of the life and strange, surprising adventures of one Samuel Pepys, who lived, far from alone, for seventy years in the island of Great Britain, and whose activities are here set down with the detail that has charmed generations since in the exploits of his antithesis, Robinson Crusoe, with all the added zest of brilliant environment.

There is, indeed, some curious kinship between these two wholly unlike productions. There is the same fascination in watching Pepys rescue from the catastrophe of the Cromwellian rule the means to make his fortune, as in seeing Crusoe rescue from the shipwreck the means of sustaining life; the same interest in observing the one build his career and the other build his house; the same suspense over the crises in the affairs of each; the same pleasure in their triumphs over adversity as they struggle with nature or with the world of men; the same satisfaction over their ultimate victory. There is even something curiously alike in the accumulation of minute and often apparently trivial detail by which, in truth or fancy, both authors produce their lifelike effects.

Pepys has, indeed, had full reward for all his pains. Since the appearance of his Diary in the first abbreviated form which printed scarcely half of its contents, much learned and loving labor has been spent on its elucidation. The ingenuity and industry of successive editors have enlarged our knowledge and understanding of the work until the two original volumes, what with inclusion of the parts at first suppressed and a great bulk of comment, have increased to ten. One editor has re-transcribed the manuscript, another has compiled a book on Pepys and the world he lived in; the family genealogy has been unearthed and a study made of one of its members

as "a later Pepys"; so far has the reflected glory shone.
The diarist's early life has been laid bare; his letters published, with his will; his portraits reproduced. A whole
book on Pepys as a lover of music has appeared; an essay
on the sermons that he heard; even the medical aspects of
his married life have been explained by a physician-
author; and there has been published lately a study of his
"soul." Essayists and bookmakers still find in him an
ever fertile subject for their pens; no biographical dictionary or encyclopædia is without a full account of the great
diarist. A memorial has been erected to him in St.
Olave's Church, a Pepys Club has been founded; and,
rising finally to the full stature of a real biography, few
names to-day in English literature are better known,
few classics more widely read or more enjoyed.

If the effect on Pepys has been so great, the influence of
the Diary on seventeenth-century history has been no less.
With the appearance of his Diary the formal, even tragic,
dignity which for a hundred years enveloped that great
revolutionary period was destroyed almost beyond repair
of the dullest historian. "It was as though in a musty library, slumbrous with solemn volumes, a window had suddenly been opened, and the spectator looked out upon the
London of the mid-seventeenth century, full of color and
movement, still breathing the Elizabethan enchantment,
. . . vehemently returned to the lust of the eye and the
pride of the flesh after the restraints and severities of the
Puritan dominion." Before the Diary appeared, the England of Charles the Second was the England of Clarendon, Echard, Rapin, Hume, a dull, tangled interlude between two revolutions; since his book it has been, for the
most of us, the England of Pepys, amusing, intimate, incredibly alive. Its obscuration has not yet been wholly
cleared away, the history of the Restoration still remains
to be written; but when it is, the secretary-diarist will
have no less a share in writing its memoirs than he had in

managing its affairs. Already from his volumes has been
evolved more than one history of seventeenth-century
manners, music, drama, literature; even political historians have used it to advantage. It has been supplemented
by other works, but to it we owe in greater measure than
to any other book the picture of a period which, even
now, makes Pepys' time nearer to us than any other
decade of English history.

When one considers what the Secretary was and did,
and how his reputation stood before the Diary appeared,
this result seems all the more extraordinary. Eminent as
he was in admiralty circles, as a patron of the arts, collector, and philanthropist; useful as his life had been and
notable for honorable success in public service, it gave
small promise of eminence in literature. His success, indeed, lies far outside that realm. However great the
quaint attraction of his phrase, however bright the light
upon his time, the Diary owes its wide appeal and deepest
charm to the infusion of a wholly different quality. It is
not merely trite to say that its fascination lies in its frankness — that is a superficial, obvious half-truth. To his
Diary, Pepys confided every thought, sensation, motive,
action, and desire, — good, bad, high, low, important,
trivial, absurd, — with a freedom beyond mere frankness. The result is unique, not merely in literature, but
almost, if not quite, in life. It seldom happens among
myriads of human relationships that anyone knows any
of his fellows, however near and dear, as well as all of us
know Pepys; most of us scarcely know ourselves as well;
few of us, or none, would dare admit even to ourselves,
much less commit to paper, in whatever decent obscurity
of cipher, all that the diarist records. His work is not
mere frankness; it is self-revelation at its highest power —
there is nothing more to tell. It is more than mere literature, it is life itself. Most of such so-called revelations are
far from what they profess to be. Some are mere pruri-

ence; some, morbid psychology; some, simple vanity; some, conscious or unsconcious pose; the most, mere formal record of an outer life, or simply "literature." Pepys' work is the delineation of a very human being, a "natural man," stripped of the *convenances* of society, who would have been at once the terror and the pride of eighteenth-century prophets who invoked such phantoms constantly, and as constantly produced imaginative figments in their place. To such vainer sophistications Pepys' Diary bears the same relation as that of frank, unashamed, and proper savage nakedness to the salacious half-revelations of a decadent stage. One has but to compare it with such outpourings from those of Rousseau to those of Marie Bashkirtseff to realize the great gulf fixed between healthy appreciation of a man's triumph over circumstances and the futile conflict with overwhelming shadows.

Being Pepys, nothing human — and very few other things which came under his observation — seem alien either to him or to his pen. First, his appearance; one reads with wonder not unmixed with awe of "a velvet cloak, two new cloth suits, . . . a new shagg gowne trimmed with gold buttons and twist, with a new hat and silk tops for my legs," — all, as it were, in one mouthful. It is no wonder that his clothes cost some five times as much as those of his wife, but it leads to serious reflection in these days.

Yet it was even more good policy than vanity which prompted this display. "I hope I shall, with more comfort," he says, "labor to get more and with better successe than when for want of clothes I was forced to sneake like a beggar." That he got more, his accounts reveal. When he went with Montagu to bring back the King, he had scarcely a penny to his name. He came back with near a hundred pounds. After seven years of office he reckoned himself worth some seven thousand pounds;

prepared to set up a coach; gave his sister, Paulina, six hundred pounds as a marriage portion; and lent his cousin, Roger, five hundred — for all of which he blessed God fervently in his Diary. When he died the Crown owed him twenty-eight thousand pounds; yet he left a comfortable fortune. And he was neither dishonest nor niggardly. During the seventeenth and eighteenth centuries, few fields of human endeavor yielded such rich returns as public office; and if Pepys took his fees like other men, unlike too many of them he gave good service in return. Nor was he ungenerous in spending money. Books, pictures, music, objects of art, furniture, plate, hangings, he purchased with almost lavish hand. Preeminently a Londoner, he was insensible to those charms of country-seat and garden which so engrossed his friend, John Evelyn; a man of weighty affairs, gambling of all kinds appealed to him even less; cautious and thrifty as became his class, no charge of penuriousness will hold against him, in the large.

His tastes, indeed, save two, were such as helped the world along. Devoted to the theatre and a good-fellowship which led him sometimes to excess, he made his frequent "vowes against wine and plays" only to break them, as men have done since. The wine at least made no inroads upon his business; the plays make his Diary the best of all guides to seventeenth-century London theatres. But at the theatre, still more in church, at home, abroad, one of his chief interests was what the eighteenth century knew as "female charms." One of his crosses was the lack of such loveliness in his own church, St. Olave's; "not one handsome face in all of them, as if, indeed, there was a curse, as Bishop Fuller heretofore said, upon our parish." What he lacked there he made up fully elsewhere. He kissed Nell Gwyn, besides uncounted others, including the face of the exhumed body of Katherine of Valois, who had been dead more than two centuries, that

he might be said to have kissed a queen! His friendship
with the actresses, especially Mrs. Knipp; the trials which
arose when she winked at him and he had trouble to make
his eyes behave as they should in his wife's presence —
are not such things and many more of like sort writ large
throughout the Diary?   These and the less creditable
story of his relations with his wife's servant, Deb, witness
something to those qualities which led the penniless
youth, but two years out of college, to espouse the pretty
daughter of a poverty-stricken Huguenot refugee ad-
dicted to invention and living chiefly upon charity.

All this and even more, in infinite variety of phrase,
men have laid stress on since his book appeared. Largely,
and no doubt naturally, this side of Pepys' nature and his
Diary chiefly appealed to a world concerned for the most
part with the trivial, or worse; and it might be supposed
that frankness such as his would win for him a place in the
esteem of those who read his book, comparable to that
which he occupied in his contemporaries' minds.   In
some degree, especially at first, thanks to the bowdleriz-
ing of his too cautious editor, this was the case.   That in-
comparable antiquarian, Walter Scott, hastened to welcome this "man of business, . . . of information if not
learning, taste and whim as well as pleasure, statesman,
virtuoso, *bel esprit*," to the world of literature, and, with
the notable — and characteristic — exception of Jeffrey,
many followed in the novelist's train. Yet, gradually, as
each succeeding issue of the Diary included more and
more of intimate, less decorous detail, omitted by the
early editors, Pepys' reputation sank. Like Lucilius,
"having dared protray himself as he found himself to
be," he proved that "no man writes of himself save to his
hurt." Generations smiled, frowned, shrugged, moral-
ized, felt superior. Critics, who frequently knew nothing
of him save his own revelations and the comments of his
editors, often sneered. Coleridge observed that he was

"a pollard man," without a top, to which Pepys might well have replied that the critic was all top. Lowell, with condescension almost worthy of a foreigner, wrote of "the unconscious blabbings of the Puritan tailor's son." Another, admitting his honesty and even a certain cleverness, laughed at his "cockney revels," and his pleasure when Lord Clarendon patted his head. Others still noted only "the strength and coarseness of the common mind," the "decomposed Puritan mind," of this "typical bourgeois, kindred to Kneller in vulgarity." A no less tolerant soul than Stevenson, following, as often, earlier lead, adduces Pepys' very appearance against him; says his face shows "no aspiration," only "an animal joy in all that comes," though he admits that "in a corrupt and idle period he played the man, toiled hard, and kept his honor bright." His severest critic elaborates at length the manifold inconsistencies of his character, forgetting the dictum expressed by Lord Rosebery that "if we accept the common and erroneous opinion that human nature is consistent with itself we find it utterly impossible to explain the character of George the Third" — to say nothing of that of other men.

Such, in general, was the judgment of the nineteenth century, hard to persuade to take the diarist seriously. Secure in its superior virtue and manners; relieved from the gay plumage of the seventeenth-century male; repressing the earlier liberties of English speech; and at least the open license of its morals; the Victorian age read, loved, despised, what seemed to it a garrulous, amusing man. It scorned the confession of his little weaknesses perhaps even more than the weaknesses themselves — his love of company, theatre, dress, diversion, deference; looked down upon his simple vanity. Above all it resented what he told of his dealings with women. He may have been bad enough, but some have written of him in terms appropriate to Sedley or Rochester — the compari-

son is Pepys' best defense — forgetting to read the Diary
and Gramont's *Mémoires*, or the Restoration drama, side
by side. Viewed thus, one may well wonder whether,
after all, the Secretary would not have preferred by far
the honorable obscurity of a dead lion, which he enjoyed
during the eighteenth century, to this contemptuously
affectionate regard for a living ass, which the nineteenth
century bestowed on him.

The difficulty of comprehending Pepys has arisen from
two circumstances: the fact that the critics have known
little or nothing of him beyond what they found in his
own pages or the comment of his editors; and the fact
that, most unfortunately for himself and for us, Pepys
ceased to be a diarist before he became a secretary. From
the eighteenth-century historians, even had the men of
literature read their books, which there is no reason to
believe they did, little could have been gleaned, and the
earlier editors, at least, were not much better. In what
spirit they began let Lord Braybrooke's own words declare. As Pepys "was in the habit of recording the most
trifling occurrences," he wrote, "it became absolutely
necessary to curtail the manuscript materially," — and
so he omitted an entertaining *half*. Bright, daring greatly,
printed some four-fifths; Wheatley, all but about thirty
pages. It was, then, nearly seventy years before the world
saw anywhere near the whole Diary. Even so, had the
critics paid more attention to the serious element and
dwelt less on those frivolities — and worse — for whose
insertion they condemned — and read — the diarist, they
might have approximated the truth more nearly.

But, as the old philosopher has said, "The pencil of the
Holy Ghost hath labored more in describing the afflic-
tions of Job than the felicities of Solomon," and we ought,
perhaps, to expect no more of the men of letters. Yet
when even the latest, and in some ways the best-informed
of them, falls in error what can we expect? He denounces

Lowell's description of Pepys as a Philistine; he reviles the historians of English literature for the amazing fallacy that Pepys lacked enthusiasm; he blames those who have made literary capital out of the diarist for the small pains they have taken to correct their "childish impressions" by the results of recent studies. And, with all this, he permits himself to say that "the diary was the one long deliberate effort of Pepys' life"! They look on him in the same light as Charles Lamb at the East India House, or Austin Dobson at the Colonial Office. So hard it is for men to realize the fundamental fact that Samuel Pepys was not a diarist who happened to be connected with the Navy Office, but was the greatest of all secretaries to the Admiralty, who happened, in his earlier years, to write a diary.

Fortunately the Diary has not been the end of the Secretary's striving against oblivion; what literature and the literary historians have failed so signally to do for him thus far, historical scholarship seems likely to accomplish. When, nearly forty years ago, the English government began to print calendars of the state papers of the Restoration period, it soon became apparent that the famous diarist had played a greater part in public affairs than had previously been recognized. The development of naval history, in particular, has gradually re-created the Secretary; and the service to which he gave his life seems likely to be the final means of securing for him an appropriate immortality. His *Memoirs of the Royal Navy* has been reprinted; the naval historians have chronicled his achievements; studies have been made of his activities in many public posts; a *Bibliotheca Pepysiana* has been begun with a catalogue of his library; and, within a decade, the Navy Records Society has begun the publication of a catalogue of his papers preserved in Magdalene College which has already reached the proportions of four stout volumes. Hereafter we shall have even more of such material, since we are promised the "Navalia" memoranda, further memoirs and calendars, filling out the record of his manifold activities. In view of all this publication, it is not too much to say that, had Pepys' Diary never seen the light, we should, in time, have had adequate knowledge of the Secretary's work, however little we should have known of the man.

The result of all this is that we have another and a better Pepys than the amusing figure which did duty for him throughout the greater part of the nineteenth century. Though even to-day few readers of the Diary will be likely to delve into this mass of calendars, inaccessible to a previous generation, and any alteration in opinion will, therefore, probably be slow, it is high time to begin to realize what the true Pepys was like, to do him the justice which he has, in a sense, denied himself.

For we are too apt to forget that to his own generation there was no such person as the diarist. Amid the silks and paduasoy of the Diary, its days of cheer and its nights at the play, its family secrets and its personal details, men have lost sight of the more serious side of him who found comfort in pouring out those things which he concealed from all the world beside into the safe cipher of his only confidant. As we go through the mass of correspondence; as we read the endless list of orders and memoranda, catalogues of ships, reports, recommendations, statements of accounts; as we observe the operation and results of his administration, we perceive the petty, childish, simple figure, evoked by literary critics from the Diary, transformed into the truer character of the historian — a man shrewd, cautious, able, conscientious, honest, brave, wholly devoted to his service and his government.

His story of naval administration and reform whence emerged the modern system of the admiralty is, indeed, no glittering chronicle. The "building of our ships more burdensome"; construction by the state rather than contractors; reform in victualing and sailors' pay; the naming and officering of the fleet and the re-rating of its vessels; the reorganization of the ordnance; long experiment in sailing and in fighting qualities; elaborate calculations of speed, strength, and seaworthiness; investigations in the source and quality of all supplies; accounting, storage; — this infinite variety of detail, much now of but an antiquarian interest even to the most technical of experts, is not easy reading and provides little enough material for epigram. But it does give us what is far more to the purpose, and that is a correct view of Samuel Pepys. If you would learn what kind of man he was, you should read his journal of the Admiralty Board from 1673 to 1679. There is to be found the real Pepys, whether you consider life or literature as the measure to be applied to him. To those who have analyzed his body, soul, mind, spirit, or whatever other attribute he possessed, from the Diary alone, may be commended a study of this greater side of the great Secretary, if they would make their portraits even distantly resemble the original.

Here is the civil servant at his best. "Æquiponderous," to his colleagues, "in moral, and much superior in philosophical knowledge of the economy of the navy," as he appeared to the men of his own day, his latest critics declare that the principles of his naval statesmanship may even now be lessons to a "sea economy as valid as they were two centuries ago." It is, indeed, almost incredible how acute and diligent he was. The single holiday of a busy life he spent in looking over Dutch and French naval establishments. Upon his first and only visit to Tangier, he found out in an hour's walk about the town what twenty years of costly statesmanship and military occupation had scarcely learned — that it was no fit place for English occupation. It would be too long even to enumerate here all the changes which he made in admiralty administration; it is perhaps enough to say that a century and a quarter after he left office, in the midst of England's struggle with Napoleon, a naval commission found in his system scarcely a thing to change or blame.

Nor was he, through all of this, a man of "sweet, uncritical mind," much less the time-server he has often been pictured. Under the transparent guise of a report to his chief, the Duke of York, which set the wheels of reform in motion, he criticized with frank courage Comptroller, Treasurer, Surveyor, Navy Board, colleagues, courtiers, contractors, every powerful interest of his service, whose alienation might well have meant ruin to him. He was, in Marvell's phrase, one of that "handful of salt, a sparkle of soul that . . . preserved this gross body from putrefication, . . . constant, invariable, indeed Englishmen." It is with high appropriateness that, in the two-hundredth year after his death, the editor of the *Catalogue of Pepysian Manuscripts* dedicates his work "To the memory of Samuel Pepys, a great public servant." After so long an interval, and through such great vicissitudes, the Secretary of the seventeenth century takes on his proper guise in the beginning of the twentieth, and appears again in something like the form he doubtless would have chosen for himself.

We must, then, in this view, re-read the Diary and revise our estimate of Pepys. As long presented, he has unquestionably antagonized many persons of highly moral minds or highly cultivated taste — and even more of those inclined merely to prudishness. The spectacle of a man who dared to set down the acts and thoughts common to many men, is so unusual in human affairs, so contrary to all those instincts of pride and shame which drive us to conceal or to condone our weaknesses not only from our fellows but from ourselves, that it has made Pepys a repulsive figure to many worthy souls. One who so far out-Boswelled Boswell as to paint not his friend's portrait but his own, has suffered accordingly.

That he was garrulous the very Diary, on which the accusation rests, disproves. The confidence reposed in him by men of every rank; his rapid rise to high responsibilities; his reputation as a safe man of affairs; the fact that only once, and then by accident, did he reveal the secret of his book, bear out his character as one not given to betrayal of his trust. That, with all his dallyings and philanderings, he was as licentious as many men of his own day, no one familiar with the period will assert. That Pepys was dishonest no one believes, or if he does, let him read the editor's informing paragraph prefacing his papers which declares: "There is no trace of anything of the kind in the official correspondence," and "even official letters, when they are numbered by thousands may be witnesses to character, for by an infinite number of delicate strokes they at length produce a portrait of the writer." Tested by this there is "no evidence of corruption."

In Pepys' case it certainly has not been true that actions speak louder than words. Bacon's saying more nearly hits the mark, that "Fame is like a river which bears up things light and swollen, but drowns things heavy and solid." Of all the charges brought against the Secretary, one of the worst is that he was not brave. Let the great crises of his life attest. A young man, new in office and affairs, dependent on the favor of Montagu, he yet ventured to remonstrate with his powerful patron for improprieties unworthy of his station and himself, in a reproof which is a model of its kind. "I judge it," he writes, "very unbecoming the duty which every bit of bread I eat tells me I owe your Lordship to expose your honour to the uncertainty of my return . . . but, sir, your Lordship's honour being such as I ought to value it to be, and finding both in city and court that discourses pass to your prejudice, . . . I shall, my Lord, without the least greatening or lessening the matter, do my duty in laying it shortly before you."

When the Plague fell on London and all who could had
fled — court and society, as usual, the first — among the
few bold spirits who remained to carry on the business of
the state, the brave, bigoted Bishop of London Sheldon;
the "best justice of the peace in England," Godfrey; the
grim Duke of Albemarle, old General Monk — amid
this courageous company of picked men, the Clerk of the
Acts stuck to his post in daily peril of his life. Read his
letter to Coventry if you would have a measure of the
man. "The sickness in general thickens round us," thus
he writes, "particularly upon our neighborhood. You,
sir, took your turn of the sword; I must not, therefore,
grudge to take mine of the pestilence."

When, following the Plague, the Great Fire of London
threatened to consume the entire city, he hastened to
have workmen brought from the dockyards, to suggest
destroying houses in the path of the conflagration, and
planned, worked, commanded, till the Navy Offices were
saved. When the Dutch fleet sailed up the Medway and
the Thames, burning and sinking helpless, laid-up English men-of-war, and threatening the capital itself; while
Monk rallied forces to resist, threw up entrenchments,
mounted guns, and sank vessels to oppose further advance, Pepys labored no less manfully to meet the clamor-
ous demands for adequate supplies by day and night,
"alone at the office . . . yet doing the king good service."
When a hostile House, hungry for vengeance, seeking a
scapegoat for a mismanaged war, fell on the Navy; when
"the whole world was at work blaming one another,"
and even the Duke advised his friends to save themselves,
Pepys, unused to public speech, alone before the Commons, defended his service, his colleagues, and himself
with such conspicuous ability and success "as gave great
satisfaction to every one." Amid the revelations of corruption and maladministration which followed the war,
he dared to beard even Prince Rupert before the Navy

Board — and to prove his point. Ten years thereafter he was accused, by no less dangerous an enemy than Shaftesbury, of being a Catholic and possibly involved in Popish plots. He lost his office and his liberty, he stood to lose his life; but he did not lose his courage or resource, and, in the Tower, prepared defense so ample as to make the absurd charge fall of its own weight.

Through all he was, he tells us, horribly afraid — but he was never too frightened to do his duty. Incredible as it seems in view of the conception of the man with which we have been instilled, his conscience was continually too much for him. Over and over again he resolves to follow the dictates of prudence and not involve himself in Montagu's affairs — but finally he does. "I was fearful of going to any house," he writes in the Plague year — but he went. "I do see everybody is on his own defense and spare not to blame another, and the same course I shall take " — but he did not. "I was afraid," he writes at another crisis in affairs, "but I did not shew it." Amid the difficulties which confronted him in the naval investigation he even found time to advise a persecuted colleague, "poor weak brother," in his defense. Proud as he was of his success in life, his house, his clothes, his coach, his dignities, his place, not all his vanity nor all his fears prevented his risking them for what he thought was right. If this be cowardice, then make the most of it.

If, finally, you would have a fairer measure of the man, compare Pepys with Gibbon, the historian, who most nearly occupies an eminence in one department of historical literature commensurate with that of the Secretary in another. Not merely does each owe his present reputation to his literary skill in that field, but the outlines of their lives show certain similarities. Both were of the middle class; both rose through their abilities from relative obscurity to distinction; both were members of Parliament; both held public office; and the private life of the historian has been approved by sober folk almost as much as that of the diarist has been condemned. Gibbon, accustomed to inherited means, refrained from marriage with one of the most attractive women on the Continent and, from prudent fear of his father's displeasure, "sighed as a lover but obeyed as a son." The penniless Pepys, with a rash unworldliness the more remarkable in a man conspicuous above his fellows for his sound judgment, married in defiance of every prudent consideration. The one, financially independent of his place, gave silent votes against his conscience for a policy which led to England's quarrel with America; the other, owing his living to his place, dared oppose the Commons' anger and his superiors' ill-will wherever he believed his cause was right. One slumbered with his colleagues of the Board of Trade over the duties of a pleasant sinecure, while the imperial policy went down to ruin; the other spent his days and, not infrequently, his nights in furthering the interests of his government. "I have entered Parliament," wrote the historian, "without patriotism and without ambition; . . . all my views are bounded by the comfortable and modest position of a Lord of Trade." "My great design," wrote Pepys, "is to get myself to be a Parliament man . . . both for the King's and Service's sake and for the Duke of York's." Reverse Gibbon, and you get Pepys.

Neither could have succeeded in the other's field: Pepys failed as much at history as Gibbon in affairs. From the desert of family and official life which the historian created and called peace, there rose, indeed, a splendid history: from the varied and fertile plain of everyday affairs the Secretary brought a no less immortal Diary. Like character, like book; the style was in each case the man himself. "The manner of the 'Decline and Fall,'" says Bagehot, "is not a style in which you can tell the truth. . . . Truth is of various kinds; grave, solemn, dignified, — petty, low, ordinary: and a historian who has to tell the truth must be able to tell what is little as well as what is amazing. Gibbon is at fault here: he *cannot* mention Asia *Minor*. The petty order of sublunary matters, the common existence of ordinary people, the necessary littlenesses of necessary life are little suited to his sublime narrative."

One may not venture to declare what the ideal style of diaries should be; but, by whatever chance, all men agree that Pepys has hit upon it; and, whatever charge may be brought against him, none can say he was not competent to tell the truth in whatever form it showed itself to him, that he failed to find an apt expression for every emotion or experience he had, or that his book does nor conform to the "necessary littlenesses of necessary life." One cannot imagine writing of Pepys that "the way to reverence him is not to read him at all, but look at him from the outside . . . and think how much there is within." Rather his book is "actually read, a man is glad to take it up and slow to lay it down; . . . once having had it in his library he would miss it from its shelves," the more so that it was not the product of "a life-time of horrid industry."

Least of all did the diarist, with the peculiar vanity of the historian, identify himself with the world's greatness. Gibbon, it has been said, confused himself with the Roman Empire; describing his pilgrimages from Buriton to London and London to Buriton in the same majestic periods that record the fall of states and empires; his amateur experiences with the English yeomanry in phrases that recall the tramp of Roman legions; his voiceless and insignificant presence in the House of Commons in a manner suited to an account of the deliberations of the Roman senators. Whatever form the diarist's egotism took, he realized his place within the universe. Nor can we well believe that the great work of the historian would have suffered from some infusion of the Secretary's qualities.

Comparisons, however invidious, are, in this case at least, illuminating; for to many minds the smug, impeccable career of the historian has seemed far to surpass the garrulous, inconsequent, vain pursuits of the gossipy diarist in all those enviable qualities which make for virtue and true success. In particular it has seemed to stand for the accomplishment of a great purpose nobly planned, idealistic, admirable, as opposed to Pepys' selfish strivings after the pleasures and profits of a worldly existence. Nothing could be much farther from the truth. If the one made a success of intellect, the other made a success of life; if the historian did much for the past and the future, the Secretary did no less for his own day and for posterity. We would not willingly give up the work of either; but, if one should fail, we could more easily replace the work of Gibbon than the work of Pepys; if we should have to choose between selfish scholar and hard-working hedonist — let each man make his choice.

That one shall ask more of life than life can give, that is the great tragedy. From it, save in perhaps a single particular, Pepys was spared. But that a man may reasonably expect of posterity an honorable remembrance for eminent service well performed, and receive instead a familiar, half-contemptuous regard as a light-minded, evil-mannered, amusing babbler, that height of fame's tragi-comic irony has been his fate too long. In the records of his service, and in the Diary read by their light, there resides the quality which the critics have found wanting and blamed him for lacking — devotion to high purpose and ideals, and a sense of duty which served as lofty patriotism or a sustaining belief in a great cause might have served to another type of mind. This does not mean that he was a perfect character, only a very human man, eminent in more than one field of human endeavor and of great service to his fellow men. To the appreciation of this world's goods and pleasures, to intellectual

and philanthropic tastes, to the doctrines of Franklin and
Polonius, he added a sense of public duty and an unre-
mitting industry, with talents which lift him far above the
level of his present reputation, as they raised him above
the generality of his own times.

He was, in short, an admirable representative of a class
not uncommon during the Restoration yet not typical of
it, the left-over Puritans, bred in the sterner, more efficient
school of the Protectorate; on whom, amid the corruption and extravagance of shifty politicians and dissolute
courtiers, rested the burden of the state. What he said of
another applies no less to himself: " It is pretty to see that
they are fain to find out an old-fashioned man of Cromwell's time to do their business for them." " If it comes
to fighting," observed one of his acquaintances when
dangers thickened about Charles the Second's path, " the
King must rely on the old party"; and this proved,
throughout, scarcely less true of administration. With all
its faults, the Cromwellian régime had one virtue which
was clearly revealed under its successor — it bred strong
men. They were not immaculate, and the most was made
of their failings by their Royalist rivals; but in morals they
were, at worst, not below the level of their generation,
and in efficiency they rose far above it. Among these
worthies Pepys holds high place. Admitting all the frail-
ties and the inconsistencies of this Puritan in Restoration
garb, his manners and his morals not untouched with
something of the weakness of his day, there yet remains a
man whom it is next to impossible to dislike, and whom
it would be wholly impossible, in the light of adequate
knowledge of his career, not to respect. His motto, which
in the half-light of his Diary has long seemed fitting, *Mens
cujusque is est quisque* — " as a man's mind is, so is he," —
may, in this view, well be replaced by one far more appropriate to his life: " Seest thou a man diligent in his
business; he shall stand before kings." Or, if you prefer a

more familiar and perhaps an even more appropriate
quotation:

> "The evil that men do lives after them,
> The good is oft interred with their bones."

Thanks to the work of scholars and lovers of the British
navy, this has not happened in Pepys' case. Yet it seems
probable that, thanks to a world infinitely less interested
in the serious than in the social Pepys, we will have still
further revelations of a life so admirable in one aspect, so
much less admirable in another, and that, in consequence,
the Secretary will again suffer at the hands of the Diarist.
For in a very different fashion from that in which his great
contemporary John Milton achieved his ambition, Samuel
Pepys, too, wrote a book "which the world will not willingly let die."

AN ACCIDENTAL VICTORIAN:
BENJAMIN DISRAELI

AN ACCIDENTAL VICTORIAN:
BENJAMIN DISRAELI

AMONG the many reflections which inevitably assail one as he lays down the life of such a man as Benjamin Disraeli, the first is that of the extraordinary processes by which human, or at least political, reputation is achieved and perpetuated. And the second is akin to the first. It is that, rightly viewed, such a career as Disraeli's, or that of any public man, is not more valuable for the light it throws upon the individual who attains distinction than for the unconscious revelation it furnishes of the times and persons among which he achieved success, the character and standards of his contemporaries, as evidenced by the qualities which they apparently most admired or feared, the services and abilities which they were most inclined or compelled to reward. For political eminence is a measure not alone of the individual, but of the society in which he plays his part; and, to many minds, the shrewdest judgment which can be passed on any people is the character of the political leaders it elects or endures.

It is now a little more than three-quarters of a century since this clever scion of a family of Levantine Jews, turned Christian and English in so far as legal and ecclesiastical conformity could accomplish that miracle, confirmed the transformation by becoming a member of

the English Parliament. He was then about thirty-three
years of age. His father had achieved some reputation
as the author of a series of studies in the by-paths of
literature, and much notoriety by his withdrawal from
the synagogue. The son, after a curiously fragmentary
and unconventional education, and a no less desultory
excursion into law, entered life — which is to say Society
— and turned to literature as his vocation. Within his
own circle he soon became conspicuous for his incredible
extravagance in dress, his eccentric manners, his egotism,
and his cleverness. To the world outside, he was known
as a romantic novelist.

Thus equipped, he aspired to direct his country's destinies. Few political careers have begun less promisingly.
He tried three times without success to gain a seat in
the House of Commons; and, when he finally succeeded
in entering that body, his first effort to address its members was smothered in laughter and contempt. His ec-
centricities of manner, dress, and speech, his exaggerated,
"un-English" qualities, his overpowering vanity, seemed
to bar him forever from the public position which he
sought. Yet within ten years he was the virtual leader
of the Tory party; in fifteen he was Chancellor of the
Exchequer; and thirty years from his advent into the
House he was Prime Minister. That office he held twice.
As chief of the Conservatives he became one of the two
great leaders of English public life; as Earl of Beaconsfield he entered the House of Lords; and save for his
own wish he would have "achieved the Abbey" as his
last resting-place.

Even from the briefest recital of such a career as this
it is evident that there must have resided in such a character some extraordinary quality, peculiarly adapted, or
adapting itself, to the times on which it fell. If we admit
with Richelieu and the great company he represents,
that "great designs and notable enterprises are to be

judged only by success"; if we are prepared to accept
the judgment of those who hold mere achievement as the
only principle which history gives to mankind, such a
life is at once its own defense, apology, and justification.
On such grounds we must exclaim with Bismarck, "*Der
alte Jude, er ist der Mann!*"

But, fortunately or unfortunately, there are those who
are not willing to regard the mere accomplishment of
one's aims as the only or even the highest test of a career.
To them there are two further considerations which must
be taken into account in the final evaluation of a man
and his achievement. The one is his character as revealed
in his motives and methods; the other is the result of his
labors on the general development of his people or mankind. If a public man's account with life ended with his
departure from it; if, when he entered his tomb and shut
the door behind him, he could by that act estop all further developments and comments growing out of his
words and deeds, the verdicts of history would be far
different. But that contingency the very nature of the
case forbids. No man lives or dies to himself; the great
current of events of which he formed a part flows on;
and the same forces which contributed to, or suffered,
or opposed his leadership while he was alive hold him to
an accounting once he is dead. "Private individuals,"
says the great searcher of the heart of politics, "may
attain sovereignty by the favor of the citizens, neither
through merit nor fortune alone, but by a lucky sort of
craft; and if they adapt themselves to circumstances
they are rarely unfortunate, provided they make themselves esteemed by great enterprises and extraordinary
actions." But for a favorable verdict from history not
even Machiavelli hazards a recipe.

For it is only too evident, as we survey human affairs,
that when a man has finally achieved place and power,
he has won only the first round of his contest with ob-

livion. He will be remembered — but how? He has still to meet the historian and the biographer. Biography, it has been observed, is the penalty one pays for fame; and the crimes committed in its name have too often been food for laughter or for tears, rather than for just appreciation of human endeavor. We may express our indifference to the opinion of posterity; but it is a pretense. And posterity's judgments are so various!

The choice between the widely divergent views of Disraeli's character and career is difficult; even the harmonizing of them has its perplexities; and when we turn from what may be called, in biographical phrase, the "public life" to the private activities of this extraordinary character — if, indeed, there is any distinction to be made — we find ourselves no less at fault. That he managed to break through the triple brass which in his day guarded English society and politics we know. That he did this by incessant advertisement of his own undoubted abilities is evident. He wore the most amazing and incredible clothes which ever gladdened the eyes of less daring or more modest males. He wrote novels. He went to endless dinner parties, made speeches, stood for Parliament, wrote poetry, even rode to hounds. And, meanwhile, from him, perhaps even in this last exploit, there poured a constant stream of words, chiefly about himself. He described himself as he wished to be, or to appear, in his stories, in his speeches, in his conversation, in letters to the newspapers. He even issued an anonymous pamphlet about himself entitled, characteristically, *What is He?* He had a passion and a genius for publicity; and through it, in large measure, he achieved his purpose. So much is evident from the full accounts of his rise to power; and, viewing the greatness of that rise, we must confess it pays to advertise.

And to what end? That he might escape from that modest private station which is the most prized possession of a normal man, whatever his rank in life; that he might have his habits and appearance become common property; his thought and speech, his personality, his daily concerns, become known to every human being he could reach; and by such means persuade his fellows to give into his hands the conduct of public affairs, as the most public of public men. So long, therefore, as men continue to make the measure of greatness the acquisition of power over each other, rather than the increase of human welfare, knowledge, capacity, or happiness; so long as history is written from the standpoint of such personal ascendancy; so long as we accept leaders on such terms as these, Disraeli must be reckoned a great man. So long, too, must the means by which his position was acquired and maintained be regarded by most people as the more interesting part of his career.

In this view, among all his biographers, Froude was the most nearly right. With the sure instinct of the novelist he realized that his hero's chief value as the subject of a biography closed with his ascent to power. The dry and dreary succession of administrative measures, the drudgery of government, what are these to the romance of achieving a position where such prosaic matters are necessary? It is the continuation into a fourth volume of a novel whose hero achieves his quest and wins the heroine at the end of the third. And, better still than Froude, Mr. Parker has put him where he belongs — in a play. There he is wholly at home and almost wholly convincing. Perhaps this is a measure of the man. There is something confessedly theatrical about him. But, whatever we may think of Mr. Gladstone, it is difficult to depict him as a character in a play!

And yet, however fascinating or sordid the details of any man's rise to power among his fellows, however depressing to the adherents of democracy it may be to see authority wielded by mere advertising in such a society as ours, the real question remains — what did he do with his power once it was obtained? What did he stand for, besides himself; what were his policies? Did he sense the great underlying movements of mankind, and help or hinder them? Did he foresee the future, and strive towards the accomplishment of the inchoate desires of humanity to better its condition; did he really lead men towards a promised land, or did he merely lend himself to the current and gain from it what impetus he could to better his own fortunes? For upon this depends, in no small degree, his place in history. To these questions we have no answer as yet beyond the cryptic utterances of his own speeches, the statute-books, the alternate panegyrics of his friends, and objurgations of his enemies; and all these are of small avail.

Yet in a measure we may, even now, come to some conclusions, for we are at the end of an epoch, and we may begin to evaluate the society which found in him the ideas and the qualities which seemed appropriate to its needs and its ambitions. It is apparent that in almost any modern state, perhaps in any age, Disraeli would have attained some eminence. His literary gifts would have provided him an audience under any form of government; his talents as a courtier would have brought him consideration in a monarchy; his abilities as a speaker would have given him a following in a democracy, which his genius for political organization might have transmuted into high office. For, unlike Napoleon, who demanded an age of war and revolution for the exercise of his talents, unlike such men as Cavour and Bismarck, who found in the situation of their own countries and the international relations of Europe a field peculiarly suited to their gifts, Disraeli's versatility and his adaptability to circumstance would have made him conspicuous anywhere. How, then, in the times on which he chanced to fall?

Despite the summary judgments of that school which finds in the word Victorian the epitome of all that is contemptible, it is no easy task to assess a period so long, so complex, so busy, and so near to us as the Age of Victoria. It not merely comprehended some sixty years of human activity; it spanned an epoch in the evolution of mankind. It still lies in that "blind spot" of our minds, the hazy borderland between memory and history, too near to give proper perspective and illumination to its characters and events, too near to see what are to be the results of the great movements which it began. It is even difficult to summarize its infinite activities; it is as yet quite impossible to determine its place in the general scheme of things.

It is evident enough that an age which began with Tractarians and neo-Catholics and ended in higher criticism; which read Dickens and Thackeray and Scott, to say nothing of Bulwer-Lytton, George Eliot, and Disraeli himself in its early years, and found its way through Carlyle and Macaulay, Ruskin and Arnold, Morley and Swinburne, Tennyson and Browning, to Kipling and Stevenson, to Gissing and Moore and Shaw, underwent some remarkable literary and intellectual experiences. It is no less apparent that an era which began life with horsehair sofas and wax flowers under glass, and came out with William Morris and open plumbing, underwent a great revolution in its habits and views of life. A people which began with wooden sailing-ships, stage-coaches, candles and gas, and emerged with steel dreadnoughts and ocean liners, steam and electric railways, cables and telegraphs and telephones, electric lights, and the countless conveniences of modern existence, was materially no less than intellectually regenerated.

In particular, a nation which began with Whig and Tory, and a sprinkling of radical, which was making its first experiments in readjusting its political and social structure to the altering facts of the material world, would scarcely recognize itself in its later phases of Liberal and Conservative and Laborite and Socialist, to say nothing of the Irish. The years preceding Disraeli's entrance on the stage of politics had been an age of revolution, agricultural, industrial, political, from which had emerged new nations, new classes, new beliefs, and new activities throughout the world. It was the peculiar province of the Age of Victoria to readjust the whole machinery of government and society to meet the altered conditions and doctrines of life and politics. It was in this turmoil of change that Disraeli was destined to play his part. In general that part was purely political; and the world of politics, as he and most of his fellows conceived it, is a realm as extraordinary as the history which records its activities.

If we reduce the transformations effected by the Victorian era to their lowest terms we see that in those fields which he most professed they tend to group themselves into three movements: political, social, and imperial. When the young Disraeli gave *Vivian Grey* to an appreciative world, England was still an oligarchy, its electoral system bound by the ties of the preceding centuries. The old rotten borough system still remained the most characteristic feature of English politics. Catholics were still excluded from office and largely from the franchise. Protestant Nonconformists voted and held place only under the sufferance of an annual bill of indemnity. All others were wholly outside the pale. And if we wish to understand how greatly the world has changed, it is but necessary to quote the observation of an English political writer that, "incredible as it may seem to the present generation, the fact that Disraeli was a Jew was a disadvantage to him when he first entered public life."

Before he took his place in Parliament, indeed, many of those ancient inequalities had been swept away. The great Reform Bill of 1832 had been passed and its provisions had been put in force. Catholic and Protestant Nonconformists alike had been admitted to a voice in government as of right, and England had entered upon that era of reform which had already set upon her statute-books the earliest measures directed towards the amelioration of social evils which had followed in the train of the Industrial Revolution. What share did he have in that great movement towards political emancipation of the masses? What was his attitude towards those masses?

It would not, perhaps, be fair to take the earliest utterances of the callow politician as the measure of his ripened convictions — let us hear the matured wisdom of the experienced public man. Eight years before his famous "leap in the dark," the Reform Bill of 1867, which virtually introduced the principles and most of the practices of democracy in English politics, he committed himself. "If you establish a democracy," he declared, "you must in due time reap the fruits of a democracy. You will in due season have great impatience of public burdens, combined in due season with great increase of public expenditure. You will in due season have wars entered into from passion and not from reason; and you will in due season submit to peace ignominiously sought and ignominiously obtained, which will diminish your authority and perhaps endanger your independence. You will in due season find your property is less valuable and your freedom less complete."

His change of heart did credit to his ingenuity. "Popular privileges," he announced in introducing his Representation of the People bill, "are consistent with a state of society in which there is great inequality of position. Democratic rights, on the contrary, demand that there should be equality of condition as the fundamental basis of the society they regulate." With these words, outbidding the Liberals, he opened the floodgates of democracy in the guise of extending the franchise and at the same time safeguarding what he called the interests of that "due influence of property, especially landed property," in public affairs. One can only wonder what form of words, if he had lived in our day, he would have found to justify his adhesion to the will of the majority of the electorate as expressed in old-age pensions, unemployment doles, and all the vast machinery of bureaucracy; and how he would have translated "privileges" into "rights."

That brings us to the question of the social issue. No one can read those descriptions of the England of William the Fourth in the pages of his early novels without the twofold realization of Disraeli's powers as a novelist, and the tremendous problem which confronted the nation in those days when the combination of the factory system and the *laissez faire* doctrine had made Great Britain what a later Liberal stateman described as "heaven for the rich, purgatory for the middle classes, and hell for the poor." Read the famous description of Devilsdust and his surroundings which darken the pages of *Sybil*, of that "other England," which saw Paradise about them — and its gates closed. No one in England, if we judge from the world of letters, saw more clearly and described more vividly the frightful results of rampant industrialism. Beside his bitter account of the "two nations" into which his country was divided by the development of factories, the pages of George Eliot and Dickens, the pronunciamentos even of the radicals, seem pale reflections. This much at least must be set to his credit — he looked deeper into the situation than even those who sought to remedy its evils. To Goldsmith's profound dictum that "honor sinks where commerce long prevails," his books add the still more discouraging reflection that wealth, unchecked by the conscience

or the authority of society, is the greatest enemy of
welfare.

What, then, did he do to correct the inequalities?
There is no better answer to that than the famous car-
toon of *Punch* which, depicting the fish dinner with
which successive ministries were wont in those days to
celebrate the end of a session, showed the Prime Minister rising to address his colleagues with a plate before
him containing a collection of fish no less remarkable
for their small number than for their extremely minute
and attenuated forms. It is a true picture. In all the long
antagonism between Disraeli and Gladstone, in all the
differences which marked their opposition of character,
none is more remarkable than their records as construc-
tive statesmen. Whatever we may think of Mr. Gladstone, we must admit that he was a great legislator, and
the statute-book remains his best monument. Whatever
we may think of Mr. Disraeli, we must admit that his
period of ascendancy is one of the most barren eras of
English legislation in the nineteenth century. To a generation surfeited with an excess of laws this may not
carry the same conviction that it would have borne to
the men of fifty years ago; but if one considers the result of the two ministries in the light of their relation to
the social progress of the past hundred years, it must
be apparent that there is some truth in the old story of
the Reform Bill of 1867. Receiving their enfranchise-
ment from Mr. Disraeli, the people replied, "Thank
you, Mr. Gladstone."

As to his reforms, the Housing Act, the Friendly
Societies Act, the bills concerned with the relations of
master and man, — all due, chiefly to Cross, somewhat
to Northcote, — these helped the workingman. The
Plimsoll Act helped the seamen, the act compensating
tenants for unexhausted improvements helped the renter.
The Public Health Act, the so-called Consolidation Act

which codified the factory acts, the Enclosure reforms,
the Rivers Pollution Act, the amendments to Forster's
Education Act relating to the universities, the encour-
agement of secondary education, the addition of four
bishoprics, these are salutary and extensive. None of
them affected the so-called "privileged" classes, it is
true; none of them went to the heart of any great problem; perhaps none of them was due to the initiative of
the Prime Minister himself. No estimate of his ministry could with any fairness omit or depreciate them.
Yet they are the last and least of those things for which
he is remembered, since at heart Disraeli was no re-
former, in the accepted meaning of the word. And to
that there are those who will add with pious fervor,
"Thank God."

For — and this is most important to the problem in
hand — however clearly he saw the misery of the masses,
he was careful not to make the mistake, which would
have been fatal to him, of attempting to alter the social
order. It is apparent that the glorious society which
appeared in the pages of his novels could only exist by
economic ascendancy, powerfully buttressed by law. It
was the fine flower of inequality. It was, perhaps, worth
all it cost. It is still a debated question whether mankind
as a whole does not, after all, gain more by the intensive
cultivation of a select few at the expense of the many
than by the almost imperceptible elevation of the mass
and the concurrent depression of selected individuals.
Laying aside the doctrine of the superman, it may be
urged with some degree of plausibility that the most
gifted societies the world has seen have been based on
the principle of inequality. But that is not the point.
Disraeli posed as the leader of the masses as well as the
champion of the classes, and as such he must be judged.

The reason for his position is not far to seek; and the
clue may be found in those same early works which so

vividly described the sufferings and the debasement of the poor. English literature boasts no more carefully written descriptions of great country-houses, parks, gardens, mansions, and palaces than those which illumine the pages of Disraeli's novels. Not Thackeray, not Bulwer-Lytton in all his splendor, compares with them. Still less do these rival Disraeli's accounts of the godlike creatures which inhabit these magnificent abodes. Never in any literature has an aristocracy been so adorned with all the graces and the talents as the glittering society which crowds his books. In his Oriental imagination that society was transfigured into something which, if it was not more than human, was at least the finest flower of humanity. Perhaps the English aristocracy of the nineteenth century was all he painted it. Some elements in it undoubtedly deserved his panegyrics as much as the houses and gardens unquestionably did. But that, as a class, it reached those heights of idealism, there is as much reason to doubt as there is that its members were all descended from the Norman conquerors.

Finally there remains imperialism. Here, at least, we seem to reach more solid ground. First, then, as to his foreign policy. If one wishes the bitterest of commentaries upon the vanity of human wisdom and prophecy, he has only to compare the utterances of Disraeli upon his return from the Congress of Berlin, with the events of the past thirty years in the Balkan peninsula, and its situation to-day. Diplomacy, like legislation, must be based not only on the experience of the past, it must be in no small degree prophecy. And, viewing Disraeli's diplomatic career, in particular his strenuous efforts to save the Turk from well-merited destruction, it is difficult to avoid the conclusion that, on the whole, Lord Salisbury's homely dictum was true. He "put his money on the wrong horse." In a labored effort to be "fair," a recent manual observes that Disraeli "showed vision and

splendid audacity," but adds with perhaps unconscious irony, "though later events necessitated a reversal of the British attitude toward both Turkey and Russia."

Against this will be urged one striking exception, that is, the famous purchase of the Suez Canal shares. While the original idea was not Disraeli's, he must be given the chief credit for the transaction, and it remains the chief monument of his career. To it, by a curious coincidence in time, may be added his project of having the Crown assume the imperial title in India. From the Suez Canal control flowed almost inevitably that long stream of events which brought England into Egypt and the Sudan, for good and ill; and, despite the ill, if we regard the old imperialism of Great Britain as a great and, on the whole, a beneficent mission, we cannot deny Disraeli whatever measure of credit the Canal purchase brought to that development. The imperial title was a gesture, pleasing to the Queen, satisfying Disraeli's own peculiar predilections, and, like the Egyptian matter, lying in the realm which most interested him, the East. Nor is it, perhaps, without significance that his great achievement was in that field which, above all others, was nearest to his heart.

But, apart from Eastern politics, was what we usually mean by "imperialism" — colonial imperialism — Disraeli's great contribution to English policy and history? Did thousands of Canadians, Australians, New Zealanders, hasten to lay their lives at the feet of the mother-country because, a half a century ago, "this old Jew gentleman sitting on the top of chaos" gave utterance to the desire, in his own words, "of responding to those distant sympathies which may become the source of incalculable strength and happiness to this land"? Was it the wand of this Oriental magician which waked England from long lethargy, and called into existence new worlds to redress the balance of the old? Was it Disraeli, rather than Pitt or Russell or Palmerston, who breathed life into the British Empire, gave self-government to her colonies, and summoned the forces of India to play a part upon the European stage?

One of the most recent manuals of modern history declares that he gave this new note to English politics, and that this is his real historic significance. One of the most widely read of modern German publicists has averred that British imperialism was the product of Disraeli's brain. One of the most brilliant of modern writers has put in the mouth of a character obviously modeled upon Lord Beaconsfield the phrases of imperialism; that England has "stretched over every continent huge embryo limbs, which wait only for the beat of her heart, the motion of her spirit, to assume their form and function as members of one great body of empire; the hearts of Englishmen beyond the seas beat in unison with ours." If it is true that he created this spirit, it is justification enough in itself for his existence and the means which raised him to place and power. If it is true only in part, it goes far to set him among the immortals.

We cannot tell. Real leadership or divination or mere high-sounding words, whatever it was, the mysteries of such a spirit are beyond the plumb-line of the historian. Legislation it certainly was not, as it was in Russell's case; nor was it the imperial leadership of the elder Pitt. It was, perhaps, more akin to the talents of Palmerston, the frank audacity, the jingoism, which invariably appeals to the self-assertiveness of a race of pioneers and emigrants. But it needs no wide acquaintance with English history to realize that, whether in word or deed, whether in spirit or statute, British imperialism was not the child of the last quarter of the nineteenth century nor was it the creature of Disraeli's statesmanship. Yet this much is true. To the rising imperialistic spirit of English democracy, as to the old Tory imperialism, he gave voice, and that was something, for that spirit had been accustomed to express itself in deeds, not words, and his opponents, in their intentness on social reform, had laid themselves open to the charge of being "little Englanders." Thus he became imperialism's legendary champion.

And thus we end as we began, in words. From *Vivian Grey* to *Endymion*, from the overdressed dandy who was howled down by the Commons in 1837 to the Prime Minister who retired full of years and honors in 1880, the line is unbroken, the course runs clear. The wit, the eloquence, the vituperation, the audacity, grow with the years. The claims to greatness mount with equal pace. But the brilliant flow of words finds slender reflection in solid achievement commensurate with those claims. One of the most scientific studies ever made in the effect of public opinion upon government in a specific case, has only revealed the gulf which yawned between the spirit of England and the policy of Disraeli during the Bulgarian atrocities and the Congress of Berlin. Its sober conclusion was that the minister appealed chiefly to the love of excitement inherent in any society, and that the so-called Disraeli-Toryism was based in large degree upon admiration not so much for the measures as for the ability of Lord Beaconsfield. This new development of Toryism, we are assured, by evidence which seems irrefutable, took temper from "his scorn of representative institutions, his idea of politics as a game where the boldest adventurer will win; his admiration for the East, and the immense importance he attached to the diplomatic and military side of politics."

It is, indeed, not easy to get at his political, still less his social philosophy, assuming that he had formulated these even to himself. Perhaps no single phrase of the multitude which Disraeli coined has been more often repeated than his answer to a too curious questioner that he "relied upon the sublime instincts of an ancient race." It has been generally regarded as one of those vague, metaphysical, flattering obscurities in which he often clothed his purpose and his thought. But it was more than that. Sublime, instinct, ancient race — there he laid bare the inmost secrets of his whole philosophy, and England laughed at the adroit evasion of a direct answer as to what he proposed to do! To him the commonplace was abhorrent; the picturesque, the dramatic, everything. To him the future was an abstraction, the past a solid reality; and instinct rather than reason the true spring of action.

Yet if one relies upon the past, if he has no other lamp to guide his feet than the lamp of experience, he must at least make sure that his past is right. Disraeli created for himself and for his followers a past which had never been seen on sea or land. He idealized the Middle Ages and sought to project them into modern society. His was an age in which popular government was making enormous strides. In the forty years between his advent into Parliament and his introduction of the second Reform Bill there had come the Chartist movement in England and the revolution of 1848 on the Continent, the abolition of slavery in the United States, and the extinction of serfdom in eastern Europe. Universal suffrage had made its appearance in France, some form of parliamentary government in every European state except Russia. Napoleon the Third had invoked the plebiscite to secure his hold upon the throne he won by a *coup d'état*; Cavour invoked it to seal the unification of Italy. It was evident to the more astute rulers of the mid-nineteenth century that popular control of popular affairs was at hand. This ill consorted with purely autocratic or aristocratic government.

In consequence two theories arose to meet the situation thus produced and to oppose middle-class liberalism.

The one was the doctrine of democratic absolutism, enunciated by that great political adventurer, Napoleon the Third, now finally Emperor of the French. The other was the doctrine first developed as "Young England," then evolved into what was to be known in later years as "Tory democracy," which was in part, at least, the product of Disraeli's fertile imagination. The one conceived of popular power delegated to an individual to be exercised for the general good by an enlightened despot, supported by the "people." The other conceived of a system, not dissimilar, in which three elements were necessary, leaders, masses, and a man. To it the classes were to supply the leaders, the masses the votes — Disraeli the man.

In this was nothing new but names. The principle had been set forth by Sieyès in his famous phrase "Authority from above, confidence from below"; the theory was at least as old as Aristotle; and whether in practice or in theory it appeals to many men. But in Disraeli's hands, whether or not he knew his Aristotle or his Sieyès, it took a mediæval form. His plan was, in brief, a democratized and nationalized feudal system, as that of Napoleon the Third was a democratized national despotism. Each embraced that oldest and most successful of all devices to secure power, the personal touch with the classes and the popular appeal to the masses. But neither was, in any sense, more than a means to stay the oncoming triumph of true democracy, of which neither Napoleon nor Disraeli was the apostle.

There is, indeed, something to be said for his policy — his praise of English character, his devotion to the Empire of England, his courage, his aggressive assertion of Great Britain's high place and destiny in the world's affairs. It appealed to a people weary of the contemplation of their weak spots as revealed by Gladstone's programme of reform; it gave them a new interest, a new

outlook, a comforting sense of their importance in and
to the world. But it had one drawback. It tended to
ignore realities — conscience among them — and it cost
money. It nearly embroiled them with Europe. It did
embroil them with Boers, Afghans, and Zulus; and Mr.
Gladstone's administration inherited, besides the Egyptian adventure, wars with all three. From the Congress
of Berlin, they were assured, the Prime Minister brought
back peace with honor; and they should have been grateful for such gifts, when joined to glory. Yet within
eighteen months they turned him out. Here is some
curious paradox. Whether democracies are ungrateful;
whether they quickly tire of this policy or that; whether
they are not willing to pay for imperialism; whether they
fear the gold is tinsel, the great magician fell at the
moment when he seemed most powerful. Yet there may
be an answer beyond these. It seems to be revealed in
that searching study of the lack of real connection between Disraeli's policy and public opinion on the Bulgarian atrocities. It shows, among other things, that
nations like England have at least two motives — conscience and interest. It was the latter to which Disraeli
appealed. It may have been the former which made
his ascent to power so slow, which made his tenure of
that power so short-lived, and which contributed to his
fall.

But, what is the use? "English politics," we are seriously informed, "relapsed into its ancient dreariness
when Disraeli died" — though that reproach, at least,
seems to have been wiped out with the progress of time.
It will no doubt always be true that Machiavelli will
attract more of the average man's attention and interest
than Malthus; that the guerilla leader will always be
more entertaining to him than the profoundest of strate-
gists. Imagination still rules the world in most men's
minds, even the world of politics; and Disraeli was one

of those rare spirits who, whatever his own personal
ambitions, contrived in that field to produce the illusion
of striving only for the public good, while at the same
time, "entertaining the crowd by his verbal cleverness
and the anticipation of what he would do next."

How did he do it? That is the question which continually confronts one in considering his life. To it no cate-
gorical answer is possible. Too much of such a *succès
d'estime* as his lies in the elusive and always mysterious
domain of personality. One cannot understand the subtle
influence of a score of political leaders, whose names
occur to one in this connection, nor can it be explained
to generations which never felt their charm.

But in Disraeli's case we can at least approximate
some of the causes of his ascendancy. In the first place
he came upon the stage at a time which was peculiarly
fortunate for his talents. He early espoused the side
to which they were most useful and where they found
the freest scope, and, unlike his great rival, Gladstone —
whom Macaulay described in his early years as "the
brightest hope of the stern unbending Tories," — Disraeli stuck to his party. That party needed him only less
than he needed its support. The attitude of mere opposition to change is never an agreeable one, and, in the
long run, it brings little but defeat. Negation is not a
policy. If the Tory party was to survive, it was necessary
to have a voice; at least the semblance of a political
philosophy; and a reason for its existence. At the beginning of Disraeli's career it was fortunate in possessing
both. But the ascendancy of Peel was far from agreeable
to many of his followers. He was too open to the newer
ideas of the times in which he lived, he was too liberal,
especially for the so-called "landed interest." When, in
the face of the increasing strength of the free trade movement, impelled by the imminent catastrophe of the Irish
famine, he undertook the repeal of the Corn Laws, and,

as the current phrase ran, "found the Whigs in bathing, and ran off with their clothes," he roused the bitterest antagonism of a small but powerful interest among his followers. This was Disraeli's opportunity, and, rejected by Peel as a supporter, he headed a secession from the minister's influence, and became the bitterest of his opponents.

In that capacity he developed rapidly the second of those qualities which made for his success in public life. His power of vituperation, almost, if not quite, unmatched in English history; his extraordinary skill in phrase-making; his unlimited audacity; his complete lack of that restraint which has marked most English political leaders in characterizing even their antagonists, gave him an enormous advantage in such a field. Whatever many of his followers may have thought in private of such tactics as he employed in his attacks upon his opponents, there is no question that those attacks were effective. As the philosopher has observed, "There is something in the misfortunes even of our friends which is not wholly unpleasing to us"; and vituperation is one of the most entertaining forms of public misfortune. It was the more effective in Disraeli's case in that it was so evidently the result of deliberate premeditation. It was not without reason that the man who allowed himself to say of Mr. Gladstone that he was a "sophisticated rhetorician, intoxicated by the exuberance of his own verbosity," came to be feared by any antagonist.

To this he added, or perhaps by this he aided, his mastery of the House of Commons, and any man who attains recognition in the House of Commons finds his fortune secure. In no other representative government in the world are the qualities which give a man ascendancy in a deliberative body so fully and so richly recognized and repaid as in England. A seat is always at his command; when his party is in power an office is always a matter of course; and, irrespective of his capacity as a campaigner or an organizer, he is sure of a relatively permanent position in public life. Such was the situation which confronted Disraeli; and, perceiving it, his first care was to secure himself in that quarter.

But to this he joined another quality. Whether as a speaker or as an organizer, he was a peculiarly gifted politician outside the walls of Parliament; and the Age of Victoria offered a fertile field for the exercise of those talents which are associated generally with the name of politician rather than that of statesman. In those practices, as in the manipulation of the Commons, Disraeli soon proved himself a master. It has been observed by one of his admirers that it was sometimes necessary to conceal from Mr. Gladstone some of the methods employed by the less hypercritical members of his party to ensure success at the polls for the principles which he championed. There seems to be no record that it was ever necessary to conceal anything from Mr. Disraeli, or even from Lord Beaconsfield. In the famous phrase of a later if not a greater statesman-politician, they were both "practical men." There were few devices of moulding his ambitions into a popular majority which were unknown to him, and the ablest student of modern politics outside of England has remarked of him that in this "he observed but one rule of conduct, that which led to success." One needs only to note the establishment of a Central Conservative Office, of local associations, of workingmen's societies, and finally a National Union in that interest, during the period of the great Gladstone ministry, to perceive the causes of the success of the Disraeli-Tory "machine" in 1874 over the "less complete organization" of the Liberals. One needs only to read his appeals for funds to "operate on a class of seats hitherto unassailed," his assurance that "I have induced my colleagues in the Cabinet to subscribe a minimum of ten thousand pounds, tho' if they follow my example it will reach a greater amount," to realize that, whatever the opinion of his statesmanship, he was an eminent exponent of the art of the politician.

And his pen was a magician's wand. Few individuals and no classes are insensible to flattery; and Disraeli was a prince of courtiers. "I do not know what we shall do," so runs the old story of Wellington's remark at the accession of Victoria, "for I have no tact and Peel has no manners." Of those deficiencies in their most practical form no one could accuse Disraeli. Whatever the contempt in which he was held by a considerable part of that aristocracy which he strove so zealously to propitiate, his talent for flattery did its work. He married a wealthy wife for her money; but, as she proudly said, if he had married her again it would have been for love! Could there be better testimony to his courtly qualities? He was as successful in attracting the attention and maintaining the regard of old Mrs. Willyums, who left him a fortune at her death, as he was in gaining the favor of Queen Victoria.

How did he do it? The answer to that he has given himself in his letters to the Queen, whom he addressed as his "Faery"; but most of all in that amazing series of more than sixteen hundred letters to two ladies of his acquaintance, written in some eight years. Here is the secret. "Except upon business," he writes, "male society is not much to my taste. Indeed, I want to see only one person, whom I never see, and I want to see her always." This person, it appears, was not his wife. She had been dead nearly two years. It was Lady Bradford, the charming wife of Lord Bradford, then past fifty years of age, and with grown children, to whom he addressed these passionate communications. "To love as I love, and rarely to see the being one adores, whose constant society is absolutely necessary to my life; to be precluded even from the only shadowy compensation for such a torturing doom — the privilege of relieving my heart by expressing its affection — is a lot which I never could endure, and cannot. But for my strange position, which enslaves while it elevates me, I would fly forever, as I often contemplate, to some beautiful solitude, and relieve in ideal creation, the burthen of such a dark and harassing existence."

Such language from a seventy-year-old Prime Minister seems, at this distance, to lack something of what one might conceivably expect of, shall we say, restraint, even though, as he says, he had "lived to know the twilight of love has its splendor and richness." "Dear darling," he writes again, "My dearest darling friend, you literally scatter flowers and fruit over my existence." But one cannot agree with his declaration that "I have no language to express to you my entire affection." That is too fearful a thought.

In some degree this was the quality which he used in other and more profitable as well as more practical fields. Were it necessary to demonstrate how sedulously and successfully he cultivated the good opinion of a powerful class, it would be necessary to read not only his novels but certain portions of his life of Lord George Bentinck. Were it necessary to prove how he obtained his ascendancy over popular audiences one need only read his speeches extolling the English character. If ever a man stooped to conquer, it was Benjamin Disraeli.

Yet all of these do not complete the tale. There is one other quality which, beside, one might almost say above, all others, contributed to his success while he was alive, and bids fair to be his chief weapon against oblivion now he is dead. It is his imagination. The Tory party, it has been remarked, needed the brains and the voice, the political philosophy and the practical qualities which it was his fortune to supply. It needed more; it needed

imagination; and this, even above his gift of what may
be called, politely, repartee, even above his gift for management, he supplied. To the English public which followed his banner he was more than a political leader,
more than an orator. He was Romance. Whether in re-
constructing that shattered vision of a Merrie England
which should somehow replace the prosaic land they saw
about them; whether drawing from his fertile brain the
mirage of an Eastern policy which somehow correlated
the dream of Oriental magnificence and the glamour of
the Crusades with the vision of imperial mission which
always appeals to any people, and so concealing the
often worse than sordid abuses of his generation, he
was successful in throwing a glamour over the most
practical of affairs. He was able to lift them into a
realm, which, however unreal, dazzled the minds of his
contemporaries.

And for this ought we not to be grateful? There is
little romance in mere reform of abuses; there is less in
the ordinary view of the means by which political ends
are achieved; there is none in the dry and commonplace
administration of the affairs of state; and there is less
than none in the official reports which chronicle the progress of modern society. Disraeli's dream of popular Toryism was only a dream; his Asiatic policy was not even a
pleasant dream, as we look upon its motives and results.
Both lacked "political substance." They were both
based perhaps on what has been termed by a wholly
disinterested observer "an illusion or a verbal juggle."
But even if this be true he managed the illusion well.
And more; he played the game of politics with courage
and with skill — nor can a race of sportsmen be insensible
to those qualities.

Thus, when all is said, he represented much in English
life in the Victorian Age; not all of it, not most of it,
perhaps not even the better part of it, or the most endur-

ing, for he had but little share in that sober, serious, plodding progress towards better living and thinking, better laws and conditions, which is its most striking and most permanent characteristic. Social regeneration was not his atmosphere. He stood for "compatibles." A landed aristocracy, an established order in church and society, and an empire, these were the pillars of his political edifice. To them he added an adventurous if unsound foreign policy, and meanwhile posed as the champion of that inchoate democracy which as yet was not wholly certain of its strength or its purpose.

When one joins such elements as these and adorns the whole with the gift of literary expression in its most fashionable Victorian form, the novel, we must recognize Disraeli as a fit representative of powerful elements of the age in which he lived. These are the permanent factors; for the rest he stood for himself, and that was no small thing. Yet in the final resolution of events and reputations, one may not be sure that all of these will weigh as heavily as his rival's more sober talents. To him life was a great adventure, politics a game; and while to many minds the soldier of fortune will always excite interest and admiration; while between Aristides and Themistocles, men will divide their sympathies; the muse of history continually inclines to be — perhaps too serious!

But was he, in all of this, sincere? That is the crux in the Disraeli problem, as it is in that of perhaps too many public men. It is idle to attempt to conceal that no inconsiderable number of his opponents, and apparently even some of his supporters, entertained serious misgivings as to his intellectual honesty. It was difficult, at times, indeed, it was impossible, for some of his rivals to suppress the fact that they regarded him as a conscienceless charlatan — and it must in fairness be said that most of them made little effort to veil their thoughts.

It was observed of Gladstone that he always took pains to convince himself that he was right, whatever side he took. Thereby he earned the reputation in certain circles of being a hypocrite. It did not always seem that Disraeli troubled to convince himself that he was right, whatever pains he took to impress the correctness of his views upon the electorate. Thereby he earned the reputation of being a scoundrel. What is sincerity in politics? "Do you imagine for a moment," says Socrates in his famous defense as reported by Plato, "that I should have managed to live all these years, had I taken part in public affairs, and, like an honest man, always stood for right, and, as in duty bound, made that my chief concern? Certainly not, fellow-Athenians — neither I nor any man!" There is, and apparently there must be, in any public man that measure of exaggeration which we associate with the word demagogue. The question of sincerity seems somehow beside the mark. In almost innumerable instances, small and great, consistency, even that higher consistency which ignores conflicting statements made at different times and under different circumstances, was denied to Benjamin Disraeli. And if this be sincerity let politicians make the most of it!

It is peculiarly difficult to attribute either sincerity or insincerity to a man who appears to so many different persons in so many different guises. The various forms which he assumes provide a measure of the problem. There is the egotistic fop who amused and defied and finally conquered the Commons; the author of *Alroy* and *Sybil*; the creator of "the Bentinck myth," and of "the Asian mystery"; the suppliant and the antagonist of Peel; the progenitor of "Tory democracy"; the purchaser of the Suez Canal; the Empress-maker.

There you have them — or most of them. But where is that elusive, Proteus-like personality, which charmed and mocked, dominated or infuriated its fellows? Where

is the real Disraeli? or was there one? The word real
seems somehow out of place. Even though politics turns
into history when it is no longer necessary to conceal
the facts; though the Age of Victoria is shrinking into
a heap of memories and documents; though it is rapidly
taking its place beside that of Elizabeth, while Cavour
and Bismarck appear scarcely less remote than Frederick the Great and Napoleon, the figure of Disraeli still
seems to evade analysis; and still, with all its vividness,
seems to lack definition.

Yet this very circumstance may contribute to his fame.
For if the great Conservative leader so long lacked an
adequate biography and if he has not greatly commended
himself to the present generation of historians, he has had
his compensations. What history has failed to do, her
elder sister has all but accomplished. His life was a
romance; it bids fair to become a legend, against whose
shadowy persistence fact is as harmless as a sword
against smoke. The veil is continually riven only to unite.
It is in vain that the shameless audacity of his early
career is laid bare, with his less creditable manœuvres
to gain and keep power and place. It is in vain that serious men like Lord Cromer, while paying tribute to Disraeli's better qualities, utter their warning against the
genius prostituted to form "a political school based on
self-seeking opportunism," and declare that he "cannot
be acquitted of the charge of having contributed towards
the degradation of English political life."

It is in vain that one party loads him with violent de-
nunciation, the other with violent praise. Each defeats
its object. Whatever his weaknesses they were not so
great as to deserve unqualified eulogy; whatever his
strength it was not so small as to require unqualified
defense; and however amazing the Disraeli legend, it is
less incredible than the facts.

He has been deified, after our modern fashion, along

with Pitt and Burke, Canning and Palmerston, each
worshiped by his cult. It is only too probable that

> A primrose by the river's brim
> A party emblem was to him,
> And it was nothing more.

If it was even that! Yet a great Conservative league has
founded itself on the pleasing and harmless assumption
that its emblem was his favorite flower. The ancient
squirearchy and the less ancient aristocracy cherished
to the end the fond delusion that they had found in him
the single-hearted champion of their interests — and their
descendants, still fighting the curtailment of those interests, revere the name of him who allowed to democracy its greatest impetus! Wiser than its opponents, that
democracy burns no incense at the shrine of the great
politician; for its members know that it was not so much
a belief in a wider franchise as the hope of more extended
power which extorted that concession. Such is the paradox of the posthumous fame of him who was himself a
paradox.

And, failing a formula of our own to explain him, let
us appeal to him to explain himself. If one seeks the
heart of his philosophy, the secret of his character and
his career, where can he find it but in the man himself?
Turn to the pages of his novel *Coningsby* and read the
words of his favorite hero, the great cosmopolitan Hebrew nobleman, Sidonia, for whose portrait, it is said,
he "looked in his own mirror." "One source of interest,"
we are told, "Sidonia found in his descent and in the
fortunes of his race." He "and his brethren could claim
a distinction which the Saxon and the Greek had for-
feited. The Hebrew is an unmixed race and an unmixed
race of a first-rate organization are the aristocracy of
nature." "Diplomatists are the Hebrews of politics;
without country, political creeds, popular convictions,"

remarks this character. And again: "You never observe a great intellectual movement in Europe in which the Jews do not greatly participate. The first Jesuits were Jews; that mysterious Russian diplomacy which so alarms western Europe is organized and principally carried on by Jews; that mighty revolution which is at this moment preparing in Germany and which will be, in fact, a second and greater Reformation, and of which so little is as yet known in England, is entirely developing under the auspices of Jews." And once again: "Since your society has become agitated in England and powerful combinations menace your institutions, you find the once loyal Hebrew invariably arrayed in the same ranks as the leveller and the latitudinarian. The Tories lose an important election at a critical moment; 'tis the Jews come forward to vote against them. . . . And every generation they must become more powerful and dangerous to the society which is hostile to them." So he continues, extolling the power of the race, visiting European capitals, he finds the Russian minister of finance, Count Cancrin; the Spanish minister, Mendizabal; the president of the French Council, Soult; the Prussian minister, Count Arnim, all Jews like himself.

Coningsby was published in 1844; and it is evident in what direction his mind worked at that early time. A quarter of a century later he could have added his own name to those he enumerated. Here, then, it may be that we can find the clue to all this mystery; for he had one formula which he applied to everything. "All," he was accustomed to say, "all is *race*." With this judgment, out of his own mouth, we must perforce content ourselves; for surely there can be no higher authority.

Prophecy is no part of the business of history; and it is doubtless still too early to appraise Disraeli's place in the eternal scheme of things. Yet the question inevitably

presents itself: What will be the future of his reputation? To this there is one clue. He has been dead a full
generation, and he has just achieved an adequate biography! It is a matter of no small significance that in six
of the more recent historical works relating to the period
in which Gladstone and Disraeli played their parts upon
the English political stage, "the model of all the virtues"
occupies rather more than twice the space allotted to "the
master of all the arts." The difference is not to be ac-
counted for by the peculiar political predilections of the
authors or the compilers of these volumes; still less is it
to be reckoned as the result of Gladstone's longer life, or
as mere accident. It seems to represent, roughly, the
relative importance, if not the relative interest, of the two
men in the minds of the historians of a succeeding generation. It may be a measure of the importance of their
careers as they will appear to a more remote posterity.
That already within forty years so great a reputation as
Disraeli's has shrunk so much in the minds of that craft is
an illuminating reflection not only upon him and his
place in the general economy of things, but upon that
portion of the English people who followed him. It would
almost seem that the appeal he made for power and fame
was to be rewarded with little more than a life interest in
either. For if this be a true test — though that may well
be denied — it seems to confirm the conclusion of those
who studied his career at the height of his power, that his
ascendancy was personal, not one of principle; that he
was fashionable rather than fundamental.

Just forty-five years ago an English historian drawing his narrative of modern Europe to a close with an
account of the Peace of Berlin observed: "Should the
Balkans become a true military frontier for Turkey,
should Northern Bulgaria sink to the condition of a
Russian dependency, and Eastern Roumelia, in sever-
ance from its enslaved kin, abandon itself to thriving

ease behind the garrisons of the reforming Ottoman, Lord Beaconsfield will have deserved the fame of a statesman whose intuitions, undimmed by the mists of experience, penetrated the secret of the future, and shaped, because they discerned, the destiny of nations." Upon this, viewing the world to-day, no comment seems necessary. It may be that this is mere accident, that, as his admirers say, his influence and reputation are greater now than ever; it may be that this spirit which conquered obscurity may prevail against oblivion. But if the same fortune follows his other views and policies we must believe that he was but a meteor, not a star — now *umbra et imago magni nominis,* "the shadow and the reflection of a great name." That is not wholly probable. Apart from the observation that "his wheat was worthless but his chaff was priceless," there is one thing which will make for his earthly immortality. It is his appeal to that spirit of high adventure, which, however ruthless, however dangerous, however unsubstantial, even at times fantastic, touches all of us more deeply than any triumph of the statute book.

A TRUE ELIZABETHAN: SIR WILLIAM MONSON

A TRUE ELIZABETHAN:
SIR WILLIAM MONSON

THE hardest thing to predicate about a man is whether he will be remembered when he is dead; and if so, for what and for how long. "It is enough," declares a great American, "if one competes successfully with his own generation," and in that view must lie whatever satisfaction most of us will ever get of fame. There is, indeed, but one sure way to keep one's memory alive. Of all the paths to immortality — an eminent ability in the destruction of one's own kind, some superhuman service to the race, some more than usual villainy, some freak of fortune, character, or birth, — all men are equal till one writes a book; and, truly, if ever man had reason to believe the pen mightier than the sword it is Sir William Monson. Among the daring seamen of Elizabeth he was by no means the least; among the counsellors of her Stuart successors his voice was not the mildest; among the upholders of English naval supremacy he occupies a not unenviable place. But were it not for the apparently inconsequential fact that in his later years the old sea-dog chanced to commit his growls to paper, we might well ask in vain of him, as of a multitude of other worthies, stout men of head and hand who in their day helped to direct the destinies of the world, "Who was Sir William Monson?"

Yet it would seem that his career might entitle him to remembrance, even had he not taken to driving quill when he left off wielding cutlass. There are greater figures than his in the stirring times when he played his part among the world's affairs, but there is scarcely one which touched those affairs on so many sides, or was so typical a product of the times. Certainly there is not one that we can now recall who managed to live long enough to fight the Armada at one end of his life and to command a Ship-Money fleet at the other; least of all one so capable of recording his experiences. Not without high lights and purple patches which make it well worth recovering from the semi-oblivion into which it has fallen, his long career has a peculiar value as a type of the successive generations which he adorned. If, then, you would make your way behind Elizabethan scenes and see how that magnificent spectacle was staged; if you would learn somewhat of its actors at first hand, and feel the stir of those days when carrack and galleon still sailed the seas, when Raleigh sought El Dorado and Drake led his handful of adventurers to sack the Treasure House of the World, — go find Sir William, sit down beside the chimney-fire and listen to the old sea-tales which have been the inspiration of two centuries of naval pre-eminence.

In nearly all of its earlier characteristics his life offers the typical features of his generation, and it is none the worse reading for that. It has been long since the boy who runs away to sea played the part in literature which he once played in life. But when as a young Oxford undergraduate Monson exchanged the Balliol quadrangle for the deck of a privateer, neither in literature nor in life was such an escapade so rare as it has since become, for the world was then crowded with great events whose principal theatre was the sea. William the Silent was leading his countrymen in that desperate revolt against the Spanish power which was to become a landmark of liberty. Henry of Navarre was waiting his opportunity amid the Civil Wars which devastated France to make his way to Ivry and the crown. And, more important still in English eyes, every port of Spain and Portugal rang with busy preparation for the mighty enterprise which, with the aid of Parma's army, then gathering in the Netherlands, was to crush England and Holland and so re-establish the ascendancy of Spain and the Vatican, now sadly shrunk beneath the strokes of the reformed communions. Hawkins and Drake and Frobisher, who had dealt some of the shrewdest of those strokes, were then in the heyday of their spectacular careers, and among the crews of those innumerable vessels then pushing out from every English port to spoil the Spaniard there were many who, like this Lincolnshire youth, were fired by the exploits of their famous countrymen to draw a sword for England and her faith and, as Monson observes of himself, "inclined to see the world," and, it might well be, make their fortunes.

To the oncoming generations each new age offers its peculiar opportunity. What the Crusades were to the young knight of the Middle Ages, what the plunder of Mexico and Peru was to the Spaniard of the early sixteenth century, what the camp was to Napoleonic France, and business to nineteenth-century America, privateering was to the Elizabethan. So, in embracing it as a profession, Monson was but an exponent of the spirit of his age when the sea and the court were the open way for the talents of an English youth. But he was not merely a type, he was the type destined to survive by its success. Not many of his fellow adventurers could boast, like him, of having helped bring back from his earliest enterprise the first Spanish prize ever seen in an English port; fewer still were able to congratulate themselves on such rapid rise thereafter. It is not likely that the parental blessing was difficult to secure for one whose professional career had

begun so auspiciously, and it was evident that this, or
some kindred influence, contributed to place the young
adventurer almost at once in command of a ship of his
own.

It must have been that seamen were developed rapidly
in those strenuous days, or that he had some extraordinary influences at work in his behalf. But, even so, when,
at the mature age of eighteen, he voyaged to the Cana-
ries, and, disguised as a Fleming, found his way into and
out of Flores harbor unharmed, he certainly justified
his choice of a career. And when, later, falling in with
a "Biscayner well-manned, sufficiently furnished and
bravely defended," from which his crew were forced by
the height of the seas to ungrapple and leave some of their
number fighting on board the stranger from eight o'clock
in the evening till eight in the morning, when she finally
struck, we must admit he had not chosen his profession ill,
if some unusual quality of adroitness and courage and
leadership and that tenacity which is reckoned a peculiar
quality of naval success be any proof. These, perhaps as
much as family influence, doubtless enabled him a year
after that wild night in the north Atlantic to embark as a
volunteer on the Queen's own pinnace in the eventful
week's fighting which ended at Gravelines and the overthrow of the Armada. With that the first stage of his long
progress came to an end.

This much is certain, that whatever star guided his
early course, thenceforth Monson sailed no longer as a
privateer but as an officer of those successive expeditions
by which Elizabeth, so long as she lived, wreaked vengeance on the power which had threatened her life and
throne, summoned her subjects to renounce her authority, fomented Irish rebellion against her rule, and supported the claims of her rival. In this long counter-
crusade, fleet after fleet put out from English ports to
harry the weakened power of Philip the Second, till that

power was no longer to be reckoned with as formidable, much less dangerous on any sea. Drake, Essex, Cumberland, in turn harassed the Spanish coasts and island ports, cut off convoys and merchantmen, and learned from them the wealth of Indian trade, the secrets of the seaways east and west. Their successors, following the track of Drake and Cavendish about the world, broke through the dangers and the prohibitions of the rich monopoly, and, with the Dutch close in their wake, poured into Europe the riches of the declining Spanish-Portuguese possessions oversea and shifted the colonial and economic balance of the world.

In this exciting, profitable pursuit Monson had his full share. "Dangers and perils by the sword and famine, by danger of the sea and other casualties, as all men are subject to that run such desperate adventures," so he writes, were his in plenteous measure. His escape from shipwreck and starvation, by which, as he tells us, he "received two lives from God"; the daring attempt that he and Captain Lister made to cut out a ship from Flores harbor with a boat's crew, "rather like mad than discreet men," and finally taking it with the help of another boat sent out to rescue them; his capture of the rich carrack, the *St. Valentine*, which crowned his achievements in this field, — such were the incidents which for a dozen years made up the sum of his adventurous life. Full of the thrust of sword and push of pike, attack, repulse, and stratagems and spoils, hair-breadth escapes by land and sea, they were busy years.

It would be too long to tell of his innumerable adventures here; how, once, when Essex was outflanked by a fortified house, Monson, with fifty "old soldiers of the Low Countries," took it with no more danger to himself, he says, "than a musket bullet through his scarf and breeches and the pummel of his sword shot from his side"; of how, again, finding himself at night amid a Spanish fleet he had been sent to spy upon, he held a dagger at the throat of his Spanish servant, compelling him to cry out that there was a strange ship among them; conceiving, as the event proved, that his enemies "having warning from me of it, of all others they could not suspect that I was she." Such was, no doubt, the daily lot of many men of those times as of all other times of wars. And if you wish a good yarn of wild doings on the "wild west coast" you will look far to find one as full of romance as that of the Admiral's suppression of the nest of Irish pirates. Not even his matter-of-fact recital of that stirring exploit quite conceals its flavor of high adventure and ingenious ruse, adroit manœuvres and dramatic end.

Yet to the man of peace to whom there comes across the centuries the echo of these long-dead rivalries, the exploits and the stratagems of old conflicts, they retain a charm not of phrase alone, they wake something of the spirit which made them possible.

> All this how far away!
> Mere delectation meet for a minute's dream! —
> Just as a drudging student trims his lamp,
> Opens his Plutarch, puts him in the place
> Of Roman, Grecian; draws the patched gown close,
> Dreams, "Thus should I fight, save or rule the world!" —
> Then smilingly, contentedly, awakes
> To the old solitary nothingness.

The more so, perhaps, in that he knows the peace that no such man as Monson ever knew. For Monson's career in those eventful days and in the darker years to come was not merely of naval interest. Scarcely was he embarked upon his second voyage when he was captured, and from his experiences as a Spanish prisoner and galley-slave brought back, among other things, some of his choicest tales, with which, to the end of his days, he was accustomed to amuse his family and his friends. That they were worth the hearing, the story of "Seignior Fernan-

dez " bears witness, if we had no other specimen. In
Monson's brief chronicle of his fellow prisoner, the unfortunate agent of the dispossessed Pedro of Portugal, whom
Englishmen once dreamed of making king again, there
lives the flavor of a real romance. From this source, too,
he drew much of that inexhaustible store of miscellaneous
information which served him and his country well
through many years. And if Sir William had only told us
how he himself was freed from his imprisonment, he
would have added to our entertainment and, perhaps to
his advantage and our own, have cleared his own memory
of the aspersion which some later biographers have cast
upon it.

But this Elizabethan, like so many of his kind, was an
amphibious creature; and, in the intervals of voyaging
against the Spaniard, he found time and opportunity to
embark on a career no less adventurous and scarcely less
hazardous than following the sea, for he became a courtier. Whatever moving accidents he had in that great
enterprise he has not told, and we shall probably never
know; but by them he gained more than by his exploits
in seamanship, which made so fine a background for one
who risked his fate at the brilliant and treacherous court
of the Virgin Queen. First attaching himself to the train
of the ill-fated Essex, he drew from this connection knight-
hood and the captaincy of a second-rate. When that
nobleman's folly and misfortune drove him towards disgrace and death, Monson, like the prudent seaman that
he was, perceived the coming storm in time and, as the
wind shifted in the royal skies, shortened sail, tacked fairly
about, and caught the favoring breeze which bore the
house of Howard to eminence; and so gained the consideration due to a safe, shrewd, and useful man. Thus commending himself to his superiors in that capacity, his un-
alterable devotion to the Queen, which he in common
with most of his fellows professed — and possibly felt —

did not prevent him, like his superiors, from mourning her death and welcoming her successor with the same loyal breath. This, no less than his conspicuous service and his well-known quality of attachment to the crown, brought him the post of Admiral of the Narrow Seas on James the First's accession, and so conducted him unwittingly to the climax and crisis of his whole career.

As the commander of the Channel Fleet for nearly a dozen years he was, as he had been before in his capacity of privateer and courtier, close to the heart of great events. In the Channel lay the center of the conflict between Spain and the Dutch which embraced the fortunes of two continents. There France, under her new king, Henry of Navarre, began to launch the first vessels of a fleet which was presently to cause England no small concern and to affect her politics in as yet unsuspected ways. There the Dunkirkers, half merchants and more than half pirates, pursued their devious ways to the exasperation of the sea-going world at large. It was a post which required more than mere vigilance; at times it became the turning-point of momentous affairs. And it was here that the Admiral was enabled to perform his crowning service to his royal master, and touch the most romantic episode of his time. For his prompt action prevented the escape to France and the marriage to her cousin of that unfortunate Stuart princess, "sweet Arabella, child of woe," which would have given the pair a claim to the English crown challenging that of James himself. This would have seemed to provide the fortunate Admiral a claim on the gratitude of his sovereign which would have outweighed any future indiscretion, however serious, and ensured his promotion to the highest post in his profession.

But that was not the nature of James, the design of fortune, nor the fate of Monson; for, with his foot almost on the last round that led to safe and eminent success, he fell. From Digby, the English ambassador to Spain, came the fatal proof of the fact that, during almost the whole term of his service as admiral, Monson had been in receipt of a Spanish pension. It was of no avail to urge that most of his fellows and superiors were open to the same charge. It was of even less use to plead past service to a man like James. Least of all could any man hope for mercy where there were so many aspirants for place; and Monson was summarily dismissed. Troubles never come singly. Scarcely was he out of office when he was accused of complicity in the most famous scandal of his day, the poisoning of Sir Thomas Overbury by the Earl of Rochester and his mistress, the Lady Frances Howard, whom the Earl designed to marry, once her divorce, in whose way Sir Thomas stood, had been secured. There was little against Monson save his attachment to the house of Howard, but he and his brother were, none the less, sent to the Tower, whence they were released some months later for lack of evidence.

Cleared of this charge, the Monsons were drawn into an intrigue by which the enemies of the Duke of Buckingham sought to replace that favorite in the royal affections with Sir William's son. But James had all the blind and obstinate attachment to unworthiness which sometimes forms the strongest characteristic of weakness. Not all the daily washing of his face in curds to improve his naturally beautiful complexion; not all the splendid costumes with which his backers adorned his pleasing person; nor ostentatious taking of the Anglican sacrament to escape the charge of Catholic tendencies; least of all his being thrust perpetually on the royal attention, availed to bring young Monson into favor. The youth, doubtless to his great relief, was commanded to desist from his attentions to the monarch. His father was virtually notified to leave the court; and the unworthy though characteristic intrigue ended disastrously for all parties concerned. Broken in spirit by successive misfortunes crowding so

thickly upon him, the Admiral withdrew to the little estate of Kinnersley, which he had managed to acquire in
the course of his long public career, there to meditate the
vicissitudes of fortune and the composition of a book.

Thereafter he lived long, but only once was he summoned from his retirement to serve his country. When,
in that long era of personal government which followed
their break with Parliament, Charles I and his advisers,
much disturbed by the threats of the triumphant Dutch,
and the increasing French sea-power fostered by Richelieu, resorted to the ill-fated policy of Ship-Money to
raise a fleet, Monson, conscious of its necessity and not
sensitive to the constitutional issue involved, supported
them with zeal. As his reward he became vice-admiral
of the Ship-Money fleet for a brief period, and in that
post found some solace for his long neglect. Thenceforth
his few declining years were spent upon those literary
labors which had always claimed his attention, and
which, when his professional career was ended, had become his chief activity. But that career was not to close
without one last look at the great events of life; for, in the
very months that he lay on what was to be his death-bed,
the forces of Parliament and King gathered to the final
test of supremacy, and scarcely was he in his grave when
the English Civil Wars had formally begun. Thus in
neglect, if not in disgrace, ended the dreams of his once
greatly promising career.

But his book was done; and, despite the ill-fortune of
his life, that, it might have been supposed, would have
secured for him at least the brief moment of fame denied
him while alive. The hard-won wisdom gained from long
command, wide knowledge of naval affairs of his own
and other lands, an infinity of "stratagems," involving
almost every conceivable possibility of attack and defense
of England's coasts, from the hand of an acknowledged
master of sea-strategy, would, he might well have im-

agined, have found an eager welcome from his countrymen, even had his writings not been enlivened with
reminiscence and anecdote, wise saws and modern instances, to say nothing of pen portraits and estimates of
his great contemporaries at first hand. With these rich
fruits of a hard and not wholly inglorious life, despite its
final failure, he might well have thought to recoup by his
pen the fortunes which his wit and sword had failed to
maintain, and gain from competition with the centuries
the recognition he had not been able to wrest from his
own generation.

Yet never was fortune more fickle in death as in life to
any man than to Sir William Monson. If he dreamed
this — as undoubtedly he did — his shade, had it been
able to observe the earliest results of his endeavor in the
field of literature, must have suffered a cruel disappoint-
ment. First he lingered over the completion of his book
till publication in his lifetime was impossible, and so he
remained almost if not quite unknown to the men of his
time as an author. Before he had become accustomed to
his grave the Civil War had broken out; and, among the
thirty thousand pamphlets which its vociferous course
produced, not even family, much less public or publishing
interest, opened the way to print.

Besides this, one even more potent and extraordinary
influence balked him in death as in life of realizing his
ambitions. Under the usual conditions of literature the
fact that one's manuscript finds no publisher argues some
defect of quality, or pocket-book, or popular taste; but Sir
William's case was so exactly the opposite of this that it
finds scarcely a parallel in literary history. Strangely
enough, it was because his manuscript was reckoned so
valuable that it failed of publication for so many years.

What this value was, an incident may illustrate. A
quarter of a century after his death, a certain rising expert
in Admiralty affairs, one Samuel Pepys, Clerk of the Acts

and on his way to the Secretaryship, called in one day to see the Duke of York, then Lord High Admiral, about some matters connected with the naval reorganization which the disasters of late war with the Dutch had made imperative. Thus he records his experience: "Beginning to talk in general of the excellency of old constitutions," so he writes, the Duke "did bring out of his cabinet, and made me read it, an extract out of a book of my late Lord Northumberland's so prophetic of the business of Chatham as is almost miraculous. I did desire," he goes on to say, "and he did give it me to copy out, which pleased me mightily." With this began Sir William's revenge on his own generation and on posterity, for this was the famous passage in his *Book of Stratagems* concerning the probable course of a Dutch attack, should one take place. Had the Dutch seen it, as it has been surmised that they or someone in their interest had done, they could not have followed its details more closely than when, two years before Pepys wrote, their fleet, passing up the Medway and the Thames to sink the helpless English men-of-war laid up at anchorage, had, for the first time and the last, affrighted London with the sound of hostile guns.

Sir William's carefully considered "stratagems" were, in fact, far too inflammable material to risk in print. They had the same value as those plans so carefully guarded in every modern war and navy office to meet the quick emergency of sudden hostilities; and so they were laid away in royal or naval cabinets or passed from hand to hand, as too useful to an enemy to be published broadcast. Not till the beginning of the eighteenth century, when Spain was no longer to be feared, when the Glorious Revolution of 1688 had set Dutch William on the English throne, and all danger from the other English foe of Monson's time had been removed, did his *Tracts* see the light in any complete form. Before that, indeed, the more innocuous part, the so-called *Early Voyages*, had been in print; but not until two hundred years were past and the old Admiral's naval writings had become a curiosity, was he to obtain the full reward of his long literary labors. Only now, at the hands of his profession, are those writings receiving final fitting form, and the recognition which he sought so earnestly.

Here, then, you have his life and works; — what, then, of his character and his place in history? The answer is not wholly obvious. Everything about him and his long career presages romance, yet that is a word one scarcely associates with Sir William and his kind. In the ordinary course of human affairs we should expect that from such an eventful and adventurous life would have emerged a bluff and hearty sea-captain, redolent of forecastle and quarter-deck; a courtier versed in the devious ways which lead to worldly eminence; a volume full of wild tales of hair-breadth escapes, fierce encounters, daring adventures, romantic episodes. In some degree this is the fact. Whole sections of his book are made of such material, the pages are thick with sea-spray and powder smoke. And yet as one reads on and on, and, if his time and patience endure, still on and on, this is not the whole of the impression that he gets, nor, indeed, the greater part of it.

"A talent," says Goethe, "is formed in quiet, a character in the stream of the world," and perhaps to most of us the character and the stream seem far the stronger, if not the finer, of the two. Yet the inference is not wholly sound nor the dictum wholly true. Eminent characters have been formed in the stillness no less than in the noisy places of the world; and there are all sorts of characters! Surely if ever they were formed in the worldly stream it was in the days of Elizabeth. But run through the public men reared then to play their part under her successor, — Cecil and Nottingham, Coke, Bacon, Somerset, — almost alone the old soldier, Suffolk, was not touched with that defect of morality based on the text over which the divines then busily engaged in translating the Scriptures must have lingered long, "The love of money is the root of all evil." The great Elizabethan period, with all its splendor of achievement, its professed chivalry, its gorgeous settings, its picturesque figures, its able men, was preeminently an age when the qualities of the ape and the tiger were the touchstone of success. Behind the mask of courtly usages too often lurked sycophancy and intrigue, with their attendant vices of envy, jealousy, and treachery; beneath the gallantry of exploits by sea lay the unpleasant fact that English privateer and Moorish pirate were often not far apart in their methods of acquiring wealth. Never was there a time, not even our own, when wealth at any cost was more passionately sought, when place and power and riches more effectually concealed the loose morality which gave them birth.

It is, then, no peculiar weakness of Monson's character, as some have assumed, that his pages, like his life, contain some of these elements. Periods, like men, have the defects of their qualities. The England of Elizabeth and James was no less frankly money-mad than great sections of society to-day. Monson was a child of his age; and in nothing more than in that which led to his downfall. Of all the accusations against him the most damning is that as commander of the Channel Fleet he took a Spanish pension; in the opinion of many it admits of no defense. A statesman or officer to-day, convicted of such an act, would, it is true, be irretrievably disgraced; and it is, doubtless, no excuse for Monson to say that England was not then at war with Spain, and so no treachery in the ordinary sense could be alleged. It is more to the point to note that in his day even ministers were subject to like influence; that judges — Bacon himself — were guilty of similar practices; and that the custom was so notorious that Sully wrote that "every considerable personage about the English court was in receipt of a French pension." Pensions from foreign powers were, in fact, proofs of one's importance in the world.

Standards, like temptations, alter from age to age. We cannot foretell how public men of to-day may be judged by the generation of 2100 A.D. Yet we may well conceive that if the public conscience maintains its present rate of development, by that time — if not much sooner — a senator of the United States interested in a public service corporation; an English cabinet-minister owning shares in property whose value might be enormously increased through territorial annexation or government adoption of mechanical devices; or a Continental official involved in furnishing information to the manufacturers of war supplies, to take no further and no more definite instances, may well be looked upon in the same light by which the virtuous present regards Sir William Monson's Spanish pension. Something of this changing public sentiment we have already seen; and we may, therefore, be the better judges of the later years of Elizabeth and the reign of James the First, in comparison with our own experience. For they form, like our own time, the climax of a long period of injustice and fraud, of corruption in high places, and an era of change with the awakening of a new public conscience. It happens when such a development culminates and the pendulum begins its backward swing, that many suffer who have but done what their fellows had done according to the custom of their predecessors. This, if there is any excuse, must be Sir William Monson's, and surely in this generation, if anywhere, he should find sympathizers.

Yet, whatever the old Admiral's defects of character as developed in the stream of the world which was his environment; whatever his misfortunes as a scapegoat; or his vices and weakness as judged by the immutable standards of absolute right and wrong; despite his evil reputation, which lived after him so long, and which his biographers

of the past generation and our own have again revived;
whatever the lack of relation between the idealized portrait of himself which he drew in his book and the more
unsavory facts of his career, — if they are really true, —
with these we are far less concerned than with the good
which was not buried with his bones. As "the first English seaman who has left on record not only an account of
the events in which he took part but a critical examination of the seamen of his own time and of those who preceded and followed him," surely for this we may be to his
faults a little blind. Few, even among naval men, can
pretend to passing interest in six volumes of naval tracts,
and a confirmed Elizabethan may be pardoned for hesi-
tating to engage so formidable an adversary. Yet, despite
forbidding title and bulk, if you find time to listen to the
tale, however long, of a sometime colleague of Drake, the
quaint narrative of moving accident by flood and field,
the shrewd reflections on life and the world generally as it
was made manifest to an Elizabethan-Jacobean sea-captain and courtier, you will find your reward.

It is no easy task, and it has not been made the easier
by Sir William's editors. The very title is discouraging:
*A Treatise of Sea Causes: A Yearly Observation of the English
and Spanish Fleets that were set forth* —[observe the admirable restraint!] — *one to annoy the other. By W. M. who hath
done it to better his experience.* This is not promising. Worse
is to come. The solemn purist who, two centuries ago, in
the most formal period of English literature, composed
the preface to the first edition, did one good thing — unlike the later editor, he made his preface short. Otherwise — again unlike the latest editor — he did his best to
damn the book. "Some nice persons," he begins engag-
ingly, "will perhaps at the first reading of this work find
fault with the language and wonder that Sir William, who
was a gentleman by birth, and so great a man as an Admiral," could write so badly. No one, least of all his in-

troducer, can vindicate the language. "But it must be remembered," he goes on to say, that the author, "though born a gentleman, spent most of his time at sea, a very unfit school for a man to improve his language"; and besides, he adds in a triumph of fatuous complacency, "we must not expect that the days of Queen Elizabeth could form a man to the language of our time." "Not so pleasing in style as some might desire," he continues in a desperate endeavor to save the rash reader from an untimely fate, "full of oversights, mistakes, or, to speak plainly, falsehoods. . . . What I have said is not to apologize for the work or to prepossess the reader, but only to prevent his being too hasty in condemning." In that laudable object he fails by anticipation, for surely never was any book so badly introduced. He may have rewritten much, as we are told he did, but Sir William's eighteenth-century editor never let his admiration for the original run away with him.

Escaping the delights of the introduction we are confronted by another barrier, the first of six dedications to the successive parts into which the work is divided. The mere list of them throws much light on the author's character. First he writes to his eldest son; then to such "Gentlemen and Commanders as were Actors in the wars with Spain in the days of Queen Elizabeth"; then an "Epistle to all Captains of Ships, Masters, Pilots, Mariners and Common Sailors"; then simply to "the Reader"; then to "the Projectors of this Age"; and, finally, to "the King's Excellent Majesty." Here lay his heart — his son, his service, his fellow adventurers, small and great, his sovereign, and those who read his book. His seems a simple creed. Yet that he was far from as simple a seaman as these titles indicate, one soon perceives if he reads but a little way into these entertaining prefaces.

Take the first, — it might well have been written by Polonius. To his heir he commends three things, "that

after so many pains and perils God has sent life to your
father to further your education; by the second you may
value his recompenses and rewards with his deservings;
that by the third you shall have just cause to abandon
the thoughts of such dangerous and uncertain courses."
Thus, in his advancing years, speaks the man who, from
about the age of the son whom he now addressed, followed the most hazardous of all professions for a full third
of a century and gave it up from compulsion, not from
choice.   Surely the generations do not greatly change
parental admonition to shun the course one has one's self
pursued.

Still less do they alter the advice one gives and gets, and
the ensuing warnings, however tinctured with his own
spirit and that of his times, are not merely a comment on
Sir William's character, they are the principles of life as
old as society itself. Love soldiers for your father's and
your country's sake, he says, but for yourself, shun arms,
since even "a wretched lawyer" has more profit than a
soldier. Above all, shun quarrels, "of two evils it were
better to keep company with a coward than a quarreler;
the one is commonly friendly and sociable, the other dangerous in his acquaintance." Shun drinking and drunk-
ards, swearing and women, take exercises of mind and
body, the latter not merely to "increase health and
agility, make a man sociable, . . . draw acquaintance,
. . . bring a man into favor with a prince and prove a
preferment to one's marriage," but because they are
peculiarly useful "in running and escaping an enemy."
Tobacco, he condemns unmercifully, since "it dries the
brain and many become fools with the continual use of
it," and there, if nowhere else, does he join hands with
James. Shun curious and costly clothing, he goes on to
say; shun too much solitude and too much court; be
choice of company but friendly to all. Shun idleness; and
if you marry "choose a wife as near you in calling, years

and condition" as possible, "for the greatest fortune a
man can expect is in his marriage" — which last observation, in any view, is a profound remark. Finally, "if
God be pleased to give you children, let them make you to
abandon the delights and pleasures of the world in respect
to the comfort and joy you receive by them. Make account then that summer is past and that the melancholy
winter approaches, for a careful and provident father cannot take delight in the world and provide for his children" — whatever the old Admiral's discreet silence concerning mothers may portend.

There, in a way, you have him, cautious, prudent, with
knowledge of the pitfalls of the world, a careful father and
a wise and not unlikable man, with more of kindness than
you might otherwise suspect. So, too, he later advises his
second son in the same strain, especially commending to
him patience and temperance. And, amid wise advice
from ancient instances, to the gentlemen adventurers, he
bids them, though "time and ingratitude are the de-
stroyers of all noble and memorable acts, and have
caused you to be forgot, though it be scandal to a commonwealth where princes make more of favourites than
of well-deservers, it behooves you not to approve or
repine at it but to hope that act of his will not stand as a
precedent." It is as well, perhaps, that James the Pusil-
lanimous, at whom this not obliquely hints, was safely
dead before this came to print. Finally, to the men of his
own kind he rises almost to eloquence. "What," he in-
quires," would it avail that all boughs of trees were oaks,
or every stalk of hemp a cable, or every creature a perfect
artist, to frame and build a ship . . . were it not for you?
She were like a sumptuous costly palace, nobly furnished,
nobody to inhabit it. How should we know France, Italy
and Spain produced wine out of the grape . . . the Indies
and the wealth therein . . . but for your skill and labour?
. . . What subjects make their king and country more

happy than you . . . what honour have your adventures and your valour brought to England above all other nations!" There speaks the Admiral.

And to the reader, having commended his book first to his friends, then to his fellow adventurers and mariners generally, now he "prohibits none but the perverse Puritans, whose stomachs are so faint and feeble that any praise that can be attributed to a Spaniard or a Papist will make them sea-sick," from reading what he has written. So much for the stout Anglican, suspected of Catholicism — and so much, too, for a generous enemy. One thing he disliked more than a Puritan. "If I could think of a more proper word than *Project* to entitle this ensuing book," he writes by way of preface to the fifth collection, "I would do it; for the names of projects and the inventors of them are grown so hateful and contemptible that all honest men abhor and detest them. There are no burthens which the sharpness of lewd brains can invent to vex the commonwealth with but they style by the name of projects, when indeed the name of *Promoter* were more proper. . . . Such men are a curse to the country that breeds them, to their friends and parents that nourished them, and to God himself that created them. . . . They pretend evil under the colour of good, set a fair countenance on a foul face, smile on those whose throats they would cut." It was, indeed, an age much like our own.

There you have him on many sides, most of them personal. But every man touches the universal at some point, and in proportion to the degree of that contact he becomes of interest to the rest of us. Nor is Sir William an exception to the rule. First, and indeed last, and most of the intervening time, he is the naval expert. Courtier, adventurer, seaman, politician, admiral, every page reflects above all the professional commander and strategist. This, you may imagine, is the precise quality which is likely to repel the general reader, and to confine the appreciation of his book to men of like profession with himself. Yet in this resides, after all, the universal element, for in the contrast between the amateur and the professional spirit which he here reveals there lies the old eternal conflict between the real and the ideal in its acutest form. For the "patriotism of the soldier," so writes a modern Englishman of no less zeal for his country and his service than Sir William Monson, "is hardly the patriotism of the citizen; no deep longing to die for his country; no nonsense about great issues. Rather it is a purely technical interest. The soldier is not concerned with defending the sacred cause of freedom against its oppressors. The psychology of the situation is a fierce desire to outshine the enemy in technical skill. . . . Equal or superior skill on the part of his opponents provokes his admiration rather than an increased hatred for the enemies of his country. . . . The patriotism of the soldier, is, in a word, just the sheer joy of the craftsman."

To the amateur alone is it given to look on his achievements in the light of romance; the professional demands not merely brilliant and heroic endeavor but results. To him heroism is all in the day's work; brilliance, enthusiasm, and their kind are but elements in the imperative success. For him the emotional value and appeal which mould popular opinion have little charm; with him romance no place. And this is true in every line of human activity forming the indissoluble bond of brotherhood between all men who really achieve.

To such the dry savor of Sir William must inevitably appeal. Take one instance of many in his book. Who has not read in prose or verse the fight of the *Revenge*; how Sir Richard Grenville with his single ship fought a whole Spanish squadron, till of his entire crew scarce more than half were left alive, and with his powder gone, six feet of water in his vessel's hold, himself wounded to the death, he begged his master gunner to blow up the ship! From Raleigh to Tennyson the tale has thrilled the centuries, like that of the Spartans at Thermopylæ, the Song of Roland, the charge of the Light Brigade at Balaclava.

Now hear Sir William! " Upon view of the Spaniards," he begins, "Sir Thomas [Howard], like a wary and discreet general, weighed anchor and made signs to the rest of his fleet to do the like. . . . But Sir Richard Grenville, . . . imagining this fleet to come from the Indies and not to be the Armada of which they were informed, would by no means be persuaded by his master or company . . . to follow his Admiral, as all discipline of war did teach him. . . . But the old saying that a wilful man never wanteth woe could not be more truly verified than in him. For when the Spanish ships approached nigh unto him and he beheld the greatness of them he . . . would gladly have acquitted himself of them. Which then to the best of his power he endeavored, but too late, for he was left a prey to the enemy."

And so ended Sir Richard Grenville, after a desperate resistance against, not the fifty-three of Tennyson's poem, but what was perhaps equally hopeless if not so spectacular, fifteen of the enemy's fleet. So, too, he made a gallant end — " at the expense of his men and the needless loss of a ship." Always the professional comment is the same. "Ah, yes," observed the great strategist of Thermopylæ, " the Spartans paid the penalty for their inexcusable carelessness in neglecting to secure their flank." " It is magnificent, but it is not war," declared the French commander, as he watched the Light Brigade ride into the jaws of death at Balaclava. We do not know Charlemagne's comment on the captain of his rearguard who allowed himself to be cut off from the main body at Roncevaux, but, expressed in forcible Frankish, it was doubtless to the same effect.

With all their valor the heroes of literature are far from

being the heroes of real war. It is glorious to die for one's country, but it is no less glorious, and far more to the point, to destroy the enemy and save your own men as much as possible. The stubborn courage of the fighting human animal caught in a trap is almost as common as the spirit of martyrdom. Compared with the weakness of those willing to exchange honor or faith for life, it cannot, perhaps, be too highly praised. But when it is set beside the temper which joins to emotion the intelligence that leads to ultimate success it seems unconvincing. When folly is redeemed with life it becomes, indeed, heroic, in the usual meaning of the word. But only when courage is joined to intellect does it reach the level of true greatness, even though literature does so often find its heroes on the lower levels. Such is the lesson that Monson and his kind are set to preach to a too heedless world.

And, lest you may think that the old Admiral with his caution was a coward at bottom, take a not dissimilar adventure of his own. The Earl of Essex, having intelligence of a hostile fleet, detached Monson to reconnoiter with one ship. "About twelve o'clock in the night," so runs his story, "I fell in with . . . twenty-five sail; whereupon I put myself into my boat . . . resolved to discover what they were . . . hailed them in Spanish . . . and knew them to be the Indies fleet; and having as much as I desired . . . performed so much as I was commanded, in shooting of my ordnance and making false fires; all the hurt that happened to me . . . beside the hazzard of shot from the castles and the fleet, my ship being shot through fifteen times, was foul words and railing language." And so, with the necessary information, he rejoined his admiral — and failed of Grenville's immortality.

From which, and an infinity of incident beside, it is apparent that Sir William's chief concern was not personal glory but "intelligence" in every meaning of the word. To him, as to his kind generally, whatever their profession, there are three unpardonable sins, cowardice, stupidity, and insubordination. From him one gets, in consequence, what is so useful a corrective to the legendary history of his age, the reduction of heroic deeds and characters to their proper size and their relation to the real circumstances of their time. To him the struggle of England against Spain was no war of pygmies and giants, where success was given to the incredible heroism of the weaker power. The Spaniards, for the most part, were, he says quite frankly and truthfully, overmatched in ships, ordnance, seamanship, crews and commanders, as every naval expert and most historians are now fully aware. From the day when, with the loss of not a single ship and scarcely sixty men, the English destroyed the Invincible Armada, to the time when, two generations later, Spain's efforts on both sides of the world to crush the Dutch sea-power brought her to ruin, England had every advantage over her unwieldy rival save the one to which mistaken popular opinion attributes her success, that of physical courage. And, as Sir William recognizes, it is poor praise to one's own prowess to enlarge upon the cowardice of one's enemy — a lesson which should be well digested by too strenuous partisans at all times.

Yet he was not, on the other hand, a mere iconoclast, nor did he lack a proper sense of true greatness, when it came his way. He only demanded, as we ought all to demand, that it should not be the false glitter of the charlatan by whom the multitude is most commonly deceived. Read but his estimate of Drake. "There is no man so perfect," he begins, "but is fit to be amended, nor none so evil but he has something in him to be praised. And, comparing the imperfections of Sir Francis Drake with his perfections, the world, not I, shall truly judge of his merits. His detractors allege to his blemish and imputation the baseness of his birth and education, his ostentation and vain-glorious boasting; his high, haughty, and insolent carriage; and except against his friends' and favourites' answer in his behalf that the meanness of his birth was an argument of his worth; for what he attained to was by no other means than merit. They say that every man is son to his works, and what one has by his ancestors can scarcely be called his own; that virtue is the cause of preferment, and honour but the effect. . . . In excuse of his ostentation and vain-glory they say it was not incident to him alone but to most men of his profession and rank. It is true that he could speak much and arrogantly, but eloquently, which bred a wonder that his education could yield him those helps of nature. . . . And though vain-glory is a vice not to be excused, yet he obtained that fame by his actions, that facility in speaking, and that wisdom by his experience, that I can but say no more but that we are all children of Adam. . . . A General ought to be stern towards his soldiers, courageous in heart, valiant in fight, generous in giving, patient in suffering, and merciful in pardoning. And if Sir Francis Drake was to be praised for most of these virtues, let him not be blamed or condemned for one only vice. . . . No man had truer trial of the inconstancy of fortune than he. For the nature of fortune is to bite when she flatters, and to strike when she is angry . . . and fortune did much for him, but at his death she was angry."

Surely, he who so unsparingly condemned the Grenvilles of his time was at least capable of appreciating what he conceived to be true greatness. He was, indeed, no hero-worshiper; but who can doubt, if he had had a hero, who that hero would have been? And where, in the light of this and other passages of the kind, now *lies* the editor who said that Sir William could not write? For it is difficult to believe that, with all his talents as an editor, any man of letters in the Age of Anne could ever catch that great Elizabethan strain which echoes through these lines.

Not that, even so, is he, or like to be, a famous man. "Reputation," we are told, "rests upon long accumulation of character and service, fame springs out of the deed of the moment," — with a reporter at hand to immortalize it; and, in default of such, he must remain a man of reputation rather than of fame. Nor is that reputation so great as he desired; perhaps not so great as it is like to be. The men of his own service have re-discovered him; perhaps the men of letters may follow in their train. Even in an age when publishers — possibly too credulous — proclaim almost from day to day new masterpieces to a certainly too credulous public; and when old literary monuments are apt to suffer the fate of all monuments, a hasty glance from hurrying travelers; even in such an age, though it be our own, six stout volumes concealed in the publications of a learned society may not prevent some courageous souls from giving Sir William his chance to escape oblivion.

And more; once the rose glow of romance is somewhat withdrawn, and the clear light of truth is allowed to play upon the spacious days of great Elizabeth, we may be able to perceive that Monson is no unfit representative of his times. He was, indeed, no Sidney; he was far from reaching the heights of Drake; and, whatever we may think of James, his predecessor's reign still seems to most of us both splendid and heroic, while Sir William's character does not greatly commend itself in either quality. He has appealed as little to one editor's sense of greatness as to the other's sense of style — and to whom shall one be a hero if not to his editor? Yet this may not be wholly due to his defects compared with the perfections of his time. He may not touch its highest peaks, yet he is far from sinking to its lowest levels. He was by no means the wisest, brightest, meanest of his age, yet all the more its typical product. Like man, like book. No Shakespeare or Bacon, scarcely a Raleigh, his too fluent pen has drawn for us his portrait with his times. His faults are blazoned large by both his editors, yet there is little reason for their often expressed fear of his attempt to deceive posterity as to what sort of man and book we have. No one who reads him largely can possibly be misled. For in his pages, all unconsciously he is what everyone must recognize, — seaman-courtier-author, strange compound of greatness and littleness, cautious, brave, crafty, secretive, voluble, worldly-wise and simple, ambitious, greedy of wealth and power, still greedier of honors and of fame, proud, loyal, prejudiced, stubborn, subservient, — a true Elizabethan Englishman.

COLONEL THOMAS BLOOD:
CROWN–STEALER

COL: BLOOD.

COLONEL THOMAS BLOOD
CROWN–STEALER

THE great event of the winter of 1670–1671 in English politics and society was a circumstance unprecedented in European affairs, the visit of the head of the House of Orange to the English Court. The young Prince William, soon to become the ruler of Holland, and later King of England, made this, his first visit to the nation which one day he was to rule, ostensibly to pay his respects to his uncle Charles, who was then King, and his uncle James, who was Duke of York. Besides this, his journey was officially declared to have no other purpose than pleasure and the transaction of some private business. What affairs of state were then secretly discussed by this precocious statesman of nineteen and his British Majesty's ministers of the Cabal, we have no need to enquire here, nor would our enquiries produce much result were they made. The web of political intrigue then first set on the roaring loom of time which was to plunge all England into agitation and revolution and unrest, and all western Europe into war, has, for the moment, little to do with this story. There was enough in the external aspects of his visit to fill public attention then and to serve our purpose now. The five months of his stay were one long round of gayety. Balls, receptions, and dinners, horse races, cocking mains, gam-

ing and drinking bouts followed each other in royal pro-
fusion. And a marriage already projected between the
Prince and his cousin, the Princess Mary, gave a touch
of romance to the affair, only qualified by the fact that
she still played at dolls in the nursery.

The Court was not alone in its efforts to entertain the
young prince. The ministers, the leaders of the opposition, and many private individuals besides, lent their
energies to this laudable end. The work was taken up
by certain public or semi-public bodies. In particular,
the corporation of the great city of London felt that
among these festivities it must not be outdone in paying
some attention to the most distinguished citizen of the
neighboring republic, who, as it happened, was also the
most promising Protestant candidate for the English
throne. Accordingly, on the afternoon of Tuesday, December 6, 1670, as the custom then was, they tendered
him a banquet at Guildhall, where were assembled the
wealth and beauty of the city to do him honor.

The great function, apart from a subtle political significance which might have been noted by a careful and
well-informed observer, was not unlike others of that
long series of splendid hospitalities by which the greatest
city in the world has been accustomed for centuries to
welcome its distinguished guests. There was the same
splendor of civic display, the same wealth of courses, the
same excellent old wine, doubtless the same excellent
old speeches. And in spite of the greatness of the event
and the position and importance of the guest of honor,
the glories of this noble feast, like those of so many of
its fellows, might well have passed into that oblivion
which enfolds dead dinner parties had it not been that
before the evening was over it had become the occasion
of one of the most daring and sensational adventures in
the annals of crime, the famous attempt on the Duke of
Ormond.

This extraordinary exploit, remarkable in itself for
its audacity and the mystery which surrounded it, was
made doubly so by the eminence and character of its
victim. James Butler, famous then and since as "the
great Duke of Ormond," bearer of a score of titles, member of the Council, sometime Lord Lieutenant of Ireland, and still Lord High Steward of England, was by
birth and ability one of the greatest, wealthiest, and most
powerful men in the three kingdoms. He was, moreover,
scarcely less distinguished for his noble character than
for his high rank. Neither these nor the circumstances
of his career in public life gave any apparent ground for
belief that he was in danger of personal violence. During
the Civil Wars he had followed the fortunes of King
Charles the father with courage and fidelity. When the
royal cause was lost he followed Charles the son into
exile. When monarchy was restored he regained his
ancient estates and dignities; he was made the virtual
ruler of Ireland and with his two friends, the Chancellor,
Clarendon, and the Treasurer, Southampton, completed
a triumvirate which dominated English affairs during
the first half dozen years of the Restoration. When our
story opens, Southampton was dead, Clarendon in exile.
But Ormond, last of the staunch Protestants and stately
Cavaliers of the old régime, remained conspicuous in a
corrupt court for his ability and his virtues. By reason
of these, as well as his office, he had been chosen on this
occasion to accompany the Prince of Orange to the city
feast. And by reason of his years he had, before the con-
cluding revels of the younger men, left the banquet to
return home and so found his way into a most surprising
adventure and this story.

At the time of which we write, he lived in a mansion
opposite St. James' palace, built by his friend, the Chancellor, and still known as Clarendon House. His establishment, like that of most men of rank in those days,

was on a scale almost feudal. It included some scores of servants, companions, and dependents of the family. A porter sat at the gate, day and night, and when the Duke went abroad in his chariot he was attended by six footmen, a coachman, and a runner. It would have seemed that in the three kingdoms there was scarce a man who, by virtue of his position, character, and surroundings, was less likely to be exposed to violence than he. What enemies he might have made in his administration of Ireland, if such there were, could at best be men of little importance, living, besides, in a land then as distant from London as the United States is to-day. They would, presumably, not be well informed of his movements, least of all of his social engagements, and they would be helpless in. the midst of London, against the power at his command. What rivals he had in England, it might be premised from their station, would be far above the practice of personal assault as a means of political triumph. Certainly nothing could have been farther from his thoughts or those of his family than that any danger beyond a possible attack of indigestion could threaten him in connection with a Guildhall dinner. As the early winter evening came on, therefore, the porter dozed at the gate, the family and servants retired early, according to the better customs of a ruder age, and the quiet of a house at peace with itself and the world settled down on the little community within its walls.

It was of short duration. When the lumbering seventeenth-century chariot was heard making its way up the street on its return about eight o'clock, the porter roused from his nap and came out to unbar the gates for the home-coming Duke. But to his dismay there was no Duke, and neither footmen nor runner, only an empty coach and a frightened coachman, crying that they had been set upon by seven or eight men in St. James Street, almost in sight of the house, that the footmen, lagging behind on the hill, had been overpowered or put to flight, that the Duke had been dragged out of the chariot and carried off down Piccadilly way, and that he was, perhaps, already killed. The porter was a man of courage and decision. He gave the alarm and, with a certain James Clark, one of the Duke's household, who happened to be passing through the courtyard when the coach came in, hastened off in the direction indicated. They found no one at the place where the attack had been made, but, hurrying on past Devonshire House, they came upon two men struggling in the mud of the Knightsbridge road. As they approached, one of the combatants, a man of huge stature, struggled to his feet. He was immediately joined by another, who appeared from the shadows, and both fired their pistols at the prostrate figure. Then, without waiting to see the result, the ruffians mounted their horses, which had meanwhile been held by a third man, and rode off.

The rescuers, joined by many persons whom their alarm had brought together, hurried to the man in the road. He was too far spent for words and in the darkness was unrecognizable from dirt and wounds. It was only by feeling the great star of the Order of the Garter on his breast that they identified him as the Duke. He was carried home and though much shaken by his adventure was found but slightly injured and after some days he fully recovered. His account of the night's happenings added a curious detail to the history of the attack and explained why he had been found so far from where the coach was stopped. The plan of his assailants, it appeared, was not merely to capture or kill him, nor, as might have been supposed, to hold him for ransom. They proposed, instead, to carry him to the place of public execution, Tyburn, and hang him from the gallows there like a common criminal. In pursuance of this design they had mounted him behind the large man, to

whom he was securely bound, while the leader rode on
to adjust the rope, that there might be no delay at the
gallows. When, however, the others failed to appear,
this man rode back and found that the Duke, despite
his age, had managed to throw himself and his companion from their horse and so gain time till help came.

Such was the extraordinary attempt on the Duke of
Ormond, than which no event of the time showed more
daring and ingenuity nor created so great a sensation.
The assailants were not recognized by the Duke or his
men. No assignable motive for their actions could be
given, nor was any further trace of them discovered. And
this was not from lack of effort. The court, the city, and
the administration were deeply stirred by the outrage,
and the whole machinery of state was set in motion to
discover and apprehend the criminals. Unprecedented
rewards were offered, the ports were watched, the local
authorities warned to be on the lookout for the desperadoes, and spies were sent in every direction to gain information. The House of Lords appointed a committee
of no less than sixty-nine peers to examine into " the late
barbarous assaulting, wounding and robbing the Lord
High Steward of His Majesty's Household."

For more than a month this august body, aided by the
secret service officers, pursued its investigations. The result was small. The most important testimony was that
of a "drawer" at the Bull Tavern, Charing Cross. He
deposed that on the day of the assault, between six and
seven in the evening, five men on horseback, with cloaks,
who said they were graziers, rode up to the inn. They
dismounted, ordered wine, some six pints in all, and sat
there, drinking, talking, and, finally, having ordered
pipes and tobacco, smoking for nearly an hour. About
seven o'clock a man came by on foot, crying, "Make way
for the Duke of Ormond," and shortly after the Duke's
coach passed by. Fifteen minutes later the five men paid

their reckoning and rode off, still smoking, towards the Haymarket or Pall Mall, leaving behind some wine, which the boy duly drank.

Besides this, a certain Michael Beresford, clerk or parson of Hopton, Suffolk, testified that on the same evening, somewhat earlier, it would appear, than the incident at the Bull, he had met in the "Piattza," Covent Garden, a man formerly known to him as a footman in the service of the regicide, Sir Michael Livesey. This man, Allen by name, appeared much disturbed, and after some conversation in which he hinted at "great designs" on foot, was called away by a page, who told him the horses were ready. The principal piece of evidence, however, was a sword, belt, and pistol, marked "T. H.," found at the scene of the struggle and identified as the property of one Hunt, who had been arrested in the preceding August under suspicion of highway robbery, but released for lack of evidence against him. Three horses were also found, one of which corresponded to the description of the animal ridden by the leader of the five men at the Bull. In addition to this there was the usual mass of more or less irrelevant informations, rumors, arrests, witnesses, and worthless testimony which such a case always produces. After much deliberation the committee finally drew up a bill against three men, Thomas Hunt, Richard Halliwell, and one Thomas Allen, also called Allett, Aleck, and Ayloffe. These were summoned to render themselves "by a short day" or stand convicted of the assault. The bill was duly passed by both houses and fully vindicated the dignity of the Lords. But it had no further result. The men did not render themselves by any day, short or long, the government agents failed to find them, and there the matter rested.

The result, and indeed the whole procedure, was thoroughly unsatisfactory to many in authority. At the outset of the investigation Justice Morton, of London, the far-famed terror of highwaymen, was asked by Ormond to look into the matter and was furnished with the names of certain suspects. He reported on Hunt and his career, and went on to say that Moore and Blood, concerning whom his Grace had enquired, were in or about London. A month later, Lord Arlington, the Secretary of State, who had charge of the secret service, reported to the Lords' committee that of the men suspected, Jones, who wrote *Mene Tekel* (a famous "fanatic" pamphlet against the government), Blood, called Allen, Allec, etc., young Blood, his son, called Hunt, under which name he was indicted last year, Halliwell, Moore, and Simons, were desperate characters sheltering themselves under the name of Fifth Monarchy men. "Would not this exposing of their names by act of Parliament," he asked, "make them hide themselves in the country, whereas the Nonconformists with whom they met, and who abhorred their crime would otherwise be glad to bring them to justice?" Apparently not, in the opinion of the Lords, and the result was what we have seen. Neither Arlington's advice nor the men were taken. And though in the minds of Ormond, Morton, and Arlington, apparently little doubt existed as to the authors of the outrage, no way was found to put their opinions into effect. It needed another and even more daring exploit to demonstrate the truth of their conjecture and bring the criminal into custody. And it was not long until just such a circumstance confirmed their surmise that the man guilty of the assault was the most famous outlaw of his day, long known and much wanted, many times proclaimed, and on whose head a price had often been set. He was, in short, Thomas Blood, courtesy-colonel of conspiracy, plotter, desperado, and now, at last, highwayman, a man hitherto not much known to the world at large, but a source of long-standing anxiety to the government and now on his way to a place in history.

Who was he and what was the motive of this apparently foolhardy and purposeless piece of bravado? The answer to that question lies deep in the history of the time, for Blood was no common rascal. Unlike the ordinary criminal he was not merely an individual lawbreaker. He was at once a leader and a type of an element in the state, and the part that he and his fellows played in affairs was not merely important in itself and in its generation, but even at this distance it has an interest little dimmed by two centuries of neglect. The story of his life, in so far as it can be pieced out from the materials at our command, is as follows:

In the reign of James I, that is to say, in the first quarter of the seventeenth century, there lived at an obscure place called Sarney, County Meath, Ireland, a man named Blood. He was by trade a blacksmith and ironworker and seems to have been possessed of some little property, including an iron-works. He was not a native Irishman but one of those north English or Scotch Presbyterians colonized in that unhappy island according to the policy which had been pursued by the English government. Of him we know little more save this. About 1618 there was born to him a son, christened Thomas, who grew to young manhood unmarked by any noteworthy achievements or qualities of which any record remains.

But, if the circumstances of his own life were of no great importance, the times in which he lived were stirring enough, and, remote as he was from the center of English political life, he could hardly have failed to know something of the great issues then agitating public affairs, and be moved by events far outside his own little circle. When he was ten years old, the long struggle between the English King and Parliament blazed up in

the Petition of Right, by which the Commons strove to
check the power of the Crown. Thereafter for eleven
years no Parliament sat in England. There, supported
by royal prerogative, the Archbishop Laud sought to
force conformity to the Anglican ritual on multitudes of
unwilling men and women, while the Attorney-General,
Noy, and the Treasurer, Weston, revived long-lapsed
statutes and privileges and stretched the technicalities
of the law to extort unparliamentary revenue. Then it
was that the Great Emigration poured thousands of
settlers into the New World and established finally and
beyond question the success of the struggling Puritan
colonies oversea. Such matters touched the boy in the
Irish village little. But when the greatest of the Royalists, Thomas Wentworth, Earl of Strafford to be, was
transferred from the presidency of the English Council
of the North to rule Ireland, Blood, like all others in
that troubled province, was brought face to face with
the issues of the time. He, like others, saw in that administration the theory and practice of the enlightened
despotism which English Parliamentarians said it was
the aim of this man and his master to force upon England when English liberties should have been crushed
with the Irish army then forming.

Whether young Blood enlisted in that army we do
not know, but it is not improbable. In any event, when
the Civil War finally broke out, the Blood family seem
to have been in the thick of it. Years afterwards Prince
Rupert said that he remembered the young man as a
bold and dashing soldier in his command. And, later still,
Blood himself wrote King Charles II, in behalf of his
uncle Neptune, for thirty years dean of Kilfernora, not-
ing among his virtues that he had been with Charles I
at Oxford. Thus it would appear that the Bloods first
sided with the royal cause. Besides this we know that, in
the year before the execution of the King, Blood married

a Miss Holcroft, of Holcroft in Lancashire. And we know further that then or thereafter, like many another stout soldier, like the stoutest of them all, General Monk himself, the young Royalist changed sides, for the next time he appears in history it is with the rank of lieutenant in the Cromwellian army.

Before that, however, many great events had taken place, in war and politics. The Royalist resistance in England had been beaten down, and the King was dead. The very title and office of king had been abolished, the House of Lords had been done away with, and England was a commonwealth with a Huntingdonshire gentleman, Oliver Cromwell, at its head. The war had shifted to Scotland and Ireland. Charles II had been proclaimed in Edinburgh, and Catholic and Royalist had risen in Ireland. Thither Cromwell hastened with his invincible Ironsides, to crush the Irish before they could gather head. His stroke was swift and merciless. The chief strongholds of his enemies, Drogheda and Wexford, were stormed and their inhabitants put to the sword after the manner of the Old Testament. The Irish army was overpowered and Cromwell hurried back to crush the Scots at Dunbar and Worcester, leaving his son-in-law, the lawyer-general Ireton, to stamp out the embers of rebellion. Thereafter, he sent the ablest of his sons, Henry, to hold the island for the Commonwealth.

With him Blood came into touch with the house of Cromwell. The young Irishman had probably been among the troops which were brought over to conquer the "rebels" serving under the Lord General and Ireton after him. For when the new government, following the example of its predecessors, confiscated the land of its enemies and the fair domains of Royalist and Catholic passed into the hands of the hard-hitting and loud-praying colonels and captains and even common soldiers of the Commonwealth, Blood not only acquired estates, but was further distinguished by being made Justice of the Peace under Henry Cromwell.

Thus with his fellows, and in greater proportion than most of them, he prospered and after an adventurous career seemed about to achieve the ambition of most Englishmen then and since, and become a real country gentleman. For a space of seven years, under Commonwealth and Protectorate, he lived, like many others of his kind, satisfied and secure in the enjoyment of the fruits of his share in saving England from the tyrant, little moved by the great events oversea. And, had it not been for circumstances as far outside his little sphere as those which had raised him to this position, he might well have finished an obscure and peaceful existence, with little further interest for the historian or moralist. But at the end of those seven fat years Fate, who had been so kind to Blood and his fellows, changed sides, and he, like many others, missing the signs of the times, or moved by conviction, could not, or would not, at all events did not, change with her.

On September 3, 1658, Oliver Cromwell died, and the fabric of government which for some years had rested on little more than his will and his sword, began at once to crumble. For a few months his son, Richard, endured the empty honor of the Protector's title. Then he resigned and the administration was left in a weltering chaos of Rump Parliament politicians and Cromwellian army generals. To end this anarchy came the Governor of Scotland, General Monk, with his army, to London in the first months of 1660. Under his shrewd, stern management the old Parliament was forced to dissolve itself and a new House of Commons was chosen. The first act of this so-called Convention was to recall the House of Stuart to the throne, and on May 29, 1660, Charles II rode into London and his inheritance, welcomed by the same shouting thousands who had so recently assembled to pay the last honors to the Protectorate.

As rapidly as might be thereafter the new régime was established. The old officers and officials were replaced by Royalists; the forces by land and sea were disbanded, save for five thousand trusty troops to guard the new monarchy; the leaders of the fallen party were arrested and executed, or driven into exile, or put under security. Some, like Monk and Montagu and Browne, were now the strongest pillars in the new political edifice. Many, like Harrison and his fellow regicides, were marked for speedy execution, while others, like Vane, were kept for future sacrifice. Many more, like Marten and Waller and Cobbet, dragged out a wretched existence as political prisoners, exchanging one prison for another till death released them. Some, like Hutchinson, were put under bonds and granted a half liberty that in too many cases led only to later imprisonment. Only a few, like Lambert, lived long in the more pleasant confinement of the Channel Islands and the Scillies. Yet many escaped. Ludlow and Lisle and their companions found protection, if not safety, in Switzerland. Many more sought refuge in Holland. Some, like Algernon Sidney, flitted over Europe like uneasy spirits. No small number joined the Emperor to fight the Turk, or took service in Holland or Sweden or the petty states of Germany. And still others, like Goffe and Whalley and Dixwell, sought and found security in the New World. The leaders of the fallen party out of the way, for the ensuing six years the government left no stone unturned to undo the work of revolution and to restore in so far as possible the old order.

It was no easy task. For twenty years England had been engaged in a civil strife where political animosities were embittered by religious dissensions, emphasized by lines of social cleavage. One section of the people had triumphed over another. Many of them, like Blood, actually entered into their enemies' inheritance and seemed likely to found a new ruling class. When 1660 came and this was all reversed, when the old party was in the ascendant, the King on the throne, what would become of them? They had been free to worship in their own way and had been largely exempt even from many forms of taxation. But all this was now suddenly reversed. The Royalists were again in the ascendant, the King was on his throne, Puritanism was discredited, its leaders gone, its organization destroyed. What were men like Blood to do?

For several months, the Presbyterians seemed likely to receive the recognition they had earned by their services to the Restoration. So far all promised well for an amicable adjustment of relations between the two great parties in church and state. But their very agreement boded ill for the third party or "sectaries" — Independents, Baptists, Quakers, and their fellows. In the days of their prosperity they had suppressed Anglican and Presbyterian alike. Now that these had joined hands the sectaries had little hope. They had early stirred to meet the danger. While the Convention debated the terms on which the King should return, their deliberations were cut short not less by the declaration of the King than by the fear of a rising of the Republicans and sects. In January, 1661, fanaticism broke out in London. A cooper named Venner, a soldier of the old army, sometime conspirator against Cromwell, sometime resident of Salem, in New England, with some threescore followers, all of that peculiar millennial sect known as Fifth Monarchy men, rose against the government, and for three days kept the city, the court, and the administration in a state of feverish alarm. But the odds against them were too great. They found neither aid nor comfort from outside, and the children of this world triumphed over those who would have restored the rule of the saints under King Jesus.

That rising helped destroy whatever chance the Presbyterians had of holding their strength in the new Parliament, and the House of Commons showed a clear majority of Royalist Anglicans. Hardly had this body begun its deliberations when the Savoy Conference met, and, after some wrangling, dissolved without reaching any agreement. Thence ensued a period of reaction whose results are writ large in religious history to this day, for this was the time when established church and denominations definitely parted company. The dominant party lost no time in destroying the strength of their rivals. The Corporation Act drove the dissenters from those bodies which governed the cities and towns and chose a majority of the Commons. The Act of Uniformity excluded all dissenting ministers from the Church of England, while the restoration of the bishops to the House of Lords, and of its confiscated property to the Church, completed the discomfiture of the Presbyterians.

They suffered most, for they had most to lose, but the new policy bore no less hardly on the sectaries; and these, joined by the more extreme Presbyterians, were little inclined to submit to the revived authority in church and state. Many moderate men, indeed, found it in their consciences to conform enough to evade the law. But many more were neither able not inclined to take this course. Deprived of their army, of their political position, of their religious liberty, even at length of their right to petition, in many cases of what they considered their rightful property, with no outlet for their opinions in Parliament, the case seemed hopeless enough. A few of the latter conformed; most began a long and honorable course of silent endurance of their persecution. Some, of bolder spirit, turned to darker ways.

These events in England had their counterpart in Scotland and Ireland. In all three kingdoms the dispossessed party was thrown into a ferment of discontent over this sudden reversal of their fortunes. The soldiers of the old army were especially enraged. They felt that they had lost by political trickery what had been won in fair fight. By a sudden turn of fortune's wheel, a bit of legal chicanery, their old enemy, the Parliament, had caught them off their guard and overthrown them. Their place had been taken by the ungodly, the Arminian, and the idol-worshiper. And these brethren of the Covenant and the sword were not men to rest quietly under such wrongs. Many, indeed, turned aside from politics and war, taking no further part in public affairs. But not a few declared they would not be led into an Egyptian bondage under a new Pharaoh. Those whom they had fairly fought and fairly conquered, those who had followed Mammon, and bowed the knee to Baal, the worshipers of Rimmon, the doers of abominations, the servants of the Scarlet Woman who sits on the Seven Hills, were these to enter upon that fair inheritance, so lately in the hands of the saints, without a blow? Surely the Lord was on the side of His servants, as He had shown them by so many signal instances of His favor, at Naseby, at Marston Moor, at Dunbar, and at Worcester, and a hundred fights besides, in the great days gone by. Was He to look on unmoved? Had He abandoned them to their enemies? Was this not rather a device of His to try their constancy and courage? Was it not their part as brave and righteous men to strike another blow for the faith that was in them and the heritage He had put in their hands? A bold stroke had once prevailed against their oppressors. Might not another restore the Covenant and give back to the afflicted saints their inheritance and the spoil of the Philistines? A new king was on the throne who knew not Joseph. But his rule was recent, his hold precarious. His father had been overthrown, though all the wealth and power of the mighty had been on his side. Now the land was honeycombed with sedition, there were thousands of bold spirits accustomed to discipline and the use of arms, and thousands more of the faithful with money and sympathy to aid in the great work of destroying the rule of grasping bishops and a Catholic king.

Thus, while the regicides fled from the wrath of the new government, or suffered the penalty of their deeds in London, while Parliament was driving Nonconformity from church and state and the greater part of the dispossessed party girded itself to endure the impending persecution, while new-fledged royalty flaunted its licentiousness in Whitehall, earnest and vindictive men plotted against the new order in England, in Ireland and Scotland and Wales, in London itself. Emissaries made their way by night along unfrequented roads, or stole from village to village in tiny fishing boats, or crept through narrow lanes of the old City and its environs, to cheer the secret and unlawful conventicles of Baptist and Quaker, Presbyterian and Congregationalist, Unitarian and Fifth Monarchist, with hopes and plans for the resurrection of the Kingdom of the Righteous.

The old Republicans were approached, the holders of land taken in the recent troubles, the members of the old Rump Parliament, the exiles abroad, the officers and soldiers of the old army at home. Proclamations were printed promising all things to all men, but chiefly toleration and lighter taxes. Tracts were smuggled from London or Holland full of the language of prophecy. The new monarchy had been measured and found wanting, the old Covenant was about to rise, Phœnix-like, from its ashes, the heavens were full of signs and portents, and prodigies everywhere indicated the fall of king and bishop. A new Armageddon was at hand, the rule of King Jesus was to be restored, "even by Blood."

Everywhere arms were gathered and men enlisted against that great day.

And everywhere, meanwhile, the government followed close on the trail of the conspirators and kept in close touch with the elements of discontent. Everywhere spies and informers were enlisted, even from the ranks of conspiracy itself, to discover and also, it was whispered, to foment conspiracy where none existed, that dangerous men might be drawn in and seized. From every county justices and deputy lieutenants poured a steady stream of prisoners and information into the hands of the administration. Under the careful direction of the Lord General the militia was reorganized, former strongholds were weakened or destroyed, troops moved here and there, suspicious persons seized, and incipient disturbance was vigorously repressed. So for three years this underground warfare went on.

Late in 1661 the government found, or professed to find, a clue to conspiracy and exploited its discovery in Parliament to secure the act against corporations. Again in 1662 another was brought to light, and was used to pass the Act of Uniformity. Some of the alleged conspirators were hanged, some were used to get more information, but for the most part the leaders remained unknown, or escaped. Thus far the disaffected had played into the hands of their bitterest enemies, and had accomplished little more than to furnish a much desired excuse for legislation to destroy Nonconformity root and branch. So useful had they been to the Anglicans, indeed, that it was more than hinted that the so-called conspiracies were in fact engineered by them for use in Parliament.

This was not quite true. Conspiracy there had been, and was, as events were to prove. And the administration learned presently that the plot they had so diligently pursued and exploited had a very real existence. By 1663 it was widespread and apparently well organized. It included the discontented Nonconformists of the west and north of England, the Scotch Covenanters, the dispossessed Cromwellians in Ireland, the London conventiclers, and the Continental refugees. A central "Committee of Six," chiefly old army officers, it was said, sat in London, whence they directed the movement from their hiding-places in those little-known regions of the metropolis where even the King's writ ran with difficulty or not at all. The scheme contemplated the surprise and seizure of Whitehall and the Tower, the capture of the King and his brother, of the Chancellor, and the Lord General. Simultaneous risings were to take place throughout the country, whereby the local authorities were to be overpowered, the Guards, if possible, decoyed away from the capital, and the central administration paralyzed and destroyed. The forces of the conspirators, under their former leaders, especially General Ludlow, were to unite, march on London, and there either exact terms from the captive King or set up another Republic, but in any event relieve the people from the burdens of religious and financial oppression. Such was the dream of the discontented, which, transformed into action, might well have plunged England again into the throes of civil war.

Meanwhile what of our friend Blood amid all these great affairs? Had he, like many others, preferred the safer course, withdrawn into private life and abandoned his property and ambitions together? That, indeed, seems to have been his first course. The Court of Claims apparently deprived him, among many others, of part or all of his new-found fortune in land, and he seems to have taken up his residence in Dublin, with or near his brother-in-law, Lackie, or Lecky, a Presbyterian clergyman, and, like his modern namesake, the historian, a fellow of Trinity College. Even so he maintained his repu-

tation as an active man, for on June 30, 1663, a Dublin
butcher, Dolman by name, is found petitioning the Duke
of Ormond for the return of an "outlandish bull and
cow" of which he had been unlawfully deprived by
Thomas Blood, lieutenant in the late army. The petition was duly granted and the animals doubtless duly
recovered. But before the worthy butcher petitioned
against him he had come under the direct attention of the
Lord Lieutenant in a much more serious connection.

It was not to be supposed that such a man was over-
looked in the assignment of parts for the great conspiracy. A committee had been formed in Dublin to
organize and enlist the old Cromwellians in the design,
and of this committee Blood and his brother-in-law were
prominent members. They were, in fact, the chief means
by which correspondence was maintained with the north
Irish Presbyterians in Ulster, and the so-called Came-
ronians in Scotland, as well as the Nonconformist group
in Lancashire and north England, with whom Blood's
marriage had given him some connection. The local design, as evolved by this committee, was most ingenious.
A day, the ninth or tenth of May, was set for its execution, men and arms were collected, and the details carefully arranged for the seizure of Dublin Castle and the
person of Ormond. According to an old usage the Lord
Lieutenant was accustomed from day to day to receive
petitions in person from all who cared to carry their
troubles to him in this way. Taking advantage of this
custom, it was proposed by the conspirators to send certain men enlisted in the enterprise into the Castle in the
guise of petitioners. Some eighty others, meanwhile, disguised as workingmen and loiterers, were to hang about
the great gate of the Castle. Another, disguised as a
baker, and carrying a basket of bread on his head, was
to enter the gate, as if on his way to the kitchen. As he
went in he was to stumble and let fall his pile of loaves.

It was calculated that the careless guard would probably rush out to snatch the bread thus scattered. The baker would resist, the pretended workmen and loiterers would gather to see the fun, and, under cover of the disturbance, rush the gate, seize the guardhouse and its arms, overpower the guard, and, with the aid of the petitioners within, occupy the Castle. Upon the news of this, risings were to take place throughout the country, and the English troops and officials were to be overpowered and brought over or killed.

It was an admirable plan. The volunteers were chosen, the disguises prepared, a proclamation to the people was printed, and the whole matter laid in train. The plot, in fact, wanted but one thing to succeed — secrecy. This it was not destined to have. At the proper time the inevitable informer appeared in the person of Mr. Philip Alden, or Arden, a member of the conspirators' committee. By him and by a certain Sir Theophilus Jones, to whom some knowledge of the plot had come, Ormond was warned of the design. He took immediate steps to secure himself and arrest the plotters. But they were warned of their danger in time to escape, and under the rules of the game they should have made off at once. Instead they boldly went on with their plans, but set the time four days ahead, for May 5. Even this daring step failed to save them. The Castle guard was increased, troops and militia were called out, the other districts warned, and the conspirators sought out and arrested.

Among the first victims was Blood's brother-in-law, Lackie. He was thrown into prison, where the severity of his treatment is said to have driven him insane. His wife petitioned for his release, and there is a story that his colleagues, the fellows of Trinity College, joined her in begging that his life be spared. They were told that he might have his liberty if he would conform, which, however, even at that price, he refused to do. This much is quite certain, his wife was promised, not her husband's liberty, but his body. And this, after his execution in December, was accordingly handed over to her. The other conspirators suffered likewise in life, or liberty, or property, and every effort was made to include Blood in the list of victims. A proclamation he had issued was burned by the hangman. He was declared an outlaw, his remaining estates were confiscated, and a price was set on his head. But the government was compelled to satisfy itself with this; the man himself disappeared. Among the brethren of his faith he was able to find plenty of hiding places. It would be too long to recount here the tale of his evasion of justice, protected largely, it would appear, by his Presbyterian brethren. But, according to his own story, told many years later, he scorned to skulk in corners. Disguised as a Quaker, as a Dissenting minister, even as a Catholic priest, he made his way from place to place, keeping the officers off his scent for some years. And so great, it is said, was the terror of his name and his daring, that a plot to rescue Lackie from the scaffold not only frightened away the crowd from the execution, but nearly succeeded in its object, while for months afterward Ormond was hindered from venturing out of Dublin by the fear of his friends that he would be kidnapped or killed by Blood and his companions.

Meanwhile the great design in England, like that in Ireland, found its shipwreck in treachery. Two of the men entrusted with the secrets of the design revealed it to the government. One of the leaders, Paul Hobson, was early seized, and his correspondence intercepted. The first leader chosen went mad, and the miracles which were prophesied did not come to pass. The plans for a rising in Durham, Westmoreland, and Lancashire were betrayed, troops and militia were hurried to the points of danger, and those who rose in arms during that fatal month of October, 1663, discouraged by the fewness of their numbers and the strength brought against them, dispersed without a blow. The rest was but the story of arrests, examinations, trials, and executions. By the middle of 1664 the tale of victims was complete, and the conspiracy was crushed. The alarm again reacted on Parliament, and a Conventicle Act, which made it unlawful to hold a religious meeting of more than five persons besides the family in whose house the worshipers assembled, was passed under pressure of the plot.

Blood, meanwhile, like several of his co-conspirators, flitted from place to place in Ireland and England, the authorities always on his trail. Finally, like many before and after him, he seems to have found refuge in the seventeenth-century sanctuary of political refugees, Holland. There no small number of the leaders and soldiers of the old army had preceded him, and many had taken service in the Dutch army and navy. It may be that he had some thought of following their example. He had nothing to hope from England, for his confiscated estates had been leased to a certain Captain Toby Barnes, reserving the rights of the government, based on his forfeiture by treason. He therefore made his way and extended his acquaintance not only among the English, but among the Dutch as well, and, if his story is true, was introduced to no less a person than the great Dutch admiral, De Ruyter, the most formidable of all England's enemies.

This was of much importance since, while he sojourned abroad, England and Holland had drifted into war. From February, 1665, to July, 1667, the two strongest maritime powers strove for control of the sea. In the summer of 1665 the English won some advantage in the fierce battle of Lowestoft, but the noise of rejoicing was stilled by a terrible catastrophe. In that same summer the Plague fell upon London. The death list in the city alone swelled from 600 in April to 20,000 in

August. Business was suspended, the court and most of
the administration and the clergy fled, and the war languished. A few bold and faithful spirits stuck grimly to
their posts. But they were few among many. Amid the
terror and confusion the Nonconformist clergy came out
of their hiding-places, ascended the pulpits which had
been deserted by their brethren of the Anglican church,
few of whom followed the example of their brave, intolerant old bishop, and ministered to the spiritual needs
of the stricken people. Conventicles sprung up everywhere, and conspiracy again raised its head.

This time new plans were devised. Hundreds of old
soldiers were reported coming to London, and taking
quarters near the Tower. Arms were collected and a
plan formed to surprise the great stronghold by an attack from the water side. In addition there was a design
for risings elsewhere, aided by the Dutch. The government bestirred itself under the direction of the inevitable
Monk. The London conspirators were seized, information was sent to the local authorities, who made arrests
and called out the militia, and the danger was averted.
Parliament met at Oxford in October and, as a sequel
to the plot, passed the most ferocious of the persecuting
measures, the Five Mile Act, by which no Nonconformist preacher or teacher was permitted to come within
that distance of a city or borough, save on a duly certi-
fied journey.

The next year repeated the history of its predecessor.
The English fleet, under the only man who seemed to
rise to emergencies in this dark time, Monk, met the
Dutch off the North Foreland and fought there a terrible battle which lasted three days, and was claimed as
a victory by both sides. Again this was followed by a
calamity. In September a fire broke out in London
which raged almost unchecked for a week, and laid the
greater part of the city in ashes. France, meanwhile, en-

tered the war on the side of Holland, and the English
government, corrupt and exhausted, seemed almost
ready to fall. It was little wonder that the sectaries,
though their arms had been lost in the fire, plucked up
courage and laid more plans. Six weeks after the fire the
Covenanters in west Scotland, maddened by persecution,
were in arms, and maintained themselves for some weeks
against the forces sent against them. During the following winter the English, short of money, and negotiating
for peace, resolved not to send out a fleet in the spring.
In June the Dutch, apprised of the defenseless condition
of the English coasts, brought together a fleet under De
Ruyter, sailed up the Medway and the Thames, took
Sheerness and Chatham, broke through the defenses
there and captured or destroyed the English ships they
found at anchor. There was little to oppose them. The
Guards were drawn out, the young gentlemen about the
Court enlisted, the militia was brought together, and
volunteers collected. Some entrenchments were dug, and
guns were mounted to oppose a landing. And the Lord
General Monk, who had done all that was done, marched
up and down the bank, before the Dutch ships whose big
black hulks lay well within the sound of his voice, chew-
ing tobacco, swearing like a pirate, shaking his heavy
cane at the enemy, and daring them to land. They did
not kill him as they might easily have done. From their
ships came a brisk cannonade, volleys of jeers and pro-
fanity, and the insulting cries of English seamen abroad,
deriding their fellow countrymen ashore. With these in-
sults the fleet presently weighed anchor and sailed away
to patrol the coasts, interrupt commerce, and attack
other ports. The negotiations then in progress having
been expedited by this exploit, the Dutch fleet withdrew,
leaving England seething with impotent rage and mor-
tification; and peace was signed at Breda a month later, on
terms influenced in no small degree by this notable raid.

And what of Blood? It is not to be supposed that the organizer of Irish rebellion, the correspondent of English revolutionary committees and Scotch Covenanters, and the friend of De Ruyter, sat quietly apart from this turmoil of war and conspiracy. Yet, working underground as he did, like a mole, it is possible to trace his movements only by an occasional upheaval on the surface. It seems quite certain that he did not, like so many of his countrymen, enlist in the Dutch service and that he was not among the four or five thousand troops, mostly English, which manned their fleet. On February 13, 1666, there is a secret-service note, that Captain Blood may be found at Colonel Gilby Carr's in the north of Ireland, or at his wife's, near Dublin, and that the fanatics had secretly held a meeting at Liverpool and put off their rising till after the engagement of the fleets. On May 3, there is a similar note concerning a man named Padshall, then prisoner in the Gate House in London, that if he is kept close he may discover where Allen, alias Blood, lodges, or "Joannes," alias Mene Tekel, and the note indicates their presence in the city. Then came the battle of the North Foreland and the failure of the Dutch to crush the English fleet. On August 24 we learn that these two men, Blood and Jones, have gone to Ireland to do mischief.

There another plot was reported forming, which contemplated the seizure of Limerick. But this, like that of the preceding year on the Tower, both of which bear a strong family resemblance to the old design on Dublin Castle, was discovered and defeated. One insurrection alone, as we have seen, resulted from this unrest, the rising of the Scotch Covenanters in October. Among them, according to advices which came to the administration, was Blood. He had evidently found the Irish plot betrayed and with some of his companions, described in the accounts of the Pentland rising as "some Presby-

terian ministers and old officers from Ireland," hurried
to the only chance of real fighting. That was not great.
The Covenanters, cooped up in the Pentland Hills, were
beaten, dispersed, or butchered, before concentrated aid
could be given them. Blood, as usual, escaped. He
seems first to have sought refuge in Lancashire among his
relatives. Thence he went to Ireland, but, landing near
Carrickfergus, was so closely pursued there by Lord
Dungannon that he turned again to England, and by the
first of the following April was reported to the government
as being at the house of a rigid Anabaptist in Westmoreland. From there he watched the government unravel
the web of conspiracy he had been so busy weaving.

Yet even here lies another mystery. In 1665, at the
time when he might be supposed to have been most active against the government, his wife petitioned, through
him apparently, for the return of certain property seized
from her father by one Richard Clively, then in prison
for killing a bailiff, and in December of that year it appears that certain men convicted of attending conventicles are to be discharged, and the order is endorsed
by Blood. More than that, there is a petition of September, 1666, the month of the Fire, noted as "Blood's
memorial," requesting a permit from Secretary Arlington that the "hidden persons, especially the spies, be not
seized till they are disposed of." From such data it has
been conjectured that Blood was playing a double part;
that he was, after all, no dangerous conspirator but a
mere informer.

This brings us to a most curious phase of this whole
movement, the relation of the conspirators to the government. It is a remarkable fact that no small number
of those who to all appearances were most deeply implicated in conspiracy, corresponded at one time or another with the administration, in many instances furnishing information of each other to the secretaries. And

this might lead, indeed, it has led, many to imagine that these vaunted conspiracies were, after all, nothing but what we should call in the language of modern crime, "plants," devised and executed by the government itself for purposes of its own. There is, in some instances, evidence of this. But in many others it is apparent that this is not a full explanation, especially of cases like that of Blood. In that doubtful borderland between secret service and conspiracy it was often possible for a man to serve both sides. Having engineered a plot and acquired money and arms and companions to carry it out, a man not infrequently found himself in the clutches of the law. The officers, because they did not have the evidence to hang him, or because they hoped to gain more from him alive than dead, were often disposed to offer him his life, even his liberty, in return for information. He, on his part, was nearly always ready to furnish information in any quantity and of any sort, in return for this favor. If he were shrewd enough, he might amuse his captors for years with specious stories, with just enough truth to make them plausible, and just enough vagueness to make them unusable, and ultimately escape, meanwhile carrying on the very plans which he purported to betray. He might even get money from both sides and make a not to be despised livelihood from his trade. If Blood were such a man, as seems probable, he represented a considerable element in the underground politics of the early Restoration. And it is to be observed that no small proportion of the men who were executed for complicity in the plots were of just this type and had at various times been in government service, only to be caught red-handed at the end. That such was the case of Blood seems to be proved by the fact that the next time he appears above the horizon his actions seem to dissipate any idea of permanent accommodation with the government.

The arrests and examinations which succeeded the abortive conspiracy of 1663 had led the secretaries of state into many dark ways of subterranean politics, and they had steadily pushed their investigations through the years of the war, the Plague, and the Fire. They had broken up one group after another, pursuing a steady policy of enlisting the weaker men as informers, and executing or keeping in prison the irreconcilables. Among those they had thus discovered had been a little group, the "desperadoes," the names of some of whom we have come across before, Blood, his brother-in-law, Colonel Lockyer, Jones, the author of *Mene Tekel*, and a Captain John Mason. The last had been taken, had escaped, and, some time during the Dutch war, was recaptured. On the twentieth of July, 1667, while the Dutch fleets still patrolled the English coast and the peace of Breda was just about to be signed, warrants were issued from the Secretary of State to the Keeper of the Tower and the Keeper of Newgate to deliver Captain John Mason and Mr. Leving to the bearer to be conveyed to York gaol. This duty was assigned to a certain Corporal Darcy, otherwise unknown to fame, who with some seven or eight troopers proceeded to carry out his instructions.

The little party thus made up rode north by easy stages for four days without incident. On the fourth day they were joined by one Scott, a citizen of York, apparently by profession a barber, who, not much fancying solitary travel in that somewhat insecure district, sought safety with the soldiers. About seven o'clock on the evening of the twenty-fifth of August the little party entered a narrow lane near the village of Darrington, Yorkshire, and there met a most extraordinary adventure. As they rode along, doubtless with no great caution, they heard behind them a sudden rattle of horses' hoofs. They turned to meet a pistol-volley from a small body of well-armed and mounted men, and a demand for their prisoners. Several of the guard were wounded at the first fire, and the surprise was complete. But Corporal Darcy was not a man to be thus handled. He faced his little force about, delivered a volley in return, charged his assailants briskly, and in a moment was the center of a sharp hand-to-hand fight. He was twice wounded and had his horse shot under him. Three of his companions were badly hurt. Of the attacking party at least one was severely wounded. But when they drew off they carried Mason with them. Leving, feeling discretion the better part of valor, took refuge in a house near by and after the fight surrendered himself again to the stout corporal. Scott, the innocent bystander who had sought protection with the soldiers, was killed outright, the only immediate fatality in either party, though some of the troopers died later of their wounds. The corporal, despite his disabled condition, managed to get one of his opponents' horses in place of the one he lost, and rode hurriedly into the near-by village for help. But the fearful villagers had barricaded themselves in their houses, and were moved neither by his promises nor his threats to join in the pursuit of the desperadoes. He had, therefore, to be content with giving information to the nearest justice, sending after them the hue and cry, and making his way to York with his remaining prisoner.

This, it will be remembered, was one Leving. And with him we come upon a character, and a plot beneath a plot, which well illustrates the times. William Leving, or Levings, or Levering, or Leonard Williams, as he was variously called, was far from being the man his guards thought him. It must have been a surprise to them after the fight to see one of their prisoners, instead of making off with the rescuers, render himself again into their hands. But the explanation, though the good corporal and his men did not know it, nor yet the governor of

York gaol to whom Leving was delivered, was only too well known to Captain Mason's friends, and explains the strange conduct of the Captain's fellow prisoner on other grounds than mere cowardice. Leving had been deeply implicated in the plots of 1661 and 1662, perhaps in that of 1663 as well. He had been caught, and, to save his life, he had "come in," to use an expressive phrase of the time. He was, in short, one of the most useful of the government's spies. It was he who had given news of Blood and his companions in Ireland. It was he who had furnished some of the information on which the government was then acting, and who proposed to furnish more, acquired, possibly, by this very ruse of sending him north with Mason. It was he who now gave to the justice and officers the names of the principal rescuers, Captain Lockyer, Major Blood, and Timothy Butler, and wrote to Secretary Arlington suggesting that the ways into London be watched, as they would probably seek refuge there. It was little wonder that Mason's rescuers had sought to kill Leving, or that he had sought refuge in flight and surrender.

These, indeed, availed him little. He was kept a prisoner at York even after it appeared from his examination who and what he was. This was doubtless done more for his own safety than for any other reason, but even this was not effectual. Not many weeks later he was found dead in his cell. Some time after, another informer, similarly confined there, wrote Arlington a terrified letter begging protection or release, "that he might not, like Leving, be poisoned in his cell." Thus, it appears, his enemies found him out even there. And that you may not think too hardly of the poor spy, it may be added that on his dead body was found a letter, apparently one he was engaged on when he died, completely exonerating certain men then in hiding for the great conspiracy. It would, perhaps, be uncharitable to hint that this was part of an even more subtle plot beneath the other two, and that his murderers sought to shield their friends outside by this device. York gaol, in any event, was no place to keep men disaffected towards the government. From the Lord Lieutenant down the place was thick with discontent and conspiracy. Indeed, no great while before the Council had arrested the Lord Lieutenant himself, no less a person than one of their own number, the great Duke of Buckingham, on the charge of corresponding with the sectaries, and had confined him for some time in the Tower.

But what, meanwhile, had happened to Mason and his friends? On August 8 they were proclaimed outlaws by name and a hundred pounds' reward was offered for Lockyer, Butler, Mason, and Blood. But they had disappeared, as usual. Blood, it was said, had been mortally wounded, and was finally reported dead. That part of the story, at least, was greatly exaggerated, and was, no doubt, spread by Blood himself. He seems, in fact, to have retired to one of his hiding places and there recovered from his injuries, which were severe. The rest dispersed, and Mason, we know, found his way to London where three years later he appears in the guise of an innkeeper, still plotting for the inevitable uprising.

To us this seems strange. Our minds conjure up a well-ordered city, properly policed and thoroughly known. But the London of Charles II was a far different place from the city of to-day in more ways than its size and the advances wrought by civilization. The City itself was then distant from the Court. The long thoroughfare connecting them, now the busy Strand, was then what its name implies, the way along the river, and was the seat of only a few great palaces, like the Savoy, and the rising pile of Buckingham. Beside what is now Trafalgar Square stood then, as now, St. Martin's in the Fields. But the fields have long since fled from Piccadilly and Whitehall. Beyond and around in every direction outside the purlieus of the Court and the liberties of the City, stretched great collections of houses and hovels, affording rich hiding places for men outside the law. The inns abounding everywhere offered like facilities. Beneath the very walls of St. Stephen's where Parliament devised measures to suppress conventicles, those conventicles flourished. Among their numbers; among the small and secluded country houses round about; among the rough watermen and sailors along the river; in wide-stretching districts where the King's writ ran with difficulty or not at all, and a man's life was safe only as his strength or skill made it so; or, it was whispered, even among some of the great houses like that of the Duke of Buckingham, men flying from justice might find safety enough.

Later Mason seems to have been joined in London by Blood, and the old practices were renewed. But the Major, for Blood had now by some subterranean means arrived at that title, was apparently not wholly content with this. He retired, it would appear, to the little village of Romford, in Surrey, and there, under the name of Allen or Ayloffe, set up — amazing choice among all the things he might have chosen — as a physician. His son-in-law was apprenticed to an apothecary, and thus, with every appearance of quiet and sobriety, the outlaw began life again. But it was not for long, at any rate. Most likely, indeed, this whole business, if it ever existed at all, was a sham. For on May 28, 1670, we find Secretary Trevor, who had succeeded Arlington in office, ordering the Provost Marshal to search out and take in custody Henry Danvers and William Allen, alias Blood. In December of that same year came the assault on Ormond, with which our story began, and Blood, under his alias, was for the third time proclaimed an outlaw, and for the third time had a price set on his head. Surely,

you will say, this is enough of that impudent scoundrel
who so long disturbed the slumber of his Majesty's
secretaries, and flouted the activities of their agents.
And, in spite of the stir raised by the attempt on Ormond, if Blood had disappeared after that for the last
time, he would not have lived again in the pages of history. For that he is indebted to the great exploit which
at once ended his career of crime and raised him above
the ordinary herd of outlaws and criminals. By it he
made good once and for all his conflict with oblivion.

At the time of which we write the Tower of London
served even more numerous and important purposes
than it does to-day. It was then, as now, a depository of
arms and ammunition, and the place where the state regalia, the crown, the orb, and the scepter were kept, and
the quarters of a considerable body of troops, to over-
awe possible disturbance in the city. But in 1670 it was
also the principal prison for political offenders. Then, as
now, the various functions of the great fortress were
quite distinct. The visitor of to-day passes through a
wide courtyard to the main edifice, the White Tower of
William the Conqueror, whose chambers are filled with
curious weapons and armor. He may climb the stone
stairs to see the grim apartments once reserved for men
reckoned dangerous to the state, and gaze with what awe
he can muster upon the crown jewels. Everywhere he
finds in evidence the guardians of these treasures, the un-
obtrusive attendant, the picturesque beef-eater, the omni-
present policeman, and if he looks down from the high
windows he may see far below him the red tunics or
white undercoats of the soldiers on parade or at work.
In some measure this was true in 1670, and to this spot
we must now turn our attention. We have already seen
some of the characters in this story taken to or from
the custody of the Lieutenant of the Tower, and our
steps in trace of our hero or villain, as you choose to call

him, have often led perilously near its grim portals. At last they are to go inside.

Among the various functionaries in and about the Tower in the year 1670 was one Edwards, the Keeper of the Regalia, an old soldier who lived with his wife and daughter within the walls, his son being away at the wars on the Continent. Some time after the attack on the Duke of Ormond there appeared one day, among the visitors who flocked to see the sights of the stronghold, a little party of strangers from the country, a clergyman, his wife, and his nephew. They visited the usual places of interest, and presently, under Edwards' guidance, were taken to see the regalia. They were pleasant folk and much interested in what they saw. But unfortunately while looking at the royal paraphernalia the lady fell ill with some sort of a chill or convulsion. Her husband and nephew and Edwards were greatly alarmed. They carried her to Edwards' apartments, where his wife and daughter took her in charge, and administered cordials and restoratives until she recovered. The clergyman was deeply grateful. He rewarded Edwards generously for his attention and they were all profuse in acknowledging the kindness of the Keeper's family. Nor did the matter end here. From this little incident there sprang up an acquaintance which rapidly ripened into friendship between the two families. The clergyman and his nephew came in from time to time on visits. The nephew was young and dashing, the daughter was pretty and pleasing. They were obviously attracted to each other, and their elders looked on the dawning romance with favor. So rapidly did the matter progress that the clergyman presently proposed a marriage between the young couple. Edwards was not unwilling and on the ninth of May, 1671, the clergyman, his nephew, and a friend, with two companions, rode up about seven in the morning to make the final arrangements. Mrs.

Edwards, however, was not prepared to meet guests at so early an hour and some delay occurred. To fill in the time the clergyman suggested that Edwards might show the regalia to his friend, who had never seen it.

So the four mounted the steps to the room where the treasures were kept. Edwards went on before to take the regalia out for exhibition. But as he stooped over the chest to get them he was seized suddenly from behind, a cloak was thrown over his head, he was bound and gagged, knocked on the head with a mallet, and, all these measures having failed to prevent his giving the alarm, he was finally stabbed. One of the men with him seized the crown and bent it so that it went under his cloak. The other put the orb in the pocket of his baggy breeches, and began to file the scepter in two that it might be more easily carried. But as they were thus busied, by a coincidence, surely the strangest out of a play, at this precise instant Edwards' son, Talbot, returned from the wars, bringing a companion with him. They accosted the third man, who had remained as a sentinel at the foot of the stair. He gave the alarm, the two men ran down the stairs, and all three hurried off towards the Tower Gate. But there fortune deserted them. Edwards roused from his stupor, tore out the gag and shouted, "Treason and murder!" The daughter hurried to his side and thence to Tower Hill crying, "Treason! the crown is stolen!" Young Edwards and his companion, Captain Beckman, gaining from the Keeper some idea of the situation, rushed down and saw the thieves just going out the gate. Edwards drew his pistols and shouted to the sentinels. But, though the warders were apparently terrified, young Edwards, Beckman, and others who joined the pursuit closed in on the outlaws. They in turn aided the confusion by also crying, "Stop, thief," so that some were deceived into believing the parson a party to the pursuit. Beckman seems to have caught him and wrestled with him for the crown, while a servant seized one of the other men.

Beckman had a most "robustious struggle" with the parson, who fired one pistol at Beckman, and when they grappled drew a second and fired again, but missed both times. Two of the three principals having been taken almost at the gate, the third might have got away, but was thrown from his horse by running into a projecting cart pole, and captured at no great distance. Their accomplices, two apparently, seem to have escaped. The prisoners were brought back to the Tower at once and identified. To the astonishment of their captors the clergyman was found to be our old friend Blood, the so-called nephew was his son, or son-in-law, the third man an Anabaptist silk-dyer named Parret. Warrants were immediately made out to the governor of the Tower, Sir John Robinson, for their imprisonment; Blood's on the ground of outlawry for treason and other great and heinous crimes in England; young Blood's and Parret's for dangerous crimes and practices.

Thus fell the mighty Blood in this unique attempt at crime, which, among its other results, had one which even he could scarce have realized. His "stroke for a crown" was his crowning stroke against oblivion. By it he was set among the immortals, and from the moment of his capture his place in history was secure. His reputation was made once and for all, for the sensation caused by his extraordinary undertaking was naturally tremendous. News-letters and correspondence of the time are all filled with the details of the exploit and for the moment the gravest affairs of state sank into insignificance before the interest in this most audacious venture. An infinite number of guesses were hazarded at the motive for the theft, for it was felt that mere robbery would not account for it. It was even suspected that it was a prelude to the assassination of the King and the proclamation of a usurper who hoped to strengthen himself by the possession of the regalia.   This view was reinforced by the fact that the Chancellor's house was entered at about the same time and nothing taken but the Great Seal.   The darkest suspicions were afloat, and the relief at the capture of the noted outlaw and the failure of his attempt on the crown was intensified by the sense of having escaped from some vague and terrible danger which would have menaced the state had he succeeded. Broadsides and squibs of all sorts were inspired by the exploit.   Among others the irrepressible Presbyterian satirist, Andrew Marvell, characteristically improved the occasion to observe that:

> When daring Blood his rent to have regained
> Upon the English diadem restrained
> He chose the cassock, surcingle and gown,
>   The fittest mask for one that robs the crown:
> But his lay pity underneath prevailed.
> And whilst he saved the keeper's life he failed;
> With the priest's vestment had he but put on
> The prelate's cruelty, the crown had gone.

The proceedings in Blood's case, therefore, excited extraordinary interest, which was not lessened by the unusual circumstances surrounding it.   The prisoners were first brought before Sir Gilbert Talbot, the Provost Marshal.   But Blood refused absolutely to answer any leading questions put him by that official as to his motives, accomplices, and the ultimate purpose of his exploit.   This naturally deepened the interest in the matter, and increased the suspicion that there was more in it than appeared on the surface, especially as the outlaw declared he would speak only with the King himself.   To the further astonishment of the world this bold request was granted.   Three days after his arrest he was taken by the King's express order to Whitehall and there examined by Charles, the Duke of York, and a select few of the royal family and household. The proceeding was not quite as unusual as it seemed, for in the earlier years of the Restoration such episodes had been fairly common, and the King had proved a master of the art of examination. But it had been given up of late and its revival seemed to indicate a matter of unusual gravity. "The man need not despair," said Ormond to Southwell when he heard that the King was to give Blood a hearing, "for surely no king would wish to see a malefactor but with intention to pardon him." But this opinion was not general and his conviction was never doubted by the world at large. A few days after his examination Secretary Williamson's Dublin correspondent wrote him that there was little news in Ireland save the talk of Blood's attempt on the crown, and he voiced the prevailing sentiment when he "hoped that Blood would receive the reward of his many wicked attempts." The coffee-houses talked of nothing else and all London prepared to gratify itself with the spectacle of the execution of the most daring criminal of the time.

But in this, at any rate for the present, they were to be disappointed. Blood was remanded to the Tower, and there held for some time while steps were taken to probe the case deeper. Two months later Sir John Robinson wrote to Secretary Williamson that Lord Arlington had dined with him the Saturday before, and had given into his hands certain warrants, not, as everyone supposed, for Blood's execution, but for his release and that of his son. Two weeks later a grant of pardon was issued to him for "all treasons, murders, felonies, etc., committed by him alone or with others from the day of His Majesty's accession, May 29, 1660, to the present," and this was followed by a similar grant to his son. Later, to complete this incredible story, his estates were restored to him, he was given a place at Court, and a pension of five hundred pounds a year in Irish lands. Not long after-

wards that indefatigable diner-out, John Evelyn, notes
in his diary that, dining with the Lord Treasurer, Arlington, a few days before, he had met there, among the
guests, Colonel Thomas Blood. It is no wonder that a
Londoner wrote in early August of that same year: " On
Thursday last in the courtyard at Whitehall, I saw
walking, in a new suit and periwig, Mr. Blood exceeding
pleasant and jocose — a tall rough-boned man, with small
legs, a pock-frecken face with little hollow blue eyes."
By September Blood had acquired enough credit, apparently, not only to get a new grant of pardon confirmed for himself and his son, but others for certain of
his former companions as well.

What is the explanation of this extraordinary circumstance? It is a question no one has yet answered satis-
factorily, and it has remained one of the many unsolved
mysteries of the period. If we knew fully we could clear
up many dark ways of Restoration politics. We have
certain second-hand accounts of what took place in that
memorable interview between the vagabond King and
the Irish outlaw, from which we may get some light on
the matter. The latter " as gallant and hardy a villain
as ever herded with the sneaking sect of Anabaptists,"
in the words of a contemporary, we are told, " answered
so frankly and undauntedly that every one stood
amazed." Snatches of Blood's comments on his most
recent exploit have floated down to us. " It was, at all
events, a stroke for a crown," had been his remark to
Beckman when he was captured, a cool witticism which
must have pleased the wittiest of monarchs when it was
repeated to him. " Who are your associates?" he is said
to have been asked, to which he replied that he " would
never betray a friend's life nor deny guilt in defense of
his own." Blood explained to the King, it is said, that
he thought the crown was worth a hundred thousand
pounds, when, in fact the whole regalia, had he known it,

cost only six thousand. He told the story of his life and adventures with much freedom, and it must have been a good story to hear. He confessed to the attempt on Dublin Castle, to the rescue of Mason, and to the kidnapping of Ormond. There was found on his person a "little book in which he had set down sixty signal deliverances from eminent dangers." And one may remark, in passing, that it is a pity that it, instead of the dagger with which Edwards was stabbed, is not preserved in a London museum.

Several about the monarch contributed their information of Blood. Prince Rupert, in particular, recalled him as "a very stout, bold fellow in the royal service," twenty years before. But the thing to which rumor credited his escape and which was reported to have made his fortune, was a story in connection with the King himself. A plot had been laid by Blood and his accomplices, according to his account, to kill the King, while he was bathing in the river at Battersea. But as they hid in the reeds, said the outlaw turned courtier, with their victim before them, the majesty of royalty was too great, he could not fire the shot. But, he continued, there was a band to which he belonged, three hundred strong, pledged to avenge his death on the King, in case of his conviction.

Doubtless truth lurks amid all this. It may all be true. Even so there is hardly material here for pardon, much less for reward. Other reasons not known at that time must be assigned for such royal clemency. One, perhaps, lies in this letter written six days after the examination:

"May 19, 1671. Tower. Col. Blood to the King.

"May it please your Majesty these may tell and inform you that it was Sir Thomas Osborne and Sir Thomas Littleton, both your treasurers for your Navy, that set me to steal your crown, but he that feed me with money was James Littleton, Esq. 'Tis he that pays under your treasurer at the Pay Office. He is a very bold villainous fellow, a very rogue, for I and my companions have had many a hundred pounds of him of your Majesty's money to encourage us upon this attempt. I pray no words of this confession, but know your friends. Not else but am your Majesty's prisoner and if life spared your dutiful subject whose name is Blood, which I hope is not that your Majesty seeks after."

Surely of the two qualities then so necessary in the Court, wit and effrontery, a plentiful supply was not lacking to a man who could write such a letter in such a situation.

Another reason for the treatment Blood received was, strangely enough, his powerful influence at Court. It will be remembered, in connection with the rescue of Mason, that the great Duke of Buckingham, Lord Lieutenant of Yorkshire, and one of the men highest in favor at Court and in the country at large, had been arrested on a charge of conspiring with the fanatics against the throne. He had been released, and was now not only again in the royal favor, but was one of the leading men in the ministry of the day, the so-called Cabal. It was he who secured the interview with the King for Blood, and he doubtless lent his influence for mercy.

And there was, perhaps, a deeper reason for this. Buckingham was the bitter enemy of Ormond. The King, whatever his inclination, could not, in decency, pardon Blood, after his confessing to the attack on Ormond, without at least some pretense of consulting the man who had been so maltreated. He sent, therefore, to Ormond to ask him to forgive Blood. Lord Arlington carried the message with those private reasons for the request which still puzzle us. Blood, meanwhile, under direction, wrote a letter to Ormond, expressing his regret in unmeasured terms. The old Duke's reply was at once a lesson in dignity and loyalty. "If the King could forgive an attempt on his crown," he said proudly to Arlington, "I myself may easily forgive an attempt on my life, and since it is his Majesty's pleasure, that is reason sufficient for me, and your lordship may well spare the rest of the explanations." But Ormond's son, and his biographer, took refuge in no such dignity. The latter declares roundly that Buckingham instigated the attempt on his master. And not long after the affair, the former, the gallant young Earl of Ossory, coming into the royal presence and seeing the Duke of Buckingham standing by the King, his color rose, and he spoke to this effect:

"My lord, I know well that you are at the bottom of this late attempt of Blood's upon my father; and therefore I give you fair warning if my father comes to a violent end by sword or pistol, or if he dies by the hand of a ruffian, or by the more secret way of poison, I shall not be at a loss to know the first author of it; I shall consider you as the assassin; I shall treat you as such; and wherever I meet you I shall pistol you, though you stood behind the king's chair; and I tell it you in his Majesty's presence that you may be sure I shall keep my word."

These were brave words, and had they come from other lips than those of the Restoration Bayard, might have been regarded as mere bravado. But he had proved his courage on too many occasions to ignore this challenge. The word of such a man was not to be lightly set aside. And whether this threat was the cause or not, or whether Buckingham was really not responsible for an assault which might have been attributed to Blood's desire for revenge on the man who had confiscated his estates and hanged his brother-in-law, the old Duke was not further molested.

But, apart from these matters, there is another and a more serious reason for Blood's pardon and reward, a reason which has been concealed for more than two centuries, and which has only now, with the publication of the archives of the times, become a matter of public knowledge. It lies in the political situation of the time. This was, in many ways, peculiar. Some four years before the events we have narrated in connection with the theft of the crown, the administration of Clarendon had fallen and had been succeeded by that of a group called the Cabal, whose chief bond of union lay in the fact that they were none of them Anglicans and they were all opposed to Clarendon. With the aid of the King, they had relaxed the execution of the Clarendonian measures. The Anglicans in Parliament had been insistent that the old policy be maintained. The King was eager to revive the dispensing power, whereby the toleration of Catholic and Protestant Nonconformist alike would rest in his own hands. This situation was complicated by the fact that king and ministers alike were bent on another war with Holland. It seemed highly desirable to them to pacify the still discontented Nonconformists before entering on such a struggle, particularly since the government had little money and must rely on the City, which was strongly Nonconformist in its sentiments. It seemed no less necessary to destroy, if possible, that group of extremists whose conspiracies were doubly dangerous in the face of a war.

To gain information of the feelings of the dissenting bodies, and discover what terms would be most acceptable to them, to track down and bring in the fierce and desperate men from whom trouble might be anticipated, to discover if possible the connection that existed between the sects and those in high places, — these were objects of the highest importance. They needed such a man as Blood. And it seemed worth while to Charles to tame this fierce bird of prey to his service to achieve such ends as he contemplated. Some such thought evidently occurred to the King during the examination. "What," he is said to have asked bluntly at its close, "What if I should give you your life?" Blood's reply is almost epic, "I would endeavor to deserve it."

This, in consequence, became his immediate business. Almost at once it was reported that he was making discoveries. The arrest of three of Cromwell's captains is noted among the first fruits of his information; and close upon the heels of his pardon came the arrest and conviction of some twenty-four or twenty-five irreconcilables. Throughout the winter of 1671–1672 Secretary Williamson was in close consultation with Blood over the situation and the demands of the Dissenters, and he filled many pages of good paper with cryptic abbreviations of these long and important interviews, in which are to be found many curious secrets of conventicles and conspiracies, of back-stairs politics and the underground connections of men high in the councils of the nation. From Blood, from the Presbyterian ministers, through one or two of their number, and from sources to which these communications led, the Court and ministry gradually obtained the information from which a great and far-reaching policy was framed. It found form in the beginning of the following year in the famous Declaration of Indulgence. This took the control of the Nonconformist situation from Parliament, and placed it in the hands of the King. Licenses were issued to ministers to preach, to meetinghouses, and to other places for worship not according to the forms or under the direction of the Anglican Church. The policy, owing to the ·bitter opposition of Parliament, lasted but a few months, but it marked an era in English history. The rioting which had accompanied the revival of the Conventicle Act, and which had encouraged the government to try the licensing system, disappeared. The Dissenters went their way undisturbed. For a few months entire religious toleration prevailed, and, though Parliament forced the

King to withdraw his Declaration, the old persecution was never revived.

In this work Blood's share was not small. He not merely furnished information, he became one of the recognized channels through which licenses were obtained, and in the few months while they were being issued he drove a thriving trade. And with one other activity which preceded the Dutch war he was doubtless closely connected. This was the granting of pardons to many of those old Cromwellians who had sought refuge in Holland a dozen years before. No small number of these, taking advantage of the government's new lenience, came back from exile with their families and goods, and took up their residence again in England. Thus Colonels Burton and Kelsey, Berry and Desborough, Blood's brother-in-law, Captain Lockyer, Nicholas, Sweetman, and many others found pardons and were received again into England. "Through his means," wrote Mrs. Goffe to her husband, then an exile hiding in New England, "as is reputed, Desborough and Maggarborn [Major Bourne?] and Lewson of Yarmouth is come out of Holland and Kelsi and have their pardon and liberty to live quietly, no oath being imposed on them." "The people of God have much liberty and meetings are very free and they sing psalms in many places and the King is very favourable to many of the fanatics and to some of them he was highly displeased with." It might have been that the regicides in New England could have returned, but the cautious Mrs. Goffe warned her husband not to rely on the favorable appearance of affairs. "It is reported," she wrote, "that Whally and Goffe and Ludlow is sent for but I think they have more wit than to trust them."

In the third great measure of the period, the Stop of the Exchequer, Blood naturally had no part, but when the war actually broke out, he found a new field of usefulness in obtaining information from Holland, in ferreting out the tracts which the Dutch smuggled into England, and in watching for the signs of conspiracy at home. Thus he lived and flourished. His residence was in Bowling Alley, now Bowling Street, leading from Dean's Yard to Tufton Street, Westminster, convenient to Whitehall. His favorite resort is said to have been White's Coffee House, near the Royal Exchange. There he established, according to report, a little group, the least reputable of the four "Whig" organizations, "Colonel Blood's Club," ready to do the bidding of, it was whispered, whichever party paid him best. That he had some connection with the Duke of Buckingham's intrigues seems certain; and only less certain that he was paid by the government as well. His sinister face and ungraceful form became only too familiar about the Court. His bearing was resented by many as insolent. He was both hated and feared as he moved through the atmosphere of intrigue by which the Court was surrounded, getting and revealing to the King information of the conspirators, of the Dutch, and of the other enemies of royalty. His was not a pleasant trade and there were undoubtedly many who, for good reasons of their own, wished him out of the way. There were many who contrasted his reward with the neglect of the unfortunate Edwards, and who railed at Blood and the King alike. Rochester allowed himself the usual liberty of rhymed epigram:

> Blood that wears treason in his face
> Villain complete in parson's gown
> How much is he at court in grace
> For stealing Ormond and the crown?
> Since loyalty does no man good
> Let's steal the King and outdo Blood.

There were doubtless many more who regretted that the King had not bestowed on him a reward that was

at one time contemplated, the governorship of a colony,
the hotter the better. In that event America would have
had some direct share in the career of England's most
distinguished criminal. But Blood was far too useful at
home to be wasted on a distant dependency; and, on the
whole, he seems to have justified his existence, and even
his pardon, as an outer sentinel along the line of guards
between King Charles and his enemies. That he was so
hated is, perhaps, in some sort a measure of his usefulness. For the times when men in the ministry or just
out of the ministry conspired or connived at conspiracy
against the government and held communication with
an enemy in arms to compel their sovereign to their will
are not those in which a ruler will be too squeamish about
his means, least of all such a ruler as Charles.

In such wise Blood lived until 1679. Then he seems to
have fallen foul of the Duke of Buckingham, who had
played such a great part in his career. He, with three
others, was accused by the Duke of swearing falsely to
a monstrous charge against his Grace and sued for the
crushing sum of ten thousand pounds. A most curious
circumstance brought out by this trial connects our story
with the literature of to-day. In Scott's novel, *Peveril
of the Peak*, it will be remembered that the villain is one
Christian, brother of the deemster of the Isle of Man,
who was executed by the Countess of Derby. This man,
a most accomplished scoundrel, is there portrayed as the
familiar of the Duke of Buckingham, who plays a part
in the romance very like that which he plays in this story
of real life. With the appearance of the later editions
of the novel the author, in response to many enquiries
concerning the authenticity of the various individuals
there delineated, added some notes in which he gave
some account of the originals of many of his characters.
Concerning Christian, however, he declared that, so far
as he knew, no such man had ever existed, and that he

was purely a fictitious character. Strange as it may seem,
one of the men indicted with Blood in this action at law
was, in fact, named Christian, and Scott knew of him.
And while he may not have played the part assigned to
him in the story, he seems to have been in the service of
the Duke, and to have had a reputation, if not a character, which might well have served as a model for the
villain of the novel.

The motive of Buckingham in beginning this suit is
obscure, but it was suspected that he thought by this
means to hush up certain accusations which might have
been brought against his own machinations, then scarcely
to be defended in the light of day. Among those accusations, perhaps, was the story that he had hired Blood
to steal the crown. The curious and unusual procedure
and the absurdity of the charge which one might suppose
it beneath the dignity of so great a nobleman to press
in such fashion against such men, lends a certain color
to this suspicion. In any event the suit was tried and
Blood was duly found guilty. But he was never pun-
ished. He fell sick in the summer of 1680 and, after two
weeks of suffering, died on August 24. He was firm and
undaunted to the last, and looked death in the face at
the end with the same courage he had exhibited many
times before.

All England was then in the throes of the excitement
of the Popish Plot and the Exclusion Bill, and civil war
seemed almost in sight. Whig and Tory stood arrayed
against each other, with the crown as the prize between.
It would not be supposed that the death of the old adventurer could have caused more than a passing ripple
of interest. Quite the contrary was the case. Strange end
of a strange story, the mystery which surrounded him
during his life did not altogether end with his death and
burial. Even that, said many, was but one of the old
fox's tricks. And to prove that it was not his body which

had been interred in the adjoining churchyard of New Chapel, Tothill Fields, the grave was opened after some days, the corpse carried before a coroner, and identified by the curious fact that one of the thumbs was twice the natural size, a peculiarity which it seems would have betrayed Blood many times during his life.

Thus ended the troubled life of a mysterious man. If his end was not peace it certainly was not worse than his beginning. Not a few persons must have breathed easier at the final burial of the secrets which died with him. He was not without some literary remains, chief of which was a Life, which, though not written by his own hand, gives evidence of having been composed either under his direction or from material furnished by him. It contains, as perhaps its chief matter of interest outside the facts here included, — not many of which adorn its pages, — a story of which Blood seems to have been very proud. It is that on one occasion some of the men in his following of desperadoes proved unfaithful. He caused them to be seized and brought before him for trial in a public house. There, after the case had been set forth and the arguments made, he sentenced them to death, but later reprieved them. This, of all the good stories he might have told, is left to us as almost his sole contribution to the account of his adventures.

For the rest, his memory was promptly embalmed in prose and verse, mostly libellous and wholly worthless, from any standpoint. Of these memorials the following sample may suffice.

> At last our famous hero, Colonel Blood,
> Seeing his projects all will do no good,
> And that success was still to him denied
> Fell sick with grief, broke his great heart and died.

But there is still one curious circumstance about his family which it would be too bad not to insert here. It concerns one of his sons whom we have not met — Holcroft Blood. This youth, evidently inheriting the paternal love of adventure, ran away from home at the age of twelve. He found his way, through an experience as a sailor, into the French army. After the Revolution of 1688 he became an engineer in the English service, owing chiefly to his escape from a suit brought against him by his enemies, which was intended to ruin him but by accident attracted to him instead the notice of the man with whose visit to England our story began, now William the Third of England and Holland. This became the foundation of his fortunes. He served in Ireland, and in the West Indies. In the English service young Blood rose rapidly through the long period of wars which followed. He gained the praise of the great Marlborough, and ultimately became the principal artillery commander of the allied forces in the War of the Spanish Succession, dying, full of honors, in 1707. Meanwhile Ormond's grandson and heir, the second Duke, distinguished himself likewise in that same war in other quarters, and bade fair to take high rank as a commander. But on the death of Queen Anne he took the Jacobite side, was driven into exile, and died many years later, a fugitive supported by a Spanish and Papal pension. Thus did Fate equalize the two families within a generation.

Nor is this all the story. It is not necessary here to elaborate the long and distinguished career of the descendants of Colonel Blood's brother, the dean of Kilfernora. They are a part of English history. It is more difficult, it is, indeed, all but impossible, to trace the descendants of the Colonel. The name is not unknown in the United States: and some of its bearers are apparently the descendants of that Edmund Blood who was a resident of Albany in the first years of the eighteenth century, and who, according to tradition, was a grandson of Thomas. That tradition seems not to have been, like so many such, without foundation in fact; and it appears probable, therefore, that the land to which he was once destined as a royal official contains many of his descendants. And if one may be permitted a further reference to the career of the Bloods in the new world, though the story is too long — and too recent — to tell here, at the beginning of the twentieth century the newspapers of New York were as full of the romantic exploits of one of the family, who stole away a beautiful heiress from these shores, as those of London at the end of the seventeenth were full of the adventures of the crown-stealer. So it seems that, even after so many generations, blood will tell!

THE FAME OF CROMWELL

OLIVER CROMWEL

FROM A PROBABLY UNIQUE COLORED ENGRAVING OR MEZZOTINT
IN THE AUTHOR'S POSSESSION

THE FAME OF CROMWELL

O F ALL the characters in English history there is not one who is more vividly remembered, whether for good or ill, than Oliver Cromwell. Go where you will throughout the British Isles, you will find many to whom the period of the Civil Wars, the Commonwealth and the Protectorate is still real and still alive; to whom it is not merely history but is still politics; in whom Charles I and Cromwell still evoke emotions almost as intense as if they were living political leaders. The reason is not far to seek, and the events of the last few years have made it clearer than ever. It is that, say what we may to the contrary, the Civil War was not merely a struggle between the Crown and the Parliament, between Anglican and Dissenter, but between classes. To this conclusion the events of the past two decades, which have altered political status and opinion so greatly, seem to give point. It appears, therefore, appropriate at this time to review the evolution of the historic Cromwell, for in the vicissitudes of his fame are bound up not only changes in knowledge but a political transformation at once far-reaching and profound. This, then, is not a study of Oliver Cromwell; it is rather a study of his reputation; and, beyond that, of the evolution of English opinion and of English affairs, as expressed in its regard for one of its greatest figures. It is, in short, the biography of a biography.

IT IS now a little more than two hundred and fifty years since Oliver Cromwell died. No great space of time to those who deal in eternities and immensities, a quarter of a millennium is none the less a substantial period in human affairs; and especially in the last two centuries and a half men have traveled far. They have done much and they have forgotten much. Among the rulers of the Protector's day few, even of the greatest, are still remembered. But from that time to our own a stream of biographies has kept Cromwell's memory alive. They are numbered now by hundreds; they continue to appear; and that circumstance, were there no other, bears witness to an extraordinary and continued interest, most unparalleled in history. "Bewildered, interminable rubbish heaps," Carlyle declared — while contributing another stone to the pile — "the dreariest perhaps that anywhere exist still visited by human curiosity," "stupid, worthy of oblivion, of charitable Christian burial," they represent no less the permanence than the changing fortunes of Cromwell's memory.

And, poor as most of them are, they have their uses. They help to answer the question of how and why the great Protector's memory has been preserved. "What can be more extraordinary," said his contemporary, Cowley, "than that a person of private birth and education, no fortune, no eminent qualities of body, which have sometimes, nor shining qualities of mind, which have often, raised men to the highest dignities, should have the courage to attempt and the ability to execute so great a design as the subverting one of the most ancient and best established monarchies in the world?" He had accomplished the impossible. He had been granted that "marvellous distinction of breaking through the charmed circle which among European nations hems in the private man." In an age of divine right, this English squire became the ruler of three kingdoms, wielding an authority which had no precedent and no appropriate name. Pretenders based their claims on royal blood; Italian despots exercised at best a petty tyranny. Cromwell thus seemed a prodigy of superhuman, if not supernatural, powers, so great that no merely mortal explanation seemed credible. The superstitious declared that he had made a compact with the devil, who carried off his soul in the great tempest which accompanied his death, while he and his followers believed his success was due to divine influence. Yet neither his opponents nor his followers could have dreamed that, however great this achievement, it would have provided him so great and so shifting an immortality.

What, then, is the peculiar character of this immortality? The first stage in the evolution of a historic personality is the opinion of a man in his own lifetime — and there is no lack of that in Cromwell's case. From the beginning he impressed his fellows as more than an ordinary man. The rector who recorded the death of Cromwell's son, notes the father, then a simple gentleman, as *vir honorandus* — a man to be honored. To the Royalist, Sir Philip Warwick, he first appeared speaking in Parliament as a "gentleman ordinarily appareled in a plain cloth suit which seemed to be made by an ill country tailor, with plain and not very clean linen, a speck or two of blood upon his band, no hatband, a man large in stature, of swollen and reddish countenance, sharp and untuneable voice," yet, he admits, of "fervid eloquence." This was the man he lived to see, "by multiplied escapes, and a real but usurped power, having had a better tailor and more converse among good company appear of great and majestic deportment and of comely presence." And, though the tailor may have played too great a part in this great transformation in Sir Philip's mind, it is apparent, even from his words, that more than apparel went to make the man.

Those intervening years while Cromwell grew from a country gentleman to European stature, brought reputation with it in a hundred curious forms. From its first peculiar product, a satirical "Panegyrick" published while he was still lieutenant-general, to the elegies which followed his death, the Revolution literature was notably swelled by the pamphlets relating to this new Star of the North. Strange words were invented to describe him, like "Tyranipocrit"; strange titles were devised for tracts concerning him — "*A Sad Sigh with some Heart-Cracking Groans*"; "*Jonah's Cry out of the Whale's Belly*"; the "*Dutch Student beseeching the English Professor in the Great School at London.*" A splendid German folk-song, a symbolic dialogue between Cromwell and Charles, sounded democracy's challenge to divine right; and, at his death, the elegists burst forth into verse, and the historians began to commemorate his deeds. Waller and Dryden were rivaled by Slater and his *Rhetorical Rapture*; while Carrington compared him to Alexander, and Dawbeney to Moses.

Grown to such greatness, he was admired rather than loved by his immediate followers; hated and feared, even when most respected, by his enemies. What his soldiers thought of him; what those voiceless thousands whose banner he bore believed, we can only surmise from their actions. His cofferer, Maidston, declared that to him the Protector's head "seemed a storehouse and a shop of a vast treasury of natural parts, his temper fiery but kept down . . . compassionate, fearless, a larger soule hath seldom dwelt in a house of clay; religious, yet his temptations were such as it appeared frequently that he who had grace enough for many men might have too little for himself, the treasure that he had being but an earthen vessel and that equally defiled with original sin as any other man's is" — an appreciation which the Protector might well have read with mingled amusement and humility.

Of whole-hearted literary defense by writers of first
rank he had little enough in his own time, save that the
greatest pen of Christendom was on his side. That
counted for much, indeed, — more in our day, perhaps,
than in his own. To Milton at the outset of the great experiment of the Commonwealth he was

> Cromwell our chief of men, who through a cloud
> Not of war only, but detractions rude,
> Guided by faith and matchless fortitude,
> To peace and truth thy glorious way hath ploughed.

Yet even here the warning does not fail; already fear —
or is it doubt? — intrudes.

> . . . much remains
> To conquer still: Peace hath her victories
> No less renowned than war; new foes arise —

Two years later, when that experiment had failed,
Milton's prose appeal to Cromwell to take the supreme
power touched the high level of English eloquence. Yet
when Commonwealth and Protectorate alike were over
and the Protector dead, the great Puritan's pen was still.
Not so that of the splendid sycophant, Dryden, who sung
at the Protector's funeral —

> His grandeur he derived from Heaven alone,
> For he was great ere fortune made him so;
> And wars, like mists that rise against the sun,
> Made him but greater seem, not greater grow —

Even when royalty was restored Dryden spoke of him
as that

> . . . bold Typhœus . . . who had scaled the sky,
> And forced great Jove from his own Heaven to fly.

Yet, on the whole, that candid friend, Andrew Marvell,

perhaps best expressed the more moderate view of his own party.

> And well he therefore does, and well has guessed,
> Who in his age has always forward pressed;
> And knowing not where Heaven's choice may light,
> Girds yet his sword, and ready stands to fight.
>
> .   .   .   .
>
> He seems a king by long succession born,
> And yet the same to be a king doth scorn;
> Abroad a king he seems and something more,
> At home a subject on the equal floor.

In the main, however, the recorded judgments of his contemporaries, when not mere libels or panegyrics or, as in Milton's case, identification of the Protector with a cause, were hostile or extremely critical. Nor is this surprising. His enemies were numerous, able, and gifted in tongues; and, occupying as he did in later years, a middle ground, he was assailed on every side. First came the Presbyterians, who damned him with faint praise. "He meant honestly in the main," wrote Baxter, "and was pious and conscionable in the main course of his life till prosperity and success corrupted him. Then his general religious zeal gave way to ambition, which increased as success," though, he adds, with somewhat labored fairness, "it was his desire to do good in the main, and to promote the interest of God more than any had done before him."

Fiercest of all were the Republicans, who felt themselves betrayed by this apostate to the Commonwealth, who had led them to the borders of the Promised Land only to seize it for himself. "In all his changes," declared Ludlow, "he designed nothing but to advance himself, sacrificing the public cause to the idol of his ambition." To such men England seemed about to enjoy the millennium; "to attain in a short time that measure of happiness which human beings are capable of, when, by the ambitions of one man, the hopes and expectations of all good men were disappointed."

The Royalists, however bitter, entertained no such fond imaginings of the perfectibility of human nature. "Had his cause been good," said Reresby, Cromwell would have ranked as "one of the greatest and bravest men the world ever produced." To Clarendon he had, it is true, "all the wickedness against which damnation is pronounced and for which hell-fire is prepared." Yet he had, too, "some virtues which have caused the memory of some men in all ages to be celebrated"; he was a tyrant, but not "a man of blood"; he had a "wonderful understanding in the natures and humours of men . . . a great spirit, an admirable circumspection and sagacity, and a most magnanimous resolution"; he was, in short, "a brave, bad man."

Such were the judgments of the great Protector passed on him by the men of his own time. And if it may seem that of the three opposed to him, the Royalists, whom he harmed the most, held him in higher esteem than the Republicans, we must remember that though he had destroyed their power he had, at worst, not taken away their dreams.

Meanwhile to Continental minds he loomed huge, portentous, threatening, "the boldest enemy Europe ever had." Little loved even by those Protestants he championed, less by Mazarin, who sought the useful if unholy aid of the heretic regicide, he was hated and feared as much by Calvinistic Holland as by her recent mistress and antagonist, Catholic Spain, since on each, for trade or empire or religion, or all three, his blows had fallen impartially. To each of these he wore a different guise, to none of them the same he took to friend or enemy at home. The Dutch represented him as an ogre, the French as a bravo, the Spaniards as a fiend. But, for the most part, while England sought parallels for his career in

Warbeck and Simnel at the best, and Wat Tyler and Jack
Straw at the worst, the Continent found apter analogies
in the ancient world, or, where men dared voice the comparison, in those tyrannies for which the Sforzas, the
Borgias, and the Medici furnished more recent and more
striking examples.

To Europeans he seemed less a popular champion or a
fanatical enthusiast than an aspiring regicide, a tyrant
in the older sense, who by his arts, ambition, and ability,
raised himself to power on the ruins of a monarchy, and
ruled his country, not, perhaps, to its great harm; in
some measure for its good; certainly for its glory; by surpassing skill in statesmanship. To them, especially to their
rulers, his power rather than his character or circumstances made appeal.   Such different personages as
Condé and Queen Christina of Sweden expressed their
admiration and regard for him; and to the boy Louis
XIV, dreaming of the despotism he was to build and
wield, he seemed "the greatest and happiest prince in
Europe." Thus, under such widely varying auspices, the
first stage of Cromwell's reputation came to an end with
his death; and his fame, under such different aspects, set
forth upon its long and chequered career.

Its first adventure was with the returned Royalism of
the Restoration period; and scarcely had Church and
Crown come to their own again when the long-pent flood
of execration burst upon the tyrant's memory. The first
biography of any worth, Fletcher's *Perfect Politician*, indicated its character by its title, and might well have taken
for its motto the pungent line of the *Iter Boreale* — "That
meteor Cromwell, though he scared, gave light." It was
soon followed and largely superseded by that "chief fountain of lies concerning Cromwell," Heath's *Flagellum*.
This, long the most widely read of his biographies, allowed its subject no qualities save those of evil; vilified his
family; accused him and them of all the basest vice and

crime; pictured him as a monster no less despicable in private life than damnable in public action; and stripped him of every shred not merely of virtue and ability but of even common decency.

It found echo abroad; for there, no less than in England, the demand was for unlimited invective. At home Cowley's *Vision concerning his late Pretended Highness*, and Perrinchief's *Agathocles, or the Sicilian Tyrant*, its frontispiece a caricature of Cromwell crowned with twisted snakes instead of laurel, typified the spirit of the time. Abroad the Latin *Comparison of Cromwell and Tiberius*, and the German *Narrative of the Meeting of Cromwell and Master Peter in Hell* strike the same note. Of these one voice may speak for all, that of Winstanley's *Loyal Martyrology*, with its characterization of Cromwell as "the English Monster, the Center of Mischief, a shame to the British Chronicle, a pattern for Tyranny, Murther and Hypocrisie, whose bloody Tyranny will quite drown the name of *Nero, Caligula, Domitian*, having at last attained the height of his *Ambition*, for Five years space he wallowed in the blood of many Gallant and *Heroick* Persons."

Now that reviling had become not only safe but profitable, it was small wonder that many lesser spirits were inspired. While the lighter-minded of the Royalists vented their feelings in a famous tavern-song which commemorated his fabled origin as a brewer, and the splendid copper color of his nose, we may judge the hatred he inspired when even sober gentlemen like John Evelyn could record: "Died that arch-rebel called Protector . . . the joyfullest funeral I ever saw, for there were none that cried but dogs. . . . This day (O, the stupendous and inscrutable judgments of God!) were the carcasses of those Archrebels, Cromwell, Bradshaw and Ireton dragged from their superb tombs. Look back and be astonished! and fear God and honour the King! but meddle not with them who are given to change." "And yet," said Pepys, prophetically, "it do trouble me that a man of so great courage as he was, should have that dishonour, though otherwise he might deserve it well enough."

This period of unchallenged invective was to last but six years. Then the Dutch fought the English on nearly equal terms; the English government by maladministration, extravagance, war, plague, and fire, was brought close to bankruptcy and put up its fleet; the Dutch sailed up the Thames; the unprotected English men-of-war were sunk or burned; London heard the thunder of Dutch guns, and every English port felt their insulting presence. And "It is strange," wrote Pepys, "how everybody do nowadays reflect upon Oliver and commend him, what brave things he did, and made all the neighbors fear him, while here a prince, come in with all the love and prayers and good liking of his people . . . hath lost all so soon." Thus his courage and ability which had made him what he was while he was alive, had begun to protect his memory once he was gone; for within a year the first defense of his rule appeared in print.

That reaction found no echo on the Continent. There, meanwhile, a Cromwell legend had arisen. It is significant that the most considerable writers who essayed his life were all Italians. The spirit in which they wrote is best expressed in the title of a later German work *Arcana Dominationis* — the secrets of governing. To Machiavelli's countrymen this was the chief appeal of the English Puritan, his mastery of men and of the "mysteries of state." Dear to the heart of earlier, empiric statesmanship, versed in the arts of management, and the means by which individual fortunes were advanced and subjects kept submissive, these were the lessons to be learned from this master of statecraft. In such spirit Galardi wrote his *Tyrannie Heureuse, ou Cromwell Politique, avec ses Artifices et Intrigues*. Thus Modena's secretary of state, Gratiani, composed his most popular play, "Il Cromwele Tragedia," of even greater vogue. It was reflected in Paioli's *Cromwell et Mazarin*; and was summed up in the most famous of this group, Gregorio Leti's *Life*, the longest account of the Protector which had yet appeared, and the one which largely determined the Continental conception of him for a century.

The author was no less notable than his book. A bishop's nephew, bred to the church, but turning Calvinist, he lived successively in Rome, Switzerland, England (where he became royal historiographer), and in Amsterdam. The historian of Geneva, the foe of the Papacy and of Louis XIV, he would have seemed the ideal biographer. But he was obsessed by Cromwell's regicide and tyranny; and his work partakes in equal measure of picturesque romance, Machiavellian statecraft, and Royalist-Republican vituperation.

In Leti's view Cromwell was a prodigy, conceiving and executing the subversion of royalty with courage, ambition, and prudence; and compelling fortune by his marvelous ability. He dominated the most fiery, subdued the most obstinate. None knew better how to assume a mask of hypocrisy to conceal ambition; to make the barbarous, unjust, and violent maxims of his rule recognized, respected, and loved, for no prince ever had such great talents, nor better understood the art of governing. Now assuming the fox's skin, now the lion's, no friend was ever so false, no foe of Europe ever so bold. He gave usurpation the appearance of public good; kindled rebellion under pretense of public safety; roused others to drive out royalty and free the nation that he might seize tyranny for himself. He reversed the order of government, and even replaced the laws of religion with others better fitted to his absolute rule. Like all tyrants he was faithless and suspicious, vindictive, bloodthirsty, and a hypocritical demagogue. He abused Parliament, destroyed the upper house, drove out the bishops, overawed the council, and sustained himself only by a powerful army wholly under control.

But Leti was not content with depriving Cromwell of all human virtues. He declared that the Protector was that rare thing in the world, a tyrant without vices, save those of state, — ambition and hypocrisy. Under his rule men lived in England as in a cloister. He hated learned and literary men; destroyed the Oxford libraries, sacked her colleges, discouraged philanthropy, religion, and education, let public edifices decay, and distributed contributions for the persecuted Vaudois among his "red brethren." Such was the character of an English tyrant which did duty for Cromwell's portrait on the Continent for more than a hundred years, and with which Catholic Europe, "seeing in him a scourge and anti-Christ," rested for the most part content.

Leti's book appeared three years after the Revolution of 1688. Whether publishers are right in their contention that popular interest runs in cycles of about thirty years, so that each generation sees a "revival" of historic characters, or whether, as Chasles declares, the Revolution gave rein to "Nonconformist and Republican sentiments" — though the latter would certainly not have helped Cromwell — this much is true. The most astute of English author-publishers took this occasion to bring out a little life whose success in England rivaled that of Leti abroad, and ushered in a new school of Cromwellian biography destined to last for half a century.

"Robert Burton," born Nathaniel Crouch, was a tailor's son. Early apprenticed to a famous publisher, Livewell Chapman, whose name and book proclaimed his Puritan proclivities, he became the most prolific and popular book-maker of his day. Being a publisher nothing human was alien to his pen. The works he wrote as Robert Burton and published as Nathaniel Crouch ranged from *A Devout Soul's Daily Exercise in Prayer* to

A Winter Evening Entertainment of Relations and Riddles.
Twenty-second in the list of forty-five volumes credited to
his industry, his *History of Oliver Cromwell* appeared two
years after Leti's book.

Burton's life was not, indeed, a defense of the Protector's memory, but it challenged those who invaded "the
Almighty's province of judging the Hearts and thoughts
of Men, attributing all to Hypocrisie and Ambition." He
gave no credit to the calumnies of Heath regarding Cromwell's private life. Leaving "every Man to his own
Opinion," he "thought it not unacceptable to his Country men to give a plain and impartial Account of Matters
of Fact." He quoted documents, Cromwell's own words,
including his pathetic death-bed prayer, and an elegy of
him "whose Valour amounted him to that height by
which he raised the Nation to that Glory that Forreign
Princes feared and envied him."

The numerous editions of this little book testify to
Crouch's prescience as a publisher. Opinion was changing. Within three years one writer reckoned the advantages of Cromwellian rule, and, upon the appearance of
Ludlow's memoirs, another published a *Modest Vindication* of Cromwell's character against the Republican's as-
persions. Then, four years after Ludlow, Clarendon's
History of the Great Rebellion first saw the light of print; and
there was thus projected into the literary field that Royalist-Republican antagonism which had earlier dominated
politics. With this the stream of Cromwellian opinion
perceptibly divides; yet not to his advantage. United in
nothing else, they were at one in denouncing him. To
both, in Pope's words, the Protector was "damned to
everlasting fame." Rejected by the Tories, who condemned him as a usurper of authority, and by the Whigs
as having exercised a tyranny, he seemed equally obnoxious to the champions of power and the upholders of
liberty.

"Like a Mahomet," wrote the Tory Echard, "with transports of Fancy, a crafty understanding, deep thought, resolute, aspiring Temper, ready to head any faction, a radical original Hypocrisy, mighty genius, prodigious Address, having usurped three Kingdoms, governed by councils of Rapine and courts of Murder, by the severest Vengeance of Heaven he died impenitent, hardened and raving mad, with the Curses of the present and the Detestation of future Ages." Echard quoted Cowley; his Whig rival, Oldmixon, repeated Baxter, with a collection of adjectives and nouns, "hypocrisy, treason to Parliament, eloquent, arbitrary, care for trade, glorious," and Leti's phrase, "a Tyrant without Vice, a Prince without Virtue." Surely where Whig and Tory so agreed it would have seemed enough to dispose of the Protector's fame forever.

On the Continent, indeed, as yet undisturbed by revolution and dominated by the ideals of the Grand Monarque, this was in a measure true, and, save for the advance of skepticism and common sense, Leti's portrait remained unchallenged. Though the lofty spirit of Bossuet, sensing something of Cromwell's religious feeling, rejected it, Voltaire found it not incredible. To him Cromwell remained tyrant, parricide, and hypocrite, "the most terrible of charlatans," who "under Elizabeth would have been hanged, under Charles II ridiculed." Thus the saint saw deeper than the cynic. In England, meanwhile, the new revolution had provided perspective; the rule of Charles II and James II had provided comparison. The generation which had felt his power had passed; and religious feeling as expressed in Dissent, with a conception of the "people" unknown on the Continent, permitted the rise of another school of thought.

In consequence, thirty years after Burton, one Isaac Kimber, a "General Baptist" minister, "impartially collecting material from the best *Historians* and several

Original *Manuscripts*," produced for the first time a frankly favorable biography. He reproduced Cromwell's own words; he adduced documents; he enumerated the sources and examples of the Protector's greatness. Above all, he replaced the repulsive effigy of a tyrant with the image of a man among his fellows. He recorded the human traits, the humor, the tenderness, the clemency, the strength and weakness of Cromwell's character, restoring those qualities which, denied by earlier biographers, cut the Protector off from human sympathy.

On the Continent, indeed, this creature of flesh and blood could not compete with Leti's monster, but in England it evoked response. Fifteen years later John Banks, in a new biography, added two contributions of his own. The one was a defense of the doctrine that a "private man" might hold the sovereignty; the other was a shrewd attack on those who had denied Cromwell the very qualities by which alone he might have risen to eminence. It is absurd, he said, to try "to persuade us that a man without the capacity requisite in a common justice of the peace should be not only too hard for the royal family but even for his own masters and all the ministers and crowned heads with whom he had anything to do." There echoes the doctrine of eighteenth-century common sense, the logic of Locke, the prophecy of democracy. Yet with it, strangely enough, we come not to the beginning but to the end of an era. For three-quarters of a century after Banks no life of Cromwell of any note appeared, and the four Cromwells — Leti's, Ludlow's, Clarendon's, and Banks' contended in men's minds for mastery.

Not that men had lost interest in the Protector; on the contrary they were never so busy investigating his character and career. For his fame, as its next adventure, had fallen among a very different kind of folk, the antiquarians. A long succession of them drew from the archives of the seventeenth century a mass of historical material —

Thurloe's correspondence, Milton's state papers, Sidney's memoirs, Cromwellian letters, anecdotes, and panegyrics; while Green ventured the first of English plays based on Cromwell.

Midway of this antiquarian period, William Harris published a *Life of Cromwell* in his Stuart series, written "after the manner of Bayle." A curious manner it was, ancestor of a later and pretentious school of scholarship, whose soul, even to-day, it might well fill with envy, not unmixed with awe. Its first hundred pages contain less than two hundred lines of text; the rest is fine-print notes. Page after page has but a single line; some — triumph of editorial art — have no text at all. Characteristically, his opinion is contained in the last lines of his final note. "Time," he says, "the great friend of truth, has, in some measure, cleared up his character and done justice to his abilities — if he cannot be ranked among the best, he is undoubtedly to be placed among the greatest princes."

As the climax of this antiquarian school, in the year after the American Revolution, Mark Noble issued his *Memoirs of the Protectoral House of Cromwell.* Wholly uncritical as it was, it did no small service in clearing up that "cloud of distractions rude" by which the real Cromwell had been hidden from the world. His reward was small. Few writers have been more used, and more abused — especially by him who used him most. "Devoid of imagination, style, philosophy, good-sense and sagacity," "imperfectly educated, vulgar-minded, puerile, silly," as he was described by later writers, Carlyle's "reverend, imbecile friend," has had his share of contumely. Yet while judgment was not the worthy parson's strongest point; while truth and error were often confounded in his pages; while he regarded Cromwell as "an exercise in archaeology," pursuing his career with an industry which did not even overlook the shape of the windows in his house, he brought together a huge, if undigested, mass of material, and laid the foundations of future study.

Lamely enough, he takes Smollett's character as his own; "An amazing conjunction of enthusiasm, hypocrisy, and ambition, courage and resolution, penetration and dissimulation, the strangest compound of virtue and villainy, baseness and magnanimity, absurdity and goodsense, we find in the annals of mankind." There spoke the representative of eighteenth-century common sense; and we must admit that its opinion scarcely kept pace with its knowledge. Between the liberal Huguenot refugee historian, Rapin, who wrote in the first quarter, and the skeptical Scotch Jacobite, Hume, who wrote in the last half, of the century, there is less difference than might be imagined from the difference in time and temperament. Each admitted the now commonly accepted opinion of Cromwell's great ability, denied by earlier writers; but the one denounced him for faithlessness, regicide, and usurpation, and the other, seeing nothing remarkable in his career once in command of the army, declared that he was "A frantic enthusiast at bottom, an unequal and irregular genius, defective in no talent save elocution, praiseworthy for his private character, he tempered absurdity with penetration, ambition and fanaticism with justice and humanity. His home administration showed ability, partook neither of liberty nor arbitrary power, his foreign policy was harmful to English interests, while his usurpation was probably necessary and unavoidable."

It is hard to see why later writers have resented such a character so much. When one compares it with the concurrent portrait drawn by the female Republican historian, Mrs. Macaulay, compounded as it is of the worst of Heath and Leti, Holles and Ludlow, heightened by her own considerable gift of invective, it rises almost to the dispassionate dignity of Thucydides. Goldsmith was not

so severe; and even Dr. Johnson, who gave up his project
of writing a biography of Cromwell because "everything
worth saying about him had been said," seems to have
disliked him as a fanatical tyrant less than he admired
him as a great Englishman. It would have been well for
Johnson's editor, Murphy, had he followed the Doctor's
example, in that highest-paid piece of literary mediocrity
of the century where he declares that the Protector, "guilty
of deserting every honest principle, acted the tyrant, and
with vile hypocrisy told the people he had consulted the
Lord and the Lord would have it so." Yet Horace Wal-
pole declared, characteristically, that Cromwell had been
no more despotic at the height of his power than Pitt, and
that he had not thought at the time he raised his regiment
of rising to the head of the state, when "the King lost his
head and the Colonel his rest."

It could not be supposed that political leaders would
commit themselves to such a delicate subject as an opinion of Cromwell; and we scan the Parliamentary debates
of the eighteenth century almost in vain for reference to
his name. Not till the century was far advanced, not till
scholarship and revolution had done their work, do we
find much trace of him. Shelburne, indeed, under whose
patronage Noble worked, declared that "justice had not
been done his career, he was not always a hypocrite, and
though he had not been able to settle government at
home, England had never been so respected abroad, nor
ever revealed so many talents, and he had set more things
forward than any English king" not excepting William
III. Such sentiments may help explain why Shelburne
was looked on askance by the silken barons of the Whig
oligarchy; but his dictum sums up the conclusions
reached by the end of the century.

Then, emerging from the antiquarians, his fame suddenly met with another and thus far its greatest adventure. It fell among a new generation of revolutionists.

Twice since his death had it been affected by the vicissitudes of politics, both times to its advantage. Now, even
while Noble and his patron Shelburne wrote, the American colonies threw off the English yoke; the French
people overturned monarchy; the new world and the old
were convulsed with war; great popular movements made
way in the world; new revolutionary leaders made their
appearance on the stage; and for the first time it seemed
that an adequate basis of comparison with Cromwell and
his times was available.

Nothing would, then, have seemed more probable than
that his character and career would find able and eloquent defense. But what happened? When Patrick
Henry strove to rouse his countrymen to resist, he invoked,
indeed, the spirit of Cromwell. But when, the Revolution
over, the Americans turned to frame a constitution, proposals to increase the power of the executive brought
prompt protest from those who feared the danger of "a
Cromwell or a Catiline." In France, however much the
early agitators invoked his great memory, once the movement neared success the fear of the usurper replaced the
inspiration of the revolutionary leader. Against Marat,
bent on Girondin overthrow, Guadet cited the dissolution
of the Long Parliament, "whose crimes served the pretext
of the usurper." To Brissot, pleading for respect for the
King, the Jacobin, Saint-Just, retorted that "Cromwell
respected royalty but conspired against Charles." Robespierre, who adduced him as an example of "tyrants who
sacrifice their equals not for the people but for their own
ambition," was taunted with attempting to use Cromwellian methods to bring himself to power. Danton, in a
famous burst of eloquence, denounced those scoundrels
who interrupted him with cries of "Cromwell," and indignantly repudiated the implied resemblance. Through
all their fiery speeches ran the menace of the usurper, and
across the Assembly, in its guise, lowered the advancing

shadow of Napoleon. With reason; for in the crisis of his
fortunes at Brumaire, amid the shouts of his opponents,
Bonaparte was heard to mutter brokenly of Cæsar and
Cromwell.

Yet, incredibly, there stood forth a great champion —
Edmund Burke. However great his reverence for social
order, his hatred of French revolutionary excesses proved
greater still. Against them he invoked a famous parallel
between their leaders and the Puritans, "men of great
civil and military talents, at once the terror and the ornament of their age, who advanced the fortunes of their
country no less than their own, not so much usurping
power as asserting their natural place in society." Yet
while on one side the Channel French leaders disavowed
resemblance to Cromwell, and on the other Burke disavowed their resemblance to him, agreeing on this point,
though no other, only in Germany and — prophetically
perhaps — in Marseilles did men publish lives of the
Great Protector. England was too busy with the new
revolution and the new usurper to hark back to her own
dictator, and for the time being the fame of Cromwell
languished among his countrymen.

Yet whether Continental wars roused England to revive the glories of the past, or whether the influence of
eighteenth-century antiquarians remained untouched by
war, the era of Napoleon gave fresh impulse to the collection of materials for history. A new and better Parliamentary history embodied the debates; new collections of
State Trials and of the Statutes of the Realm; the Journals of the Lords and Commons; and a whole regiment of
memoirs, served to illumine the darkness of the past,
and with it the figure of its greatest character.

Its first effect was not on England but the Continent.
There it was heightened by another circumstance.
Among the incidental results of Napoleon's career doubt-
less none would have surprised him more, had he known

of it, than his effect on Cromwell's fame. For the first time Europe had felt a tremendous popular convulsion in the French Revolution. The fears of the revolutionary leaders had been more than justified; for they had seen a private man rise to dictatorship. That served in some measure to explain Cromwell to the Continental mind. The parallel was too obvious to be missed and, from the first year of the Consulate to Waterloo, pamphleteers were busy in pointing it out.

Then, with Napoleon's fall, the streams of knowledge and of experience combined. Within five years appeared Villemain's life of the Protector, the first of any consequence since Leti, which revealed Cromwell to the Continent. But in what a different light! The scholarship of the preceding century, the events of the preceding generation, Banks' views, Noble's notes, Hume's "inexact eloquence," the papers of Thurloe and Milton, the memoirs of Ludlow, Whitelocke, Newport, Hutchinson, the official documents, even the opinions of Voltaire and Bossuet, all contributed to his pages. And if his work echoes as much of the "penetration of genius" as of scholarship, the "sagacity of a high intelligence supplementing minute investigation of facts," this was reckoned no defect by the generations which read and enjoyed and were informed by it. For a quarter of a century it reigned supreme; and it inspired, among other things, Victor Hugo's drama of Cromwell, whose difference from Gratiani's measures a whole world of thought.

Meanwhile, in England, Byron had declared that

> Sylla was the first of victors; but our own
> The sagest of usurpers, Cromwell; he
> Too swept off senates while he hewed the throne
> Down to a block — immortal rebel! See
> What crimes it costs to be a moment free
> And famous through all ages.

And meanwhile the antiquarians pursued their steady

way, now reinforced by members of the house of Cromwell, which broke its silence of a century and a half with a biography and a selection from its archives. With them began a new crop of Cromwelliana, for while Villemain ruled the Continent some seven biographies contended in the new English heptarchy — Salisbury, Edinburgh, Manchester, Glasgow, and London's three; and it is notable that Scotland had its share for the first time.

It was too much to expect of the Age of Reform that Godwin should not expound the views of the Republicans. Still less could it be supposed that the most industrious of English literary men-of-all-work, Southey, could restrain his pen. Least of all could it be hoped that he would refrain from pious platitudes. Yet, even so, when summing up the career of "the most fortunate and least flagitious of usurpers" he might have spared quotation from the Litany against heresy and schism, and his pious conclusion that "in the world to come — but it is not for us to anticipate the judgments, still less to limit the mercy of the Almighty."

That marks the early Victorian at his worst, and Cromwell, if not the Almighty, would doubtless have felt appropriate gratitude for his biographer's magnanimous restraint. Yet, despite Southey's courteous refusal to influence that final adjudication, it is evident that, under the pressure of the oncoming wave of liberalism, opinion was changing rapidly. It was apparent in the work of the sane and able essayist, John Forster. Though Landor said that Cromwell lived a hypocrite and died a traitor; though Lodge declared that "not even a flowery Whig pen had yet tried to varnish his name with eulogy nor the fierceness of democracy to bedaub with coarse, plain-spoken praise the career of a subtle, treacherous, blood-thirsty, ambitious tyrant"; though Hallam drew his parallel between Cromwell and Napoleon, — Brougham ventured to speak of his administration as brilliant; commended, like Bright, his projects for law reform; and, like Bright and Russell both, adduced his projects for Parliamentary reforms as a model for such action. Finally, Macaulay, with his usual acuteness, summed up the case. "No sovereign," he declared, "ever carried to the throne so large a portion of the best qualities of the middling orders, so strong a sympathy with the feelings and interests of his people. He had a high, stout, honest English heart and though his memory has not been taken under the patronage of any party, truth and merit at last prevail." There spoke the voice of triumphing middle-class Liberalism, to Cromwell's virtues very kind, and to his faults a little blind.

The hour and the book were now at hand. Planning for years to write a life of Cromwell, Thomas Carlyle finally, and no doubt wisely, joined the antiquarians — on his own terms — and in 1845 reprinted Cromwell's own words, with Carlylean comment to provide a connected narrative. He undertook the task in the spirit of Banks; he carried it out in the spirit of Harris and Noble. It was received by nineteenth-century England in the spirit in which Europe received Leti. To Carlyle's generation, which had seen two revolutions and a reform, and which was within three years to experience 1848; which was in a ferment of social, political, intellectual, religious activity; which hoped all things, which believed all things, Carlyle's *Letters and Speeches of Oliver Cromwell* came like the revelation it professed to be.

It is apparent now that Carlyle claimed and received more credit than he deserved. His book contained no great amount of material not already published, save the editor's volcanic comment, which was not always good. His treatment of his predecessors was, at least, ungenerous. He used them and abused them. He condemned as worthless some books which it is charity to assume he had not read. He misquoted Noble and vilified him for his stupidity. And he did all this in the strident Carlylese, combining "the singularities of Richter, the caprice of Hoffmann, the obscurities of Swedenborg" in a commentary which is a "series of hymns and apotheoses," not unmixed with billingsgate. But, withal, he did two things of consequence. He collected a heap of valuable material in one place. He blew away much of the chaff and dust which had obscured it; he purified the rest; and danced and sang, and shouted and objurgated over the result till the world came to see. Having seen, they believed. This was the service which he rendered to Cromwell's memory. It was a great service and brought reward to both. One may not venture to reckon how many editions his book ran through, nor compute its influence. Carlyle did not, as Acton said, invent Cromwell; he did not even discover him; but thenceforth the Protector stood forth clear of extraneous matter. Called to the bar of history, his own words won for him the favorable verdict of democracy; and when Sanford and Forster had quieted forever the libels of Heath, Leti, and Dugdale, the age of rehabilitation was at hand.

Whatever else it did, Carlyle's *Cromwell* inspired a small host of followers. First in France, reinforced by the Revolution of 1848, able writers entered the Cromwellian field. The Academician, Chasles, produced a notable bibliographical and philosophical appreciation of the "successor of Luther," the "Mahomet of the North," the "militant head of Teutonic liberty." Merle d'Aubigné, the historian of the Reformation, despairing of his first design of translating Carlylese into French, wrote a brilliant, if superficial, "Vindication"; Louis Philippe's fallen minister, Guizot, followed with a history of the English Revolution and Oliver Cromwell, illuminated by his own experience with revolution. The one saw in Cromwell above all a great religious force; the latter a revolutionary despot "whose prudent genius, despite his destruction of legal order and liberty, commanded admiration, full of contradiction and mystery and paradox" as he was.

Thus was introduced a long line of biographies in half a dozen languages, all variations on the same theme. Yet in them all his reputation grew. Forster revised his earlier and less favorable verdict; Tulloch hailed him as the hero of Puritanism; Goldwin Smith as the hero of democracy. And though the opinion of the practical men changed little, though where Talleyrand had seen only a fanatical military genius, Napoleon III now beheld only the skilful pilot of a revolutionary storm and Disraeli ranked him still lower in the scale, the last march of the long pilgrimage began with a triumphal strain.

One thing remained — to give him an appropriate background and setting in his period. This the earlier biographies, hampered by lack of knowledge and insight, had done imperfectly, if at all. Godwin, Dahlmann, and Guizot had contributed something. Now, at last, his fame fell among modern historians. Of these the greatest were Professor Gardiner and his co-workers. The first volumes of Gardiner's *History of England from the Accession of James I* appeared in 1863; and, steadily progressing through the next thirty years or more, the patient genius of his scholarship gradually made clear the greater secrets of that much-vexed period. Before its revelations the Royalist conception of the brave, bad tyrant gave way, with that of the Republican, and those of their successors.

And what was his conception of Cromwell? "It is mainly this combination of interests — social and religious reform, commerce and empire —," he declares, "which has raised Cromwell to the position of the national hero of the nineteenth century. Like him modern Britain has waged wars, annexed territory, extended trade, and raised her head among the nations. Like him, her sons have been unable to find satisfaction in their

achievements unless they could persuade themselves that
the general result was beneficial to others besides themselves. It is inevitable that now as then such an attitude
should draw upon itself the charge of hypocrisy, inevitable, too, that in the eyes of foreign nations the benefits
accruing to ourselves have been more conspicuous than
those we have conferred upon the world at large."

Here, then, we have the force which made for Cromwell's rehabilitation, the feeling that, for good or ill, he
stood somehow for the English people, that he was a
symbol of the race from whence he sprung. But there was
another force which was of still greater strength. It was
the development of popular sovereignty. For, as Professor
Gardiner's work went on, England became a democracy,
prepared to see in the Cromwellian period the beginnings
of that form of government. The effect was immediate
and profound. The long search for a formula to explain
him was at an end. The result was, indeed, no formula,
but an appreciation of great underlying forces too long
ignored; and Cromwell rose to view no longer the strange,
isolated figure of an earlier day, the ambitious, earth-com-
pelling prodigy, but a product of his time, the expression
of its spirit, moved often by powers outside himself towards ends which he and his fellows saw dimly if at all.

Once this was grasped, the conclusion was obvious.
The work of great scholars from Ranke to Firth contributed to it; and with the concurrent advance of democracy and scholarship the stature of the Protector grew.
Matthew Arnold took him as the subject of his prize
poem at Oxford. The German, Pauli, and the Englishman, Harrison, writing almost simultaneously just before
1890, quoted approvingly Milton's splendid panegyric at
the outset of the Protectorate: "You alone remain, the
sum total of affairs has come back to you, and hangs on
you alone. . . . In human society there is nothing more
pleasing to God, more agreeable to reason, nothing fairer

and more useful to the State than that the worthiest
should bear rule. . . . To you our country owes its liberties . . . you have not only eclipsed the achievements of
our kings, but even those which have been fabled of our
heroes."

The ensuing decade and a half saw the culmination of
the apotheosis thus begun. In England and America
scarcely a year but saw a new and increasingly favorable
biography. German thesis-writers investigated the mi-
nuter points of his career, after the manner of their kind;
military critics, chiefly German, studied that phase of his
activities, after the manner of *their* kind. An American
president and an English statesman published biographies, at opposite ends of the scale of biographical value,
but alike extolling his virtues and his policies. His place in
history was determined by Gardiner's final dictum that
"with all his conscientious and spiritual yearnings, in the
world of action he was what Shakespeare was in the world
of art, the greatest and most powerful Englishman of all
time."

In such fashion his fame reached the end of its journey
— for the time. Gladstone, indeed, declared he could not
love him, but admitted he was "a mighty big fellow" but
"intolerant," which is, perhaps, as much a contribution
to our knowledge of Gladstone as to that of Cromwell. An
English government proposed to erect a statue to him in
Westminster Hall; and when the bitter hatred of the Irish
for his memory prevented its being placed there, the gen-
erosity of a Liberal prime minister provided for its erec-
tion in Palace Yard — so that though he was not, as the
wittiest American said, to be counted among the sover-
eigns, he could at least be reckoned among the half-
crowns.

Thus, as once none dared to praise him, so, as the ter-
centenary of his birth approached, no voice save that of
Ireland was raised to blame, and that may be, perhaps,

some measure of his fame. The old Republican opposition was turned to democratic praise; and Royalist de-
nunciation was as feeble as the royal power, only a few
sparks of it remaining to reinforce the long-smouldering
Irish hate. Meanwhile the high eloquence of democratic
statesmen filled the ear. "He was," said Lord Rosebery,
"a practical mystic, the most formidable and terrible of
all combinations, uniting an inspiration derived from the
celestial and supernatural with the energy of a mighty
man of action; a great captain, but off the field seeming,
like a thunderbolt, the agent of greater forces than himself; no hypocrite, but a defender of the faith; the raiser
and maintainer of the Empire of England."

In as lofty phrase Morley concluded: "Political ends
miscarry and the revolutionary leader treads a path of
fire. It is our true wisdom to learn how to combine
sane and equitable historic verdicts with a just value
for those eternal qualities of high endeavor, on which
amid all changes of fashion, formula, direction, fortune,
in all times and places, the world's best hopes depend."
Finally, Firth, in completing Gardiner's work, quotes
Henry IV's words to his son, which might well apply, not
alone to Richard Cromwell, but to those schools and
spirits that have inherited the fruits of the Protector's
work.

> To thee it shall descend with better quiet,
> Better opinion, better confirmation,
> For all the soil of the achievement goes
> With me into the earth.

He might have gone on in that son's words, voicing in
them what Cromwell would have wished.

> Therefore still bear the balance and the sword
> And I do wish your honours may increase
> That the great body of our state may go
> In equal rank with the best governed nation.

YET to this, as to all things human, there is an epilogue. When this essay was first written it included one passage of prophetic character. It ran somewhat as follows. "It is not too much to anticipate that with a further shifting of political ideals and practices, the popular opinion of the Protector will again be revised. Now he appeals to democracy, as he did two centuries ago to royalty, and as he must, in all ages, to masters of statecraft. But there may come another age; and fame, like times, may change with it. We have had hostile Royalist biographies in an age of monarchy; friendly biographies in an age of democracy; should the newest of popular political schools triumph, we shall have again, no doubt, at least a less favorable appreciation from the intellectual heirs of those Levellers and Diggers, whose projects, which seemed so visionary to him, the Protector so unsparingly repressed. For, however heroic the 'undemocratic hero of democracy' has appeared to the democrat, it is too much to hope that we shall not have a new Cromwell from the hand of the Socialist."

It is not often that prophecy is so justified of its early fruits. The Socialist has already invaded the field of history — and of Cromwell appreciation. To its latest prophet, Mr. Hyndman, the Protector wore another and a different guise. To him Cromwell was the representative of the "highly respectable, if sometimes hypocritically ascetic Puritans," the "powerful profiteering class." He had a "curiously complex, crafty and ruthless character," behind his "fanaticism." "He was able to gratify his ambition and determination to be master of them all because, in direct contradiction to what he said of himself, he knew quite early in his career of self-aggrandizement where he was going and how he would get there." He "never at any time had any scruples whatever." "Brutal and merciless," "the thorough representative of the English well-to-do landowning, farming and profiteering class . . . sympathy with democracy and freedom he had none." "From the moment he discovered that none of his possible rivals possessed the politico-warlike qualities that were combined in his person, he threw overboard every opinion and was false to every pledge that might encumber him in his upward climb."

So, through the revolving years, we come back to Heath again, in twentieth-century dress. But with a difference — we now know the facts, though they beat on Hyndman's intelligence in vain. It may be that this is the last and final adjudication; but if we judge the future by the past, it obviously is not. Only — and this, as Cromwell would have said, is the root of the matter — what possible school of thought is left; what can be the next adventure of his restless fame?

A SERVANT OF THE CROWN: SIR JOHN WENTWORTH

GOVERNOR JOHN WENTWORTH

FROM THE DARTMOUTH COLLEGE COPY OF THE PORTRAIT BY COPLEY

A SERVANT OF THE CROWN:
SIR JOHN WENTWORTH

AMONG those portraits which help to make up the picture gallery of Dartmouth College in Hanover, New Hampshire, none, not even the saturnine Choate, nor the Olympian Webster, impresses the beholder more than the lightest and most graceful figure of them all. A man in the early prime of life, with a keen, intelligent face, clean-cut, clear-eyed, he looks out on the world he left long since with understanding gaze, not unsympathetic, yet not deceived; serious, yet with the faintest shadow of a smile about the well-formed lips. The light, close-fitting wig, the dove-colored silk coat and waistcoat with their fine-wrought buttons and elaborate embroidery, proclaim the mode of the mid-eighteenth century, in sharp contrast to the businesslike presentment of the pious or philanthropic figures by which it is surrounded, worthy no doubt, but far from beautiful in comparison with this attractive old-world face. In the Government House at Halifax there hangs another portrait of the same man after forty years. Still serious, still regarding the world with steadfast gaze, with whitened hair and more sober dress, the same face looks out upon a very different world with undimmed spirit and unbroken charm. Between these pictures lies the life of a man, replete with human interest, dramatic circumstance, touch of romance, tragic catastrophe, and a peaceful, if not wholly happy, conclusion, — the type and symbol of a great epoch of history and a vanished race. And it seems worth while, even in these days, to tell the story of this man who, in a troubled age, played his part with courage and with skill, and, if he kept little else, kept his honor bright.

It is now a little more than a century and a half since the ill-fated ministry of George Grenville entered upon a policy which was to prove so disastrous to his country, then at the height of its earlier imperial career. That policy sought to organize, defend, and administer an empire enlarged in the preceding seven years by the acquisition of Canada and the dominance of India. And, among measures to check smuggling in America, to erect her western lands into an Indian reservation, to protect the frontier, and to strengthen the imperial authority, it embarked upon the project of taxing the North American colonies by means of a so-called Stamp Act, of evil eminence in English history.

Neither the ministry which devised it, nor the Parliament which passed it, nor even the colonial agents who opposed it, dreamed of the storm the Stamp Act would produce. But the American colonists, increased in numbers, wealth, and national sentiment, and relieved from their long-enduring fear of the French, were in no mood to see their trade crippled, their manufactures checked, their governors made independent of their assemblies, and their taxes levied by Parliament. In consequence the hectic summer of 1765 saw violent opposition to Grenville's policy. A new organization, the Sons of Liberty, welded that opposition into a fighting force. Riots and destruction of official property, including the stamps, widespread agitation, the enforced resignation of the stamp agents, and perfervid appeals to the British government, and to the colonial agents in London, combined in an attempt to nullify the hated act, with ultimate success.

At this dramatic moment in imperial history there appeared among those agents — the astute Franklin, the judicious Ingersoll, and their fellows — one of a different type from the shrewd men of business whom the British ministers were wont to see in that capacity. A young man just turned twenty-eight, handsome, agreeable, tactful, well-mannered, honest, frank, son of a wealthy merchant, nephew of a colonial governor, some two years resident in England and there received into the best society, a friend and namesake of the Marquis of Rockingham, this new-comer might well have sat for the portrait of that young Esmond whom a later novelist immortalized. Such was John Wentworth of New Hampshire, commissioned at this juncture joint agent with the London merchant, Barlow Trecothick, to adjust, if possible, the differences between his countrymen and the British government, and thus he made his entrance on the stage of history.

His appointment seemed a happy augury; for almost at once the Grenville ministry was replaced by that of Rockingham, pledged to reverse its predecessor's policy and conciliate America. The Stamp Act was repealed; and, as it chanced, — perhaps young Wentworth had been sent and kept abroad by his shrewd father with this end in view, — these measures included the appointment of a governor to succeed old Benning Wentworth, now retiring from the office he had held for a full quarter of a century. The ministry did not hesitate. Here ready to their hand was a candidate equipped by family, station, character, and ability, agreeable both to England and America, and Rockingham lost no time in nominating his namesake to the post.

Scarcely in fiction is to be found her favorite character of the Fortunate Youth so well exemplified. Wentworth was not merely appointed governor of New Hampshire. To this was added the important and lucrative post of Surveyor-General of His Majesty's Woods and Forests in

America. He was knighted; and to his degrees from Harvard, where he had graduated some ten years earlier, and from Princeton, Oxford and Aberdeen added their doctorates. Thus equipped with civil and academic dignities, he was despatched to his new post, the bearer of the tidings of Repeal, a pledge of friendship to the troubled colonies. With the servants he had engaged in Yorkshire and the horses he had bought, with testimonials of esteem from his English friends, he sailed by way of Lisbon to Charleston, where he proposed to begin his duties as Surveyor of the Woods.

The circumstances of his home-coming bore out the promise of his stay in England. From the hospitable homes of the Carolina planters he made his way to play cards with Mr. Byrd at Westover, to buy horses from Mr. Randolph at Chatsworth, to be the guest of Governor Sharpe at Annapolis, so through New Jersey to New York to hear Miss Bayard's charming songs at Weehawken, to visit his old friends in Boston, and so, after some six months, to New Hampshire. Meanwhile he attended to his office as no surveyor ever had done before, reporting as he went on hemp and tar, pitch pine and live oak, white oak and yellow pine, to the huge satisfaction of the government, approving himself no less efficient as a public servant than delightful as an ornament of society.

His province welcomed him as it had few governors. A committee of the Assembly, representatives of the Council, and two troops of horse met him at the Massachusetts line. At Portsmouth he was greeted by a militia regiment and the "independent company of enginemen" with military honors. The troops and citizens gathered in the public square; his various commissions as governor, captain-general, and vice-admiral of New Hampshire were read; the cannon at Fort William and Mary fired a salute; the militia followed suit; the people

cheered; and, after the usual public banquet, his friends
and neighbors "waited upon his Excellency to his seat,
where they took leave and left thim to receive, if possible,
a more endearing reception from his affectionate family."
Under such happy auspices the Fortunate Youth was
inducted into office — the last royal governor of New
Hampshire.

His appointment seemed more than justified. Here
was no alien proconsul set to rule a strange province.
Bone of its bone, flesh of its flesh, his family from the beginning had been identified with the colony. A century
and a half before, in that momentous decade which preceded civil war, when Charles I dismissed his Parliament
and turned to personal rule under the guidance of Archbishop Laud and the greatest of the Wentworths, Earl
Strafford to be, one of the latter's humbler kinsmen
crossed the sea among those thousands which the Great
Emigration of the Puritans poured into New England,
to secure its fortune and their own. To this man, William
the Emigrant, the intolerance of Massachusetts Bay seems
to have been as distasteful as the intolerance of Laud, and
he soon pushed beyond its jurisdiction to that palatinate
across the Merrimac but lately granted to Sir Ferdinando
Gorges and Captain John Mason.

There, almost from the time when the Laconia Company, formed to exploit this grant, had planted its first
settlement on the deep, still harbor at the mouth of the
Piscataqua to "cultivate the vine, discover mines, carry
on fisheries, and trade with the natives," New Hampshire
and the Wentworth family had flourished together. As
the colony increased from the original settlement to four
towns, Portsmouth, Hampton, Dover, and Exeter, William Wentworth and his descendants held their own. He
cleared land, built house and barn, farmed, trapped,
raised a family; became a party to the Indian deed to
Exeter; signed the "combination" which organized the

town; became an elder in the church. His eldest son, Samuel, come of age, made his way to Portsmouth, set up as tavern-keeper and merchant, married the daughter of a leading citizen, one Benning; prospered; had a son, John, who in turn married a Sarah Hunking; and in time became lieutenant-governor. Of his numerous progeny, one son, Benning, became the first governor of the separate province when, after a hundred years, its connection with Massachusetts was broken; another, Samuel, married a Deering; still another, Mark Hunking, married a Rindge, and became the richest man in the province and the father of Sir John.

Thus, as the handful of scattered trading and fishing posts and farms grew slowly to a body politic, as the simple economy of forest, field, and fishery grew into a more varied industry, this family, farmers, innkeepers, merchants, shipowners, landholders, officials, became the dominating influence in the society which it typified. Bennings, Deerings, Hunkings, Rindges, Atkinsons, Gilmans, Wentworths, a little group close bound by family ties, in a century of energy and thrift, had drawn into its hands the larger part of the young colony's goods and power. It had become the chief landed as well as the chief commercial interest, for its members had but recently bought up the claims of Mason's heirs to that part of the original grant which he divided with Gorges and named after his English home, New Hampshire. And as the province grew by an increasing flood of settlers in that century, — Scotch after Dunbar, Irish after Boyne, men from the southern New England colonies, English adventurers, — it took toll from the incoming settlers, as landholders through grants of land, as merchants through supplies and trade, and as officials through fees and salaries.

Such was the epic of New Hampshire and the Wentworth family; such the society in which he found himself;

such the oligarchic rule which he inherited; for on his council there was scarcely one who was not kin to him by blood or marriage or both. It was a characteristic feature of the period we call "colonial"; repeated in every province, the Hutchinsons in Massachusetts, the de Lanceys in New York, the great families of the south, a "natural aristocracy," based on talents, enriched by landholding and commerce, cemented by marriage. Its dominance was not, indeed, wholly unquestioned, in New Hampshire or elsewhere. Beyond it lay the "new men" of the time, chiefly the later comers and their sons; the "people" and their leaders, as distinct from the "aristocrats" of the elder line. This newer element was now rising to wealth and influence, though still denied entry into the inner circle of "those who managed." Able, ambitious, seeking place and power, it had already invaded the assemblies and the courts, challenging the authority of those who had arrived.

For while the Wentworths and their connections were predominant in Portsmouth; there and elsewhere, especially in those growing communities which resented the ascendancy of the capital, they had their rivals. In Portsmouth were the Langdons, John and Woodbury, trained in Daniel Rindge's countinghouse, now enterprising merchants on their own account, John in particular having made much money in the recent war. In Dover was John Sullivan, sometime a student in Judge Livermore's law office, son of an Irish exile, "schoolmaster" Owen O'Sullivan of Somersworth. In Exeter, which took political leadership from Boston rather than from Portsmouth, lived Captain Nathaniel Folsom, who had gained distinction in the late war; and the Gilmans, all of whom, save one, — the Speaker of the Assembly, — were in opposition. In Londonderry lived John Stark; and elsewhere were to be found others dissatisfied alike with the ascendancy of the Wentworths and of Portsmouth.

Yet withal Portsmouth remained the center of the stage. It was a thriving town of near five thousand souls and had felt the wave of prosperity which the war had brought to the northern colonies, by preying on French commerce and supplying the British — even, it was whispered, the French — with food and war material. The wharves which lined the river banks, the shipyards and ropewalk, the piles of deals and timbers, the warehouses and custom-house, the vessels which filled the harbor, revealed its principal industry. Its many handsome houses, adorned with all the taste and fancy of the period, equipped for ample hospitality, witnessed its success.

Its public institutions were no less conspicuous. It had a public library on the "tontine" plan. Besides its many taverns there was then being built the Earl of Halifax Hotel, in whose upper room met the St. John's lodge of Masons, affiliated with the Boston lodge, of which Dr. Joseph Warren was grand master. There was a work-house and a jail, however little used. A dozen years earlier an earthquake, a fire engine, and a newspaper, the *New Hampshire Gazette and Historical Chronicle*, the first of its kind in America, had made their almost simultaneous appearance in the town, and more recently there had appeared a rival to the latter, the *New Hampshire Mercury and Weekly Advertiser*, to express the sentiments of the "more zealous Whigs."

The pages of these little sheets are instinct with the vigorous life of this provincial society, and their character reveals the interests and the activities of its members as nothing else can. Proclamations regarding town-meetings, taxes, roads, quit-rents, proprietors' rights, boundaries of townships, compete with advertisements of lotteries to promote settlement, to encourage education, notably in Harvard College, ship entries and clearances, strayed cattle, packet-boats to New York, deserting seamen, and the search for "maids who understand country business." Daniel Pierce fills a column with notice of his importations of English and French cloths, linens, and silks. Gregory Purcell announces that he "takes in Flax Seed." John Sherburne deals in loaf sugar, molasses, and steel; Stephen Hardy in Gloucester cheese and hair trunks — curious combination; Mendrum Janvrin in crockery and glassware, flax, powder, shot, shoes, and rum.

Sparhawk and Fowle are the rival booksellers; Hughes and Knight the rival periwig-makers and hairdressers. Griffith the watchmaker, Hickey the dyer, and Doig the painter divide interest with Sheafe, who deals in Philadelphia flour. Nor are the graces of life wanting. Daniel Humphreys opens a private school; William Crosby engages to teach music, vocal and instrumental; Daniel McAlpine opens a broadsword academy. Ammi R. Cutter has to sell not only his medical skill but a fresh assortment of medicines, a vast array of easements for the ills of the flesh, including Jesuits' Drops, British Oil, and groceries, not forgetting the most staple of all groceries then, wines, brandies, and rum.

Yet proclamations and advertisements are not the whole of the story these newspapers tell. Week by week they record the news of the world, chiefly "by letter from London," reports of the doings in Parliament, the speeches of Chatham in full, the activities of the ministry, even a good deal about the more spectacular happenings of English society. Besides these, still, are the acccounts of marvelous prodigies — of two women who perished from spontaneous combustion of their own bodies, of the "affecting history of Zunchin, the last Emperor of China," of a monstrosity born from a sheep, like a negro child with the hinder quarters of the sheep. There are moral articles on such texts as "Industry and Frugality are the hands of Fortune." There is the news of Voltaire's death and his will, with other information from the continent of Europe, not unlike that which even now misrepresents the United States in Continental newspapers. All in all, then, Portsmouth was as alive intellectually, and especially politically, as it was materially. It even produced verse — for there are columns, even pages, of poetry. Especially when Dartmouth College was founded, the whole first page was taken up with a poem written by a member of that body to Wentworth as its chief patron. Its character may be seen in its last stanza.

> May Heaven propitious in one ceaseless shower,
> Round thee her richest Store of Blessings pour;
> To thee and to the Partner of thy Soul,
> May Happiness in endless Rivers roll,
> May every Grace your noble Souls inspire,
> A numerous Offspring crown your fond Desire
> Beneath thy watchful Care thy People grow
> And Shame and Silence seize on ev'ry Foe;
> May Peace attend thy Life, and blissful Rays
> Gild the calm Evening of thy setting Days.

It was, perhaps, unintentional unkindness which made the editor print in a later issue an " Epigram."

> Thy verses are eternal, O my Friend!
> For he who reads 'em, reads 'em to no *End*.

But, besides these political, historical, and literary bonds, Portsmouth had other communication with the outside world, celestial and terrestrial. From the roof of Captain Macphaedris' mansion rose the first lightning-rod in New Hampshire, erected, it was said, by Dr. Franklin himself. A regular stage service to Boston — one round trip a week, Mondays to Fridays, fare three dollars — provided access to New England's capital. By it, or like conveyance, came visitors — Copley to paint the dignitaries of the province, the Governor among them; Benjamin Thompson, later more famous as Count Rumford; John Adams on his legal rounds; Doctor

Franklin; and President Dwight of Yale, each to record
his favorable opinion of the government in his own way.

Such was the bustling, agreeable provincial capital
which was the stage of the ensuing drama. Here Wentworth had been born and bred. Here he lived in a house
on Pleasant Street, hired for him by the Assembly, a
"good, warm little dwelling," a "small hut" as he described it too disparagingly; adorned with wall paper and
furnishings from Boston, manned by the servants he had
brought from England — a "Lilliputian Wentworth
House" after the fashion of the Rockingham seat. From
his windows he could "look over the town and down the
river to the boundless Atlantic; on the other side . . . a
garden, bounded, or rather separated from the fields by a
large sea-water pond, which enlivens the rural scene."
Thence, too, he could see the neighboring residence of his
cousin, Theodore Atkinson; and conveniently at hand
stood his stables with his sixteen horses, and the carriages,
in which he took such pride. Here, from the moment of
his arrival, he was the most distinguished and popular
figure; and here he entered upon his great adventure as
governor.   .

His position, like that of all colonial governors of the
time, was difficult. His chief troubles were inherited. His
uncle and predecessor, Benning Wentworth, had filled
the offices with his favorites, had administered his fees
and perquisites from the land grants too much to his own
advantage, and refused to change the local government.
Meanwhile the increasing inequalities of provincial life
had grown to grievances. The new settlers complained of
his incompetence and greed. The scarcity of specie and
the uncertain currency bore hardly on poor men, while
the rude if salutary check on paper money and land banks
imposed by the British government increased the discontent. The outlying settlements, so rapidly filled up, found
no adequate representation in the government. To the

earlier frontier equality had succeeded new classes, especially the poor and the professional elements, the former lacking votes, the latter place, save by the grace of those about the Governor. Complaints that "officers were appointed from abroad to please the English government rather than the people" grew to a feeling that there was "a set of men seeking to found an American nobility intermediate between crown and democracy."

The gravity of this situation was not lightened by the utterances of the palladium of public liberty, the press, which, threatened by the Stamp Act, had not only opposed it, but encouraged resistance in others. Repeating the exaggerated tales of "near 40,000 weavers, glovemakers and other manufacturers," "with a black flag," surrounding the "R-y-al pal-c and par-mt House," in London, the *Gazette* had deplored the fact that "the whole continent is almost in despair" at the threatened loss of liberty and "the people exactly copy the example set them by their brethren at home." It urged that "the Accounts we give from Time to Time [of the Stamp Act disturbances] will not be taken as though we aim at Independence as some have in a most vile manner insinuated" — but "what ingenious mind that reflects on their ancient state can think of their present without weeping for the human species?"

Following this, two columns by "Cato" denounce the Stamp Act — and it is noted that "This piece was wrote several Days before the late Stirs in Boston." This, again, is followed by notes on similar disturbances in New Haven, once more by "Cato," in whom we somehow seem to discern the editor. The *Mercury* appeals in a serial editorial to the printers against the Stamp Act; and with these appears an account of the burning of the "Effigies of a Distributor of the Stamps pendant behind who hung a Boot newly soled with a Grenville Sole out of which proceeded the Devil," together with the office built for stamps. In such fashion resistance came to New Hampshire, and was chronicled. In such fashion was the none too grateful task of colonial governors made more difficult by a blundering home government and an aggressive colonial spirit.

Every colonial grievance had been reflected in the Stamp Act disturbances in which Portsmouth had shared. "Every one that was in distress," the officials quoted bitterly, "and every one that was in debt, and every one that was discontented" had joined in them; and though the moderates had prevented New Hampshire's representation in the Stamp Act Congress, the dissatisfied element had expressed itself. Of the new Governor's instructions but three remain — one as to attendance of the councillors, one in regard to a province survey, one relating to freedom of debate in the Assembly, and from the first meeting of that body the divergences appeared. For it refused to vote him a "permanent" salary; and while it approved his "benevolence and amiable qualities," his fitness for his post by "birth, fortune and education," it called attention to his "remarkable opportunity of hearing every Branch and part" of the British Constitution "pass the most critical Examen any age has ever seen," and thanked him for his services in that "critical conjunction of affairs when it was threatened and in danger of irreparable Burthens." This echoed the sentiments aroused by the Stamp Act; but, like the complaints about the currency and the struggle over the division into counties, it was to have been expected; and there was nothing here, in his opinion, which could not be arranged with prudent management, if he were let alone.

But it was suddenly complicated by another element. Scarcely was he in office when that evil genius of the British Empire, Charles Townshend, now Chancellor of the Exchequer, persuaded Parliament to impose petty and irritating duties on glass, paper, tea, and painters'

colors, and so raised again the question of colonial taxation. New agitation flamed; the Sons of Liberty revived;
non-consumption and non-importation agreements were
proposed to influence English merchants and through
them the British government, whose representatives in
America found themselves again in a peculiarly difficult
situation.

Not, indeed, in New Hampshire so much as elsewhere.
There the radicals might oppose the Stamp Act; they
might restrict the Governor's salary; but they could not
dictate to the powerful commercial interest how it should
conduct its business. Partly because, in the words of the
old historian, "the improvement of the country at this
time occupied the minds of the people and took off their
attention in great measure from the view of those political
difficulties"; partly because this issue lay largely in the
hands of merchants well-disposed to Britain and ill-dis-
posed to fight; but partly because of the young Governor's
"gift of governance," Portsmouth experienced no such
disturbances as some other ports, notably Boston. Thus
Hillsborough wrote approval of Wentworth's "prudent
endeavors to suppress in their infancy the factious attempts to kindle in New Hampshire the flame in respects
to the revenue laws which has disturbed the neighboring
colonies."

His character was well exemplified in this first test of
his capacity to rule. "The grand secret of peace," he
wrote, "is to cause men to think before they act, the longer
the better; and to be steady, open and resolute, without
any mystery or intrigue. In this way there will never be
great tumults. It is impracticable to raise a dangerous
mob if all the business is understood. Men will not be led
to broken heads, gaols and gallows, unless they are somehow deceived." In consequence, when an unpopular
official came, and the "zealots from Boston notified their
more moderate brethren" in Portsmouth to drive him

out of town, the Governor gave notice of his coming; asked advice of "some warm people"; entertained the man, and made his stay not merely peaceable but enjoyable. Nor was this due to lack of courage. Not long before, a mob had formed to rescue a prisoner from execution. The young Governor, notified by the sheriff at midnight, ordered out the militia, summoned the Council, stood before the jail, and commanded his men to fire to kill, if an assault was made, to take as many prisoners as they could, and to hang them the next day. This news dismayed the mob, which presently dispersed; since which time, he wrote, "we have not had even an escape, though the prison may be knocked down by an old woman."

This was the temper of the man; and it commended itself alike to the British government and to his own people. "Johnny" Wentworth was popular, alike from his courage, his fairness, and his good temper. Whether as Surveyor he explored the forests, checking the activities of the illegal wood-cutters; or whether as Governor he presided over his Council, his spirit and conduct were equally approved. He was, indeed, the most diligent as well as the most popular of executives. In a serious attempt to strengthen his government he called to office men and interests neglected by his predecessor. He carried on the work of setting up new townships, as settlers came, attracted by the easy terms of clearing and planting five acres in five years, paying an ear of corn a year for the first ten years as rent, and thereafter a shilling a hundred acres.

The mere list of charters, grants, and incorporations in his administration, from Dublin to Berlin, from Jaffrey to Bretton Woods, some thirty in all, reveals this incoming stream of population pushing forward into the wilderness and taking form. One reads of how in the "province of New hamsher, county of Starford" (Strafford), was held the "aneuil town-meeting," where the freeholders and

"inhabetens" chose their officers — moderator, town
clerk, "selekmen," "sevairs" (surveyors), hogreeves,
fence viewers, "Dear-keepers," and constable. They
could not spell but they could found a state. And as the
original four towns were thus reinforced, the Governor
embodied them into counties whose names still echo those
of his English friends — Rockingham, Strafford, Hillsborough, Cheshire, and Grafton. Here he showed his
statesmanship; for he successfully opposed the narrow
views of the Portsmouth group who were unwilling to
recognize the newer settlements.

In every phase of this new-forming province he took an
active interest. He paid the greatest attention to the
militia in his capacity of captain-general, commissioning
"new" men like Folsom, Stark, and Sullivan. He traveled far and wide to see at first hand how his people
fared. He co-operated with the New York authorities
with a view to exploring the forests on the Connecticut
and checking the pernicious activities of Judge Wells
among them. He approved young Thompson's plan to
survey the White Mountains, offering his own books and
instruments to that end. He tried to get the Assembly to
vote £50 for a province survey, and, when it refused, took
up a private subscription to employ Captain Holland,
Surveyor of the northern coasts, in that enterprise. He
busied himself with coinage reform and abolition of the
paper currency, which he finally accomplished. He tried
to strengthen the Church of England, now in danger of
submersion by the influx of new communions. Above all,
he strove to provide the first necessity of this new society,
communications. He projected roads to the Connecticut,
to the mountains, even to Quebec, hoping to make Portsmouth, as he said, "the first provision market in New
England."

No one can read his reports — as yet unpublished —
in which he supplied the Commissioners of the Treasury

with information of the situation of the forests and his own activities, without being conscious of two things, that here was a peculiarly honest and active servant of the Crown who loved his work, and that the work was difficult in the very nature of the case. "I found," he writes from Casco Bay in 1772, "on my arrival in my District, that the greatest part was not Inhabited; and such as were, the Inhabitants could not supply us with Provisions, and with such necessaries as we should have occasion for; [and] an extensive Sea boat; the extreme fatigue we must certainly experience in exploring the Woods; and the necessity of a place for the People to retreat to, were the reasons which induced me to request the above Vessell, and Boat. These disagreeable circumstances, I have in some measure experienced in some of the Eastern parts of my District." "In the months of June, July and August, the Moskitoes and black Flies are very numerous and troublesome; which renders travelling in the Woods, at that Season, extremely fatiguing." "I considered it of the highest importance to His Majesty's interest to go up the river Androscoggin, and put a stop to the depradations they were committing. I have the satisfaction to inform their Lordships, that our appearance had the desired effect, those Invaders fled at our approach, they had cut down some Pines, for Logs to be saw'd into boards; and for Shingles and Clapboards."

Yet he recognized the natural desires and necessities of the settlers no less than the rights of the Crown. "The acts of Parliament," he writes again, "relative to the preservation of pine timber in America, being merely penal and too general, operated so much against the convenience and even necessities of the inhabitants, that, had, or could they have been strictly executed, they would have prevented cultivation, and soon put an end to the lumber trade both in the West Indies and England. . . . Hence it became almost a general interest of the country to frustrate laws, which comprehend nearly an unlimited reservation." He pleads, therefore, for regulations which would permit cultivation, and enable men to "cut into the different species of lumber requisite for their own building, or profitable at market for exportation, the proceeds supplying the poor settlers with provisions, West India produce, and British manufactures." And no one can read his statesmanlike proposals to that effect without realizing the peculiar abilities of this greatest of early conservationists.

Nor, indeed, as he goes through this correspondence, can he fail to note another fact, that even at this early date there were those who "combined against" the public service, "interested in defeating the Actions, that they may Themselves trespass on the King's Woods with Impunity." Moreover, "though the Trespassers were without Difficulty convicted, yet they escaped punishment by the unworthy Intervention of Judge Wells in becoming a Trustee in a fictitious Conveyance of the Goods and Chattels, which alone were liable." Thus, it would appear, the raid on public property and the devices to evade punishment were not unknown to our ancestors; and not in our own time only has the government been left to meet the costs of its own impoverishment.

He was especially concerned with education; for, almost alone among the colonies, New Hampshire had no college; and here he came in contact with an important enterprise. One Eleazar Wheelock, of Connecticut, a Yale graduate, backed by Colonel Moor, had set up a training school for Indians and Indian missionaries some years before at Lebanon. But Indians were scarce in Connecticut, and Wheelock sought a site nearer the wilderness. He had fallen out with Benning Wentworth, who was determined to secure the institution for the Church of England. But the new Governor met his terms. A township on the Connecticut was set aside; the Governor subscribed to an endowment, the Assembly voted £100. A converted native, Samson Occom, was sent to England to solicit funds, and the spectacle of an Indian who read Greek and preached acceptably in English opened the English purse. The Earl of Dartmouth subscribed £50 and became chairman of the committee; the King gave £500, and there was raised £11,000 in all. Like any capable college president, Wheelock, with one eye on the Lord, the other on the main chance, drew up a charter, moved to the new town of Hanover, and set up there his school, a ferry, and a mill. And thither, in 1771, came Wentworth and his friends on horseback to the first Commencement, leaving as a souvenir of their visit a handsome punch bowl to the president.

That visit took the party through lands then in dispute between New Hampshire and New York, the so-called New Hampshire Grants — sixty-eight towns which Governor Benning had granted beyond the limits of his jurisdiction. New York protested vigorously enough to rouse even the somnolent Board of Trade, which checked his too ambitious plans and gave the lands to New York, to the disgust of their inhabitants, who, when occasion offered, set up their own state of Vermont. This had been part of young John's business in England; and when, just prior to the visit to Hanover, Benning Wentworth died, leaving his property to his widow, the "gypsy girl," whom this old provincial Cophetua had married a few years earlier, the Benning Wentworth grants came into politics. For within two months she married again, this time a Colonel Wentworth who, three years before, had brought his reminiscences of Culloden and Fontenoy to this new market with such great success. With that — whether from pique at being disinherited, or from family pride, or from reasons of state — Governor John enquired of his Council whether the five hundred acres his predecessor had retained for himself from the two hundred townships

to which he had given title, were legal. He was answered
in the negative, with one dissenting voice, and with this he
came to a great problem of his government.

That voice belonged to a newcomer in the province,
Peter Livius, of indeterminate antecedents, the husband
of a New Hampshire heiress, and through that a man of
property and position, whom Benning Wentworth had
made a justice and a member of the Council. He had already proposed, behind the Governor's back, a new system of forest administration. He now offered a minority
report, a bitter indictment of the Governor and Council,
sought support for it among the disaffected in the province, and presently took it to England to the Board of
Trade. It recited that the Governor had dispossessed
grantees of large tracts of land without process of law;
secured for himself through others the recovered grants;
prevented protest; and abused Livius personally. It
alleged further that no account of "powder-money" had
been made for thirty years, and the Assembly's vote for
an investigation had been killed in the Council; that the
Governor had changed the justices in the Common Pleas
to get a favorable verdict for himself; that he had filled
the Council with his relatives; and had failed to send a
copy of its journal to England, "to keep out of sight the
practices of himself and his council."

The Livius complaint was that most dangerous form of
accusation, a half-truth. The Board of Trade transmitted
it to Wentworth and his Council, who traversed at nearly
every point the charges it contained. The resumption of
the Benning Wentworth grants, they declared, had been
approved by the Attorney and Solicitor-Generals of England, and the Governor denied a personal interest in the
matter; the powder-money had been regularly collected;
and Livius had not been reappointed justice because of
his maladministration when in office. The change of
judges was due to the colonial practice of not permitting

men who had been counsel on either side of a dispute to sit in judgment on it; and though the council proceedings had not been sent to England, through ignorance of the law, they were kept and were available. As to relatives, the Governor averred — not quite ingenuously — that he had but one member of his family by blood upon the Council.

All this was reinforced by affidavits and certificates of character from the leading men of the province. None the less, after long deliberation, the Board of Trade found Wentworth guilty on four counts and virtually recommended that he be dismissed. It was a crushing blow; but his friends appealed to the Privy Council, which ultimately threw out the whole contention, arguing, no doubt, that a successful governorship, so rare in America, was a sufficient answer to the charges of a disgruntled office-seeker, even though some of its actions might not bear the closest scrutiny. And one might have more sympathy with Livius had he not, as a judicial officer in Quebec, presently fallen foul of its honest and capable governor, Sir Guy Carleton, in like fashion. Thus was concluded the "Livius Case," notable in the annals of colonial history, if for nothing else, because it was the last of its kind; and Portsmouth took occasion to celebrate the Governor's vindication with a great ball, while addresses of congratulation poured in from the towns.

Such were the problems and the character of this "model colonial governor" in his five years of rule; and had his history ended with his last great ball, or had it been merely the account of his official stewardship, it might have formed, indeed, a chapter in the chronicles of his colony, or in those of colonial America in general, of interest to the mere historian or the antiquarian, but of small consequence beyond that charmed, and charming, circle. But it has wider bearings and more human appeal; he "touches the universal" on at least two sides.

First, in that elemental necessity of us all, his house.

From his boyhood days he dreamed of a great country-seat, and his grand tour, if it taught him nothing else — and it taught him much — had strengthened his resolution on that point. He had long been a proprietor of the town of Wolfeborough, where his father transferred to him more than two thousand acres, which he increased to five. There he began almost as soon as he was Governor to settle tenant families, and interest his friends in his project. He incorporated it, set up a gristmill and a saw-mill, cleared ground, made roads, and began to build. There presently arose his manor house, a hundred feet in length and forty wide, two-storied, gambrel-roofed, with a great central hall. It held, according to tradition, more than fifty rooms, among them a great ballroom the whole width of the house, an East India room with wall-paper of scenes from Indian life and marble fireplaces, a green room, a blue room, a "king's and queen's chamber" with niches for statues of royalty and a gray marble fireplace, a billiard-room and council-chamber; and downstairs a kitchen and dining-room, a drawing-room, and a library with a black marble fireplace. Beside the mansion rose a barn of equal size; a stable and coach-house to hold thirty horses; dairy, chimney and smokehouse, and a joiner's shop. About it lay a forty-acre garden, bordered with elms and walled with stone. Beyond he planned a park for deer and even moose. He put in English pheasants but they disappeared; he put cusk in the pond, and took extraordinary interest in collecting animals for the great estate. There, surrounded by his friends and colleagues, among them Doctor Cutter, for whom the nearest hill was named; his uncles, Jotham and Daniel Rindge; his brother, Thomas; his attorney-general, Judge Livermore; even his sometime councillor, Peter Livius, he planned to spend the summers of his life — the first of many "summer residents" who in that delightful region have sought the same agreeable fortune.

In this he was not merely the forerunner of later generations which have dotted this "playground of America" with a myriad of like structures, less lovely in the main; he typified the times and the society of which he was so eminent a representative. From Maine to Georgia we may see them even now, those stately relics of an older day, surviving here and there the onslaughts of time and "progress" — old "Tory Row" in Cambridge, the houses on the Green in New Haven, a handful in New York, and more in Germantown, with still more farther south, and nearly everywhere in the outlying districts of the older colonies — memorials to a vanished aristocracy, then in the making, ambitious of that worldly immortality expressed in fine houses and the foundation of a "family."

But Governor Wentworth was a bachelor when he began his house in 1768, and a bachelor still when he began to live in it in the summer of 1770. Not all the beauties of the English court nor of the southern mansions, nor Miss Bayard's voice, nor the maidens of Portsmouth, seemed to touch his heart. For this there was a reason near at hand. He had loved his cousin, Frances Deering; but while he was gone to England she had married her cousin — and his — young Theodore Atkinson, his nearest neighbor in Portsmouth. Then, at the moment that his house was done, his rival died, leaving his lovely wife a widow at twenty-four. She was not long left so. The same guns which on November 1, 1770, fired minute by minute their last tribute to Atkinson, on November 10 roared their approval of his widow's marriage to the Governor; the same crowds which mourned at the funeral joined with "innocent mirth" in the wedding festivities; the same minister who laid Atkinson to rest officiated at the more joyful ceremony, with no apparent sense of incongruity. No one seemed shocked; perhaps it was then better understood than now. Four years there-

after the guns boomed again; this time a welcome to the
new-born son, Charles-Mary as he was baptized after
both Lord and Lady Rockingham at their request. "He
will," wrote his proud father, "do to pull up the stumps
at Wentworth House," a place which, as an infant of
three months, he was then seeing for the first time — and
possibly the last.

The world went very well then for Sir John Wentworth
and his lady wife. Blessed with health and wealth, with
office and estate, with home and wife and child, it seemed
that the promise of the Fortunate Youth was now to be
fulfilled. And yet the climax of his destiny was already
past. Even as he wrote, he might well have pondered the
parable of the rich man who would have pulled down his
barns and built greater. He might a few months earlier,
indeed, have read with profit the story of Belshazzar's
feast. For, at the very moment that Portsmouth had been
absorbed in the great ball to celebrate his victory over
Livius, on the night of December 16, 1773, a little group
of Boston radicals were throwing tea-chests from a British
ship new-come into the harbor, and so, among a great
variety of consequences which they did not then foresee,
altering the fortunes of Sir John Wentworth, with their
own.

The news of the Boston Tea Party reached Portsmouth
almost at once and divided interest with the comments on
the Governor's ball, though probably not wholly in the
same circles of society. In a sense the news of some such
outbreak was not wholly unexpected by the British officials in America. When, three years before, Lord North
had become chief minister, it was hoped and expected
that he might conciliate America. His utterances
breathed concession; the Townshend duties, save that on
tea, were repealed; and the American radicals were in
despair. But the East India Company presently fell upon
hard times; the ministry conceived that it could take the

stores of tea in English warehouses, ship them to America with trifling duties, and so relieve the Company's immediate necessities, provide the colonists with cheap tea, and check the smuggling of that commodity.

It seemed an admirable policy; but the "patriots" perceived in it a shrewd and subtle device to bribe the colonists to accept the principle of taxation which they had repudiated. The Sons of Liberty revived, with committees of correspondence and of safety. As early as the March preceding the Boston "outrage," the New Hampshire Assembly had received a circular letter from the Speaker of the Virginia House of Burgesses enclosing a resolution to establish a committee of correspondence to enquire into the proposed transportation to England for trial of the Rhode Island rioters who had burned the British revenue vessel *Gaspée* for trying to enforce the law. To this the New Hampshire Assembly replied by appointing a like committee, assuring Virginia they would join in "all constitutional means" to secure the rights of America, and asking the governor for a copy of his commission and other papers to see what his powers were. And three days after the Boston incident, a public meeting in Portsmouth resolved that the tea business was "artfully designed" to "raise a revenue from the colonies without our consent. Wherefore from a due sense of the value and importance of our liberties and properties, and from just apprehension of the horrors of slavery," it was resolved further that this was not only "unjust, arbitrary, and inconsistent with the principles of the British constitution," but "directly tended to hasten on the destruction of the empire." Therefore opposing "natural rights" to "arbitrary government," they resolved, finally, to form a union of all the colonies to obtain repeal, and "use any necessary method" to prevent the landing or the sale of tea.

Nothing is more characteristic of the new spirit of affairs than its reflection in the press of Portsmouth, as

elsewhere; and in it nothing more remarkable than that
as the year 1773 progressed the news from Boston begins
to take the place on the front page hitherto reserved for
the news from London. The center of gravity had begun
to shift. In June came news of the protests of the Massachusetts House of Representatives against the letters
written by Governor Hutchinson regarding the affairs in
that colony, secured in London by Doctor Franklin and
by him transmitted to America. Then, too, is quoted
from the Providence *Gazette* an address "To the American" observing that "The Union of the Colonies which
is now taking place is big with the most important advantages to this Continent." Beside this even the account of
the Harvard Commencement exercises which included
an oration in Latin, one in Arabic, and one in "Indian,"
pales into insignificance, though nowadays such a phe-
nomenon might well share honors even with patriotic
appeals.

By August the spirit had spread. An article headed,
"Britons attend! Americans give Ear!" informs us that
"The People of this Continent are awaked by the Call
of Liberty, and are now forming Plans to preserve it in
Perfection to Future Ages. The People of Britain are
alarmed. . . . No Power nor Wisdom in Great Britain
can secure the Dependence of the Colonies agreeable to
her Idea of Dependance." A Congress is urged to establish a "Union between Britain and America founded on
Equal Liberty." This article from the Boston *Gazette*
divides interest with the controversy over paper money;
and by December the Portsmouth paper notes the instructions to New York pilots not to bring in any ships
suspected of carrying tea, under penalty of the "vengeance of a Free People."

These things the Governor read; and though the issue
of December 17 noted that the Livius charges had been
dismissed and he had been "honourably acquitted," the

next week's issue contained an account of the meeting of the freeholders and others in Portsmouth to protest landing of tea. Moreover, its resolutions declared, among other things, that "a Union of all the colonies is most likely, under God, to secure repeal" of the obnoxious measures; and the resolutions were signed by a list of names beginning with John Sherburne and ending with Captain John Langdon. That issue contained the story of the Boston Tea Party, carried out by "a number of Persons supposed to be Aboriginal Natives from their Complection." By January the little town of Greenland, up the bay from Portsmouth, had resolved against tea, and a whole page is filled with obituaries, fires, accidents, and — what the Governor might have grimly noted as similar catastrophes — news of like protests. For from all parts of his government, as from America generally, came news of similar activities.

Thus warned, when Wentworth had word in June of the coming of the *Grosvenor* with tea aboard, he rode out to Dover to divert attention, while the captain and consignee landed the cargo and stored it in the custom-house, according to his directions. The next day he came to the meeting held by the radicals to protest, agreed with their committee to send the tea to Halifax, set guards over it, and so blocked a Portsmouth Tea Party. Yet he knew well that he was at the beginning, not the end, of his troubles. "Our hemisphere," he wrote, "threatens a hurricane. I have in vain strove almost to death to prevent it. If I can, at last, bring out of it safety to my country and honor to our sovereign, my labors will be joyful."

It was evident to him, as to others, that two incompatible theories of imperial administration stood face to face. The British doctrine of the supremacy of Parliament over the colonies confronted the colonial contention that its assemblies were of equal authority with Parliament, under the Crown. It was no less apparent that the great

constitutional issue was but half the case; since men seldom fight for abstract principles. There was dislike of
"oligarchic" government, however capable and benevo-
lent. There were business rivalries and social feuds. There
was the mass of later immigrants, resentful of the dominance of the older settlements and families; the antagonism of the outlying districts towards the capital. There
was widespread belief that each man's fortunes and un-
realized ambitions were somehow the fault of government,
and could be relieved by change. There were able and
ambitious men prepared to use these forces to attain to
power, and, under the guise of liberty and equality, lead
the increasing spirit of democracy to the overthrow of
the old régime.

In the face of this what could one colonial governor do;
with what weapons could he combat this "universal
frenzy" of the people? Hardly with force, for in Portsmouth the dignity and authority of British "tyranny"
was represented by a handful of officials, and by Fort
William and Mary, whose crumbling walls were now defended by an officer and five men. He had forbidden the
committee of correspondence to meet in a government
building; but it sought a tavern and summoned a provincial convention at Exeter, which presently chose Major
Sullivan and Colonel Folsom as its delegates to the first
Continental Congress, meeting in Philadelphia in this fall
of 1774. There, as in New Hampshire, a new power prepared to challenge the authority which he typified.

Thus far he had avoided an open break while, like his
fellow governors, bombarding the home government with
advice and appeals. But British patience with Boston was
at an end, and Lord North's ministry passed through
Parliament measures to close that port. General Gage
was ordered there as governor, troops despatched to
maintain his authority, the city fortified, and the Assembly dissolved. That body, in return, met as a provin-

cial congress, appealed to the other colonies, collected
stores, drilled men, and seemed to threaten war. Meanwhile the Continental Congress drew up protests to the
King, to Parliament, and to other colonies; signed an
Association to prevent commerce with Great Britain till
America's grievances were recognized; and entrusted its
execution to local committees of safety, or of "ways and
means."

Wentworth's position became daily more difficult; but
thus far, while other governors were seeking safety where
they could, his enemies had been unable to shake his
popularity. Then Gage found his efforts to get carpenters
to build barracks blocked by the Boston radicals. He
appealed to Wentworth for assistance, and the Governor
employed an agent to secure them secretly. The Portsmouth committee discovered this act of "treachery," denounced the Governor's "cruel and unmanly" conduct,
pronouncing him an "enemy of the community," compelled his agent to beg forgiveness on his knees, and
frightened the New Hampshire carpenters from their jobs.
With this "discovery" his chief asset, his popularity, was
gone.

Worse was to follow in this winter of 1774–1775.
Warned of the colonists' evident intent to appeal to force,
the British government forbade the export of munitions to
America, while Lord Dartmouth, as Secretary of State,
ordered the governors to prevent the landing of such supplies. The Rhode Islanders seized the stores in the harbor
fort, the news was relayed from Boston to Portsmouth by
Paul Revere, and action there developed rapidly. The
Governor sensed what the enterprise would be. There in
Fort William and Mary lay a hundred kegs of powder
guarded by six men, and he advised Captain Cochran to
defend it at all costs.

But its defense was hopeless. On December 13, a
twelvemonth almost to the day from the great vindica-

tion ball, a meeting of the patriots was held. Next day
a crowd gathered "to the beat of drum," refusing to disperse for the chief justice whom the Governor sent to read
the riot act and warn them against violence. Joined on
its way by contingents from Rye and Newcastle, the mob
of some four hundred men marched to the fort, overpowered the little garrison, and seized the powder. Next
day arrived John Sullivan from Durham to assure the
Governor that he would use his "utmost endeavors" to
disperse the crowd, while a committee waited on Wentworth to disavow the act and ask suspension of prosecution against its captors. It was agreed that if the powder
were returned the Governor would look on that as an
"alleviation" of the grave offense. But Sullivan's efforts
were so peculiarly ineffective that the following night he
led another party to seize the cannon, muskets, and some
stores, then spirited away by still another group who came
down under Folsom to share the enterprise.

Thus revolution began in New Hampshire. To force
there is but force for argument, and Wentworth appealed
to Admiral Graves at Boston, in his extremity, and got
two ships and a hundred marines for protection. Despite
his proclamation against the rioters they were not seized,
for reasons none knew better than himself. "No jail," he
wrote, "would hold them long, no jury find them guilty,
for by the false alarm raised through the country it is considered by the weak and ignorant who have the rule in
these times an act of self-preservation." He deprived the
known leaders of the mob of their commissions in the
militia; he formed a little force of fifty men to guard his
person; but within a month another convention at Exeter
had chosen the mob leaders, John Langdon and John
Sullivan, as delegates to a second Continental Congress as
recognition of their services.

That late winter and early spring of 1775 was fraught
with deep significance to him and to the cause he repre-

sented. In February a committee for carrying out the so-called "Association" recommended by Congress as a weapon against British authority issued a proclamation not merely against raising prices on account of the virtual embargo against English goods which Congress had decreed, but against gaming, especially by cards and billiards. This piece of Puritanism roused the bitter wrath of "Bystander," who protests against such hypocrisy. "Oh, my country," he exclaims, "so this is *Liberty*!" In March John Sullivan writes to deny that the militia company at Durham has been raised to escape the authority of the militia officials. But in his very denial, as in the decree of the Committee, still more in the measures of Congress, we may read the coming storm.

Still hoping against hope, the Governor played for time. The Assembly was to meet in February; he adjourned it till May, and went to Wolfeborough with his wife and infant son, born five days before Langdon and Sullivan had been elected delegates to Congress. In view of that event it is small wonder that the Governor had not, as some historians suggest that he should have done, met his antagonists at the fort. And what should he do now? That question must have pressed him sorely at this juncture in affairs; but he had not long to wait. While he was there the revolutionary spirit spread. The Loyalists were being driven from their homes, and were seeking refuge first in Portsmouth, then in Boston. Lord North's proposals for conciliation were on their way to America; but, almost before they came, Gage's incautious effort to seize his antagonists' supplies brought on conflict, and Paul Revere appeared again in Portsmouth to announce Concord and Lexington.

Wentworth hurried back to face the storm; but there was little that he could do. Twelve hundred men marched from New Hampshire to join the army forming at Cambridge to besiege Boston, and the provincial convention

at Exeter voted three regiments of two thousand men for
a year's service. Amid these distractions the Assembly
met in May, put off the Governor's appeal to consider
Lord North's proposals, and, playing still for time, he adjourned it until June. Before it met again, a quarrel between the British crews and the Portsmouth men further
embittered the situation, and when the Assembly came
together it attacked the Governor for empowering Lyme,
Orford, and Plymouth to send representatives, and deprived the members of their seats.

This apparently trifling incident precipitated the catastrophe which Wentworth had so long and skilfully put
off. For one of these members, John Fenton, sometime an
English officer, that night took dinner with the Governor.
A crowd collected and demanded him as a prisoner; the
Governor demurred; and to enforce their claim they
brought cannon to train on his house. Whatever his politics, Fenton was a gallant gentleman. He came out un-
concernedly, surrendered, and was carried in triumph to
Exeter. The ensuing issue of the *Gazette* which printed the
correspondence between the Governor and the Assembly
over the excluded representatives carried the news of the
battle of Bunker Hill, and the meeting of the New Hampshire Provincial Congress at Exeter.

This was the end. That night Wentworth took his
family to the fort, where, under the guns of the *Scarborough*, he might hope for safety for his wife and son. With
this the government of the colony passed definitely into
other hands. Its epitaph is written in the words of its historian: "He saw another authority rising in the province
founded on the broad basis of public opinion and unre-
strained representation . . . over which he had no influence or control; yet he endeavoured to preserve the
shadow of royal government and keep up its forms as long
as possible." "His temper was pacific; and whilst the
temper of the times allowed him to act agreeably to his

own principles, his government was acceptable and beneficial; but when matters had come to the worst, his faults
were as few and his conduct as temperate as could be
expected from a servant of the crown."

There, in a sense, there lies the moral of his life. He
might have echoed the words of that earlier English
statesman, "What shadows we are and what shadows do
we pursue, and how does Fortune banter us." His virtues
were his own, his faults were those of time and circumstance. His problems were set for him by other men, for
whose mistakes he was held responsible, and for them he
paid. Left to himself he might have solved them successfully; but he was, as Belknap says, a "servant of the
crown," which made success impossible. The story of
revolution in New Hampshire and his part in it brings up
the whole great issue of human conduct and character in
the most difficult of circumstances, that of a representative of authority faced by a popular uprising against the
government. There are three courses open — to stand
aside and let things take their course, preserving his own
fortunes by silence and consent; to take the lead himself
and perpetuate his power by sacrifice of his principles; or
to go down in honor. Of these the first is always possible;
the second, Wentworth, almost alone among American
governors, might have pursued with some prospect of
success, and so preserved his fortune and his family.

He chose the third, and thus determined his future once
for all. When the *Scarborough* was ordered to Boston, he
and his family went with her to join the army of loyalist
exiles within the British lines. Thence he returned but
once, when in September he came to New Hampshire soil
for his last official act, a proclamation to prorogue the
Assembly to the following April. Before that April came
he wrote Dartmouth that he had taken ship "to whatever
place the fleet and army go." First to Long Island and
New York, then finally to England, he went, while his

estates were confiscated and he was proclaimed a traitor by the men who had now risen to the head of the New Hampshire government. In the space of eighteen months his dreams had come to a tragic conclusion. Fortune, who had so long favored him and held out such high hopes, had struck hard at the height of his career.

He did not break, as he might well have done; but what was he to do? His shrewd old father, keeping clear of politics, saved from the wreckage what he could. The ministry gave the ex-Governor a pension, and his wife a place at Court. His relatives were rich and devoted, and he found a place in English society, where he might have lived a life of leisure and comfort, with possibly an office as a reward for this loyalty. In fact this last he did obtain; for, curious coincidence, Lord Rockingham was again brought in to make peace with America; and, before he died, did one last service, as he had done the first, for Governor Wentworth. The post revealed the character of the man, for it was the revival of his old office of Surveyor of the Woods, in which capacity Sir John returned to America under far different circumstances than those under which he had returned just twenty years before. This time he came to Halifax to rejoin his fellow exiles in Nova Scotia; and there he lived eight years. Then, during another visit to England, the Lieutenant-Governor of that province died, and Wentworth was appointed to the post.

For nearly sixteen years he exercised its powers, till the storm of the Napoleonic wars set Prevost in his stead. There with his wife and brother-in-law, Benning, who had followed his fortunes and was now in the Council, and presently with Charles-Mary, who came from England to a like post, he revived the shadow of his New Hampshire home. Removed from office he returned to England; but his wife died, and, his heart turning always to America, he came back to Nova Scotia, where he lived till 1820, and there lies buried beneath a tablet which records that "His unshaken attachment to his Sovereign and the British constitution was conspicuous through his long life."

It might well have added his attachment to America. For, after all, he and his fellows were American, by birth and blood and sentiment; and no circumstance in his life is more touching than his passionate desire to live his life out in his native land. The word "loyal" is not nowadays as much in evidence as it was once, and "Loyalist" is an ill-omened name in American history. Yet this was their country no less than that of their opponents; and in their fate there lies a moral as well as a tragedy. They braved the curse of history, with what effect we know. Only where their memory is preserved by adventitious circumstance, posterity is too apt to heap upon the leaders of lost causes that last measure of contempt — oblivion.

Save for the still execrated Tryon and Dunmore, or the accomplished and unpopular Hutchinson, who now recalls the greatest of the Loyalists? Here and there the zeal of antiquary or historian preserves their memory. In the neglected pages of their martyrologist, Sabin, move the shadowy figures of that earlier age, or in the monographs of those who find material for scholarship in their activities, something remains of their departed greatness. But for the most of them in the land they ruled and loved not many years ago, as history reckons time, they are as dim figures as Sennacherib.

Yet history has not yet rolled up her scroll. The painstaking industry of her devotees seeks even now the reconstruction of a period and a class long buried beneath the panegyrics of the conquerors. The wider view of the historian perceives Cornwallis and his fellows regaining in distant fields some of the laurels they lost in "that grave of reputations," America. The filial piety of the heirs of those driven from their first inheritance to found new for-

tunes and new families in another land enters the lists
against oblivion; and there will come a time when these
will right the scale.

So what of Sir John Wentworth and the fame he
sought? Beside Copley's talents what has he to show
against the long neglect of what were once his countrymen? How can he hope to defeat oblivion? A building at
Dartmouth College still bears his name; an old silver
punch bowl still handed down from president to president
— an empty symbol of its once good cheer; in Halifax
some volumes of his letters and a tomb; elsewhere in his-
tories and documents some mention of his name; in Portsmouth a handful of relics to amuse the casual visitor avid
of such memorials of "colonial" history; in Wolfeborough
the cellar of his house — these are his weapons against
oblivion.

Dramatic to the last, no circumstance in his life is more
striking than the fact that his dreams perished with him.
In the year he died his great house burned, and with it
went, according to tradition, by a stroke of lightning, the
pine which he planted to commemorate its founding.
And with it went his hopes of family; for Charles-Mary
died in England a bachelor; and thus ended the dreams
of those five busy years when the young Governor looked
forward with such confidence to the accomplishment of
his ambitions in his native land.

Yet he is coming back. Among the chief antagonists of
oblivion, the genealogist sets his lance in rest. The portrait of the New Hampshire Governor may look with
some touch of tenderness upon that huge, bald, commonplace presentment of his namesake in the Dartmouth
gallery, sometime, for his peculiar talents, mayor of a
great city in a region which when Wentworth lived was
given over to wild beasts and Indians, Chicago. For
"Long John Wentworth," amid widely different activities, devoted time and substance to revive the glory and

perpetuate the memory of the stock whence he was sprung, and among them the New Hampshire Governor.

And, again, — for in such curious fashion does history war with forgetfulness, — Sir John has found another champion among those summer residents who followed him into that lovely land where he first planned a home: for one of them, Mr. Lawrence Mayo, has written a biography to commemorate his name, inspired, perhaps, in part by the ruins of that house on which he staked his fortune. Thus, though but one town of his province bears his name, and he all but lacks that tribute of posterity; though in an age and land of monuments not even a statue now perpetuates his fame, his memory is not dead. Though he fell short of his great desire; though his work and plans were interrupted by events beyond his power to control; though even the family through which he hoped for such immortality failed him, — he has won his fight finally against oblivion, by means which he could scarce have realized, and which were far from those of which he dreamed.

A HISTORIAN-SAINT:
THE VENERABLE BEDE

A HISTORIAN–SAINT: THE VENERABLE BEDE

IT IS much to ask of a generation like ours to interest itself even for an hour in a subject apparently so remote, so erudite, and so unpractical as the life and work of a Northumbrian monk who died nearly twelve hundred years ago, and whose chief claim to distinction is that he wrote a book. But it is a well-known canon of authorship that neither knowledge nor ignorance is now reckoned a bar to literary composition; and mere interest in a subject, or a desire to write, or even the possibility of an audience, is held to be sufficient justification for setting pen to paper. And, in the present instance, perhaps the circumstance that there is to be found hardly anywhere outside of highly learned, even technical, studies, any reasonably full and accurate account of the Venerable Bede, may serve as one excuse for an essay on the first great English historian.

To most men to-day, Bede is scarcely more than a name, if that; and even to his biographers he is a shadowy figure. The history of his life is, indeed, so brief and so simple that it is difficult to construct on it any elaborate biography such as we are accustomed to reckon a part of worldly greatness. He has told it himself in words which cannot be improved upon.

"I was born," he says, "in the territory of the monastery [of Wearmouth-Jarrow] and at the age of seven I was given by my relatives to the most reverend abbot Benedict, and afterwards to Ceolfrid, to be educated. From that time I have spent the whole of my life within that monastery, devoting all my pains to the study of Scripture; and amid the observance of monastic discipline and the daily charge of singing in the church, it has ever been my delight to learn or teach or write. In my nineteenth year I was admitted to the diaconate, in my thirtieth to the priesthood, both by the hands of the most reverend Bishop John, at the bidding of Abbot Ceolfrid. From the time of my admission to the priesthood to my present [fifty-ninth] year, I have endeavored, for my own use and that of my brethren, to make brief notes upon the Holy Scriptures, either out of the works of the venerable fathers, or in conformity with their meaning and interpretation." To this it may be added that he made two journeys of which we know; one to Lindisfarne, the Holy Island, with its famous monastery; and one to the monastery at York, neither more than seventy-five miles from Jarrow; and this, even for the eighth century, cannot be considered as wide traveling.

Of all the candidates for immortality, on his own account, it would be difficult to find one more unpromising than this humble monk. Viewed from the external circumstances of his life, indeed, there seems nothing to chronicle, and still less to make him remembered now. Even that indefatigable historian, Bishop Stubbs, confesses that "there is scarcely one of the fathers of whose personal history so little is known." Compared with the eventful period in which he lived, the uneventful character of his life is still more striking. In the year of his birth the Saracens advanced to the siege of Constantinople, whence they were driven by the new invention of Greek fire. Mohammed had died but fifty years before; and Bede was nearer to him in point of time than we are to Lincoln. Mohammed's followers were beginning that great sweep across northern Africa which, before Bede died, had crushed the Visigothic kingdom in Spain and brought their armies to defeat at the hands of Charles Martel on the field of Poitiers. While Bede lived, the Merovingian dynasty was being superseded by this same Charles, whose son Pepin was chosen king of the Franks some fifteen years after Bede's death, while his son, known to history as Charlemagne, was a boy of eight or nine.

Such is the contrast between Bede and his times, which throws in high relief a life absorbed in "learning and teaching and writing" in a remote Northumbrian monastery while the world was being shaken by these great events. But what more is there to know of such a life than he has told? What more is there to know about that of any modern scholar, save that he may be, perhaps, more married and more traveled? For such careers there is little of importance in external circumstance comparable to that of more conspicuous characters like kings and bishops. In such lives as those of Bede the important things are not what offices they held, in what spectacular events they played a part, what speeches they made, and what their struggles were to have their own way in the world. The only important contests in which such men commonly take part are within themselves; they are conflicts of the spirit rather than of the sword or tongue. The greatness of these men lies in what they do for the world, not what the world does for them, or what they do to it.

Yet in its way Bede's was a busy life, even though it had little to do with that extermination of his fellow beings which makes up a great part of the history of his day. The young monastery which had been founded about the time that he was born had become one of the famous institutions of its time. The life within its walls was that common to such establishments — the daily tasks of the great monastery gardens and farms, of cooking food for its hundreds of inmates, of teaching in its school, of caring for the sick within and without its bounds, of overseeing the novices, of visiting and ministering to the physical and spiritual needs of the lands round about, of studying and writing, of entertaining visitors, and, above all, the conduct of church services.

These were no light tasks. Beginning with matins between midnight and three o'clock in the morning — and it must have been cold in winter time; with prime at sunrise, tierce half-way between sunrise and noon — and Bede observes that it was not always easy to determine the hours in a latitude so near the midnight sun; with sext at mid-day, nones in mid-afternoon, even-song at six, and complines at bedtime — these, with the allotted daily tasks, made monastic life of this period no life of idle luxury. It was, and it was meant to be, a hard existence, however preferable in many minds to the vicissitudes of the world outside.

It seems to us, none the less, peculiarly detached and isolated; much as the learned leisure and cloistered seclusion of academic circles nowadays appears to the non-academic mind, and with perhaps the same proportion of reality. There were monks then, as there have been doubtless professors since, who saw and knew little of the world from which they fled, and cared still less. But there were others who were brought into close contact with its material realities, preachers and teachers, men of business and affairs, physicians, agents, emissaries and factors of all kinds. Above all were the heads of the establishments, men of responsibility and authority, wide-traveled, experienced men of business — like some college presidents. There were the hewers of wood and drawers of water; cooks and scullions; there were teachers and writers, scribes and musicians; nurses and hostlers. There were others, like Bede, who, taking part in daily tasks and devotions, kept alive the knowledge of their day and increased it; and who, through books and correspondence,

contact with distinguished visitors, and that sense of relationship with humanity which is the product of the
spirit rather than of external circumstance, were in touch
with affairs far more than many who played a more conspicuous part upon the worldly stage. Born in another
age, these might have been the stuff of which professors of
the better sort are made. For these great mediæval monasteries, besides being a combination of church and model
farm, hotel, dispensary and hospital, publishing establishment, settlement house and fraternity headquarters,
were not unlike a modern university, with less actual —
though relative to their age as much — learning, perhaps more social service, and certainly far more pious observances.

Such was the life of this Northumbrian monk, such the
world in which he lived. In appearance it differed little
if at all from that of thousands of his kind whose bones,
like his, are dust, but whose memories, unlike his fame,
are buried with them. What, then, has he done to deserve
our recollection? He wrote books. But hundreds of his
fellows did the same; and most of his works, like theirs,
have sunk into oblivion. For, following the fashion of his
time and kind, the chief part of his labors, as he says himself, were comments on the Scriptures; on Genesis and
Samuel; upon the tabernacle, its vessels and priestly vest-
ments; those exegetical ephemeridæ of theology, whose
summer is long past, now dead beyond recall. Besides
these he composed some so-called "scientific" works —
on grammar and natural phenomena; a book, in his own
words, "concerning the nature of things"; one on "or-
thography and alphabets distinguished in order"; one on
the "metrical art, and in connection with this another
little book on figures of speech and tropes, that is, the
forms and modes of speaking, with which the Holy Scriptures are connected." Besides these, still, he composed, or
compiled, a hymnal; a book of epigrams in heroic or ele-

giac meters; a martyrology of the natal days of the saints;
a history of certain saints, one, he says, "badly translated
from the Greek"; a history of the abbots of his monastery;
and two chronologies; in all some twelve stout volumes
when printed out in modern form, no small life work as
such things go.

Of these his chronology was of peculiar significance, for
he used the so-called Dionysian system of reckoning
events from the birth of Christ, which had been devised a
century before by an Italian abbot; and so confirmed, if
he did not actually introduce, that system in English his-
toriography. To this matter of chronology, indeed, he
devoted his time and talents, and became the great champion of that far-reaching controversy between the Roman and Celtic churches, whose issue turned, in no small
part, upon the method of calculating the date of Easter,
and the proper time for its celebration. Thus he established his professional reputation, and took his first step
towards immortality; for early writers speak of him as
"Bede the Computator," the "marvelous computator,"
"most studious in the Scriptures, especially in the art of
calculating"; and, as the most industrious as well as the
most eminent of English theological authorities and the
model of monastic virtues, Bede "the Venerable."

Yet, even so, were this the whole story; had Bede's contribution to the world ended with a long and blameless
life as monk of Wearmouth-Jarrow; or with his long list
of writings on the Scriptures, his hymnals and his verse;
even, perhaps, with his great service to chronology and
the Easter controversy, — though no doubt to his mind
and to those of his fellows these were his chief achievements in this life and his chief claims to life hereafter, —
men to-day might still be wholly ignorant of his name,
save here and there a lonely scholar might recall his work.
For so he lived to nearly three score years, but little known
beyond the narrow circle of his professional brethren.

But when he was some fifty-eight or fifty-nine, he wrote a book which lifted him above the level of his times, and kept his name alive to all posterity — his great *Ecclesiastical History of the English People*. For this book he is remembered; and from it, rather than from his other works, we may derive some knowledge of him, what kind of man he was, what he thought and believed, what was his mental and spiritual stature. We may, in fact, through it, come to know him better than most men we meet day by day, whose outward semblance is well known to us, but whose true characters are less familiar to us than the character of this long-dead monk of whose form and features we have not the slightest notion. Such is the curious nature of life. Such is the advantage — or disadvantage — of authorship; for is not Job made to say: "Behold, my desire is, that the Almighty would answer me, and that mine adversary had written a book!"

It may seem superfluous, if not tiresome, to describe the book which has prolonged the memory of its author for more than a thousand years, yet not to do it would be to leave Hamlet out. The *Ecclesiastical History of the English People* is, in its essence, what it purports to be, an account of the development of the English Church from the coming of that rather unwilling apostle to the British Isles, St. Augustine, in 597, to what Bede calls in his final chapter the "Present state of the English people and of all Britain," that is to say about the year 731. It is divided into five books, the first largely devoted to an introductory account of Britain and its history before the coming of Augustine, with the story of his mission. The remaining books cover the hundred and thirty years between 600 and the time Bede closed his story.

Merely as a matter of proportion, chronologically speaking, this work, which fills perhaps three hundred pages of a modern book, is well constructed and carefully arranged. It compares, indeed, not unfavorably with

almost any similar history written at any time. It is, even
now, making some small allowance for a difference in
times and tastes, readable by a generation accustomed to
a very different kind of literature. Its vigorous style, attractive even in translation; its wealth of anecdote and
character sketches, which, though often tinctured with
the miraculous element so dear to his time and his profession, seldom sink to the level of the "Sunday-school
book" moralizing so dear to our more immediate ancestors, provide that strong "human interest" which the
most modern of modernity demands. To the men of his
own day it must have seemed a godsend, for even its mediæval readers could omit — as King Alfred actually did
when he translated the volume into Anglo-Saxon —
most of the many letters from the Popes, and so shorten
and enliven the narrative.

And in no respect does his book differ from that of most
mediæval historians more than in this. As one goes
through the work of his contemporaries, his predecessors,
and even most of his monastic successors, few things seem
more remarkable than the desire of those worthies to
leave nothing untold, to harmonize the irreconcilable,
to chronicle the utterly impossible and vain. Most of
them begin, as perhaps they should, at the beginning, for
universal history is the most ancient, if not the most honorable, form of historical activity. And as the early monastic historians had at most scarcely more than four
sources of information of events before their time — the
Bible; Virgil, and sometimes Homer; the Fathers; and
the traditions of their race — and as they belonged to the
harmonizing rather than the critical school, the results of
their combination of these are sometimes surprising in the
extreme.

This is most striking in their genealogies. There it is
not uncommon to find Adam and Noah linked with the
descendants of Priam, — Æneas and his brethren, whom

mediæval fancy determined as Britus who founded Britain, Francus who founded France, — eponymous heroes who fled from Troy to whatever shore they could make and there set up their household gods. These in turn are connected with the heroes of Teutonic mythology, so that the already incongruous family circle is enlarged by the intrusion of Woden and his descendants. And it is scarcely necessary to point out that a reunion of Noah, Adam and his family, Priam's sons, and Woden's descendants would have made an interesting occasion, in whatever realm of future blessedness it was held.

Such temptations, at least, Bede avoids. His history begins, not with the creation, whether Biblical or scientific or mythological, but where history should begin, with geography. "The island of Britain," he starts off, providing at once the scene and the conditions of his narrative, "which is sometimes called Albion, is situated to the north and west [of the continent of Europe], facing, but at a considerable distance from the coasts of Gaul and Germany and Spain, which form the greatest part of Europe. It is about eight hundred miles long to the north, and two hundred miles wide, except where promontories make it wider, and it is about 3675 miles around." Its nearest port to the Continent is Richborough, whence it is about fifty miles across to Boulogne. At the back of this island are the Orcades. Thus we know at the beginning just where we are.

And what kind of a place is it? That, too, he tells us. It grows grain and trees, it is good for cattle, it produces vines, has plenty of land and waterfowl, fish, and plentiful springs, an abundance of salmon and eels; there are seals and dolphins and whales in the surrounding waters, many sorts of shellfish, often containing pearls, and quantities of cockles, of which cochineal is made. There are salt and hot springs, which furnish baths for all ages and sexes, and, as he is careful to say, "arranged accordingly."

The land is rich in metals, copper, iron, lead, and silver; it even produces jet, which, being heated, "drives away serpents," and being rubbed, "holds fast whatever is applied to it like amber."

Once Britain contained twenty-eight noble cities, besides many castles or fortresses; and of these remnants of the vanished Roman civilization he speaks frequently throughout his narrative. Lying as it does almost under the North Pole, the nights are light in summer — or the days are of great length — and there is a midnight sun, quite unlike "Armenia, Macedonia or Italy." There are five languages spoken, "according to the number of books in which the Divine Law is written," English, British, Scottish, Pictish, and Latin, the last "by study of the Scriptures common to all the rest." The first inhabitants were the Britons, who came, it is said, from Armorica. Then the Picts, coming from "Scythia" in a few "long ships," reached Ireland, whence, encouraged by the Scots to prolong their journey, they proceeded to conquer northern Britain, whither in course of time they were followed by the Scots.

Then as to Ireland, which, though shorter than Britain, "in breadth and wholesomeness and serenity of climate far surpasses" the sister island. "For no man makes hay there in summer for the winter's provision, nor builds stables for his cattle"; "no reptiles are found there, and no snake can live there . . . on the contrary almost all things in the island are good against poison." Moreover, this favored land abounds in milk and honey, vines, fish, and fowl, and "is remarkable for its deer and goats."

Such is the scene of his story; and it is evident that Bede regarded his native land as a peculiarly blessed and delightful place — which is no bad qualification for its historian. The stage thus set, first enter the Roman hosts by sea in eighty ships, under the lead, as his Anglo-Saxon translator renders his words — incorrectly — of the "Emperor Gaius, also called Julius." The conquest made, Bede discusses at some length the history of the new masters of Britain and their rule; notes the Wall of Severus, which he himself has seen; tells of the persecution under Diocletian, and the martyrdom of St. Alban; the heresy of the Briton Pelagius — whom later scholars have determined was a Welshman named Morgan; of the invasions of the Picts and Scots on the Roman withdrawal; and the British invitation first to Aëtius, then to the Angles and Saxons, to come over and help them. Then, briefly recording the degeneration and overthrow of the Britons, with an excursus on St. Germanus, who, in the words of the famous epigram, "first quelled the tempest of the sea and afterwards that of the Pelagian heretics," he passes to his true theme, the conversion of the Anglo-Saxon conquerors.

To this introductory part of his book the ubiquitous German scholar has taken severe exception, as being both inaccurate and inadequate, especially with regard to the Britons. But Bede had neither the sources of information nor the peculiar sympathy with the British possessed by the Teutonic critic. He was concerned less with those who had fallen than with the fortunes of their new masters. Moreover it was easier to obtain material on the Britons in the nineteenth century than in the eighth — and in regard to the main body of his history even the German admits its excellence.

But once his introduction done, this is the tale he tells: how Pope Gregory sent Augustine into Britain to preach the word of God to the English nation; the adventures of his mission in Kent; how thence the faith was spread, to the East Saxons by Mellitus, to East Anglia and Northumbria by Paulinus, to Mercia first by the Scot Diuma, to the West Saxons by Wilfrid, to the South Saxons by Haedde, — devoted torchbearers of the faith, now names and less than names to most of us. Thereafter he relates the struggles of the new communion to keep what it had won, the frequent lapses of its proselytes and their reconversions; the gradual establishment of bishoprics and an episcopal succession; the foundation of monasteries; the slow and toilsome efforts of successive churchmen to lay foundations for the faith; and their final triumph.

On its face such a story would seem to have but little interest for those outside the circles of church influence; stories of missionary enterprise are seldom enlivening save to a small and select audience. But in Bede's hands it has an epic quality. Every great history is the story of a great conflict; and this is no exception. It is the struggle not merely of the white Christ against the pagan gods; it is the chronicle of the civilizing influence of the old world on the new. It has its chief protagonist, Pope Gregory the First, who conceived and directed the great enterprise; its lesser heroes, not only St. Augustine, Paulinus, Wilfrid of York, Chad and Cedd of Mercia; but, on the other side, Aidan and Cuthbert and Columba of the Celtic church, champions not only of Christianity but of that rival communion whose contest with Rome adds a secondary plot and interest to the narrative. Such history as he writes, even of what may be called half-contemptuously, missionary enterprise, has neither time nor place of fashion or of season; it is good at any time, for it is an imperishable record of human striving which is ever our chief source of interest.

It was a great and seemed like to be a dangerous enterprise, this conversion of those fierce pagan tribes which had overrun the Roman Empire and overthrown the civilization of the ancient world. It took courage and ability and self-sacrifice; and no one can read the story of the men who went forth on this great crusade without respect for their high qualities. Moreover, apart from the religious aspect of their labors, they had wide and deep worldly significance, for what Rome had finally failed to

THE VENERABLE BEDE   235

do by the sword of the flesh, she undertook with spiritual weapons and with more enduring success. Viewed merely as a political, and still more as a cultural, achievement, the conversion is a great fact in history. These missionaries were not only champions of Christianity but of civilization; the preachers taught more than the precepts of a new religion, they were the apostles of a new life. The monasteries they founded were more than spiritual centers, they were the outposts of that Roman polity and power which, through them, penetrated the remotest corner of this new Teutonic Europe, bound it to herself, and brought to it the traditions and customs of the older world.

It was Bede's own abbot, Benedict, who carried to this distant house the "treasures" which he picked up on his many visits to Rome, "never returning from his many journeys oversea without some gifts, now copies of sacred books, now relics of the blessed martyrs, now architects for building the church, now glass-makers to construct and ornament the windows, now singers, and masters to teach the church services, now a Papal letter of privilege, now pictures of sacred history." He was a type of his class, this great Anglo-Saxon nobleman turned monk, founder and benefactor of monasteries. So Theodore of Tarsus established his famous school at Canterbury which trained the scholars of Britain; so Wilfrid brought to York singers and stonecutters, glass-makers, workers in iron, gold- and silversmiths. There he established a still more famous school from which went out Alcuin to Charlemagne's court, to bear the torch of learning to that great empire. So Ceolfrid, the noble founder of Wearmouth, sent architects to the Pictish king. With these went, too, the humbler but no less necessary arts, of husbandry, of cattle breeding, of gardening, which made these great ecclesiastical establishments the foundation-stones of a new edifice of civilization in the wilderness.

How were these barbarians approached, and how did they receive the new faith? The answer is the commonplace of missionary labor; it has been repeated a thousand times and in a thousand forms, yet its beginning never loses charm, for it is the story of the childhood of our race. There is no better illustration of it than the tale of Edwin of Northumbria's conversion. Driven, when a youth, from his kingdom by Ethelfrid, he sought refuge with Redwald of East Anglia, who, refusing to surrender him, was threatened with attack by Ethelfrid. In fear of such a powerful enemy, Redwald considered for a time returning the young fugitive to the usurper. Seeking flight the prince was dissuaded from his plan by a mysterious stranger who told him of Redwald's final decision to protect him. When Ethelfrid was defeated and Edwin was restored, the stranger proved to be the missionary, Paulinus; and in return for his friendship, Edwin summoned his friends and counsellors to hear the new gospel. In the argument which followed the motives for accepting Christianity are vividly set forth. But let Bede tell the story.

Having asked the chief men what they thought of Paulinus' message, first Coifi, the chief priest, spoke. "Oh, king," he said, "consider what this is which is now preached to us; for truly I confess that the religion which I have hitherto professed has no virtue in it. For none of your followers has devoted himself more diligently to the worship of our gods than I; and yet there are many who have received more benefits from you; and more dignities, and are more prosperous in all things. Now if the gods were good for anything, they would help me more, for I have been more careful to serve them. Therefore, if you consider this new religion fairer and stronger, let us adopt it at once." There spoke the practical man.

But another of the King's counsellors, in the words of the Anglo-Saxon version of the best-known of all Bede's stories, "one of his chief men assented to these words, and took up the tale, and thus spoke: 'Oh, king, this life on earth in comparison with the time which is unknown to us seems to me as if you sat at table with your ealdormen and thanes in winter-time; and the fire is lighted and the hall warm, while outside it rains and snows and storms; and there comes a sparrow and flies swiftly through the house, in one door and out the other. And while he is inside he is not pelted with the winter storm; but that is only the twinkling of an eye, and it passes, and he soon comes from winter to winter again. So, then, this life of man seems but a little while; what goes before, or what comes after, we know not. Therefore if this new doctrine brings aught more certain or more probable, it is worth while for us to follow it.'"

Then, the others coinciding, and Paulinus having preached, the ever practical Coifi observed that, having sought truth in the worship of the old gods, and having failed to find it; and it appearing from Paulinus' words that the new faith would, as he said, "provide the gifts of this life, salvation, and eternal happiness," he proposed that they should at once set fire to the old temples and altars, "which we have consecrated without receiving any benefit from them." Asked who should begin the hazardous work of destruction — for if the old gods should, by any chance, have power it might have been unfortunate for their opponents — he showed the courage of his convictions. He volunteered to begin the holocaust; mounted a stallion, — which was forbidden to priests, — cast his spear into the temple and ordered his companions to burn it down. Which, seeing that nothing happened to him as the result of his sacrilege, they did; and thus was Northumbria brought to the true faith.

But there is one notable circumstance in this history of the conversion of the Anglo-Saxon race — there are no martyrs! It is true that Augustine was not at first allowed an indoor interview with the Kentish king for fear his magic would be more effective within four walls and a roof; that Mellitus and Justus fled from their backsliding congregations; that the Anglo-Saxon king at the battle of Chester first slew two hundred monks who came to pray for the success of his British enemies and after his victory destroyed their monastery of Bangor-iscoed. But, unlike the Romans, the Germans, and the Frisians, even the Scandinavians, the Anglo-Saxons seem to have raised no hand against the Roman priests. The history of Bede is, then, no martyrology.

Yet if it lacks sad stories of the death of saints, the tale of the conversion has its full complement of interesting incidents. Of the grand strategy of the inspiring leader of this important enterprise, Gregory the Great, who directed it from Rome; of the devices to wean men away from pagan practices, there are a hundred instances; of the adventures of his agents there are a hundred more. The identification of the Christian festivals, like Easter and Christmas, with pagan ceremonials of the approach of spring, and of midwinter, with Freya and Yuletide; the use of pagan temples wherever possible for Christian worship, so that people would not have too great a shock to their traditions of time and place of worship, — these are characteristic touches of the Roman pontiff's statesmanship. The caution of King Redwald of East Anglia, who set up altars to the old gods and the new at opposite ends of the temples, so that he might win either way; the final, conclusive argument advanced by the Roman emissary at the Synod of Whitby, that St. Peter held the keys of the gate of Heaven, sorrowfully admitted by the Celtic representative, convinced the Northumbrian king that he ought not to antagonize the church of the gatekeeper, — these are the little touches which bring the story home. The aid given to rulers by counsel in battle, as in the great victory where the British Christians put their pagan opponents into confusion and flight by singing *Alleluia* to them, after the manner of Cromwell's Ironsides as they charged; the aid given to the starving people by the missionary who taught them to fish — these are a few instances of the many services the gospel-bearers rendered outside the field of the new theology.

Such are the tales which make Bede still readable. There are the puns of Gregory the Great upon the sight of fair-haired English youths in the Roman slave market, who seemed to him more like angels than Angles; that, coming from the kingdom of Deira, they should be saved *de ira*, from God's wrath; that, their king's name being Ælla, they should be taught to sing *Alleluia*; this is the most ancient of recorded jests in English history. There is beside it the tale of Cædmon, the hostler-monk of Whitby, who in a gathering where, after the good old English fashion, each must take his share in entertainment, left the room because he saw the harp coming towards him and he could not sing; and so retiring to the stables fell asleep and was there visited by an angel who encouraged him to sing of Creation. And thus he sang:

> Now let us praise the heavenly kingdom's ward
> The Creator's power and his mode of mind,
> The works of the father of glory, how He wrought wonders,
> The eternal Lord who created marvels.
> He first wrought for the children of the earth
> Heaven as a roof, this holy Creator;
> Then this guardian of mankind
> The eternal Lord, afterwards fashioned
> The earth as a home for men, the almighty ruler.

So runs the beginning of the first English epic, and of English poetry. To the modern ear, attuned to the language and the sentiments of free verse, it may seem no great achievement; but it shows, at least, how far we have come since those early days. And it is only fair to add Bede's own comment. "This is the sense but not the words in order as he sang them in his sleep; for verses,

however well composed, cannot be translated literally out
of one language into another without losing much of their
beauty and loftiness" — a critical observation as good
to-day as then.

Such is the tale he tells, but it is not all the tale. For,
apart from the conversion of the English folk, and the
spread of the Roman church among them, there remains
the great conflict with the Celtic church, which, having
long refused to share its hope of immortality with its conquerors, was stirred to undertake the task by the advent
of the Roman missionaries. It is scarcely surprising that
the British Christians did not care to commit themselves
to the tender mercies of the Saxon tribes; nor is it probable that the latter would have looked with favor on an
effort to replace their victorious deities with the God of
the conquered — for faith and works were intimately associated in their practical minds. Here the Roman
church had a distinct advantage over its rival in this missionary field.

Yet the Celtic church was, in many ways, a worthy
antagonist. Founded during the occupation of Britain by
the Roman legions, it boasted an antiquity as great as
that of the church of Rome itself. The numerous inscrip-
tions on tombs of legionaries attest its wide sway in their
ranks; thence it spread to the Romanized Britons, and
there are still found little parishes, even in the midst of
English towns, whose names reveal their British character. It survived the withdrawal of the Roman garrisons
and seems to have gradually displaced Druidism in great
parts of the island. Besides its greater centers, York, Lincoln, and London, its followers had begun to found monasteries which became the peculiar products of its genius,
especially in the west. From that region in time came St.
Patrick, who bore Christianity into Ireland. There and
in Wales, and in the islands, there arose the great monastic establishments which, by the time of Anglo-Saxon con-

quest, numbered their inmates by hundreds, or even, it is said, by thousands; developing there customs, traditions, and ceremonies which differed in many ways from those of the Roman church.

To that region it was largely confined by the Conquest; but when the first storm of invasion had passed, with its co-ordinate communion, the Irish church, it set forth to Christianize Europe at about the same time that Rome took up the same great enterprise. For this it was well equipped. Protected from the great barbarian invasions, the Irish church in particular had maintained and even advanced the standards of culture which had almost vanished elsewhere. Thence its representatives bore them back to Britain and the Continent, where their pupils and successors were the chief agents in that Carolingian renaissance, which, during the eighth and ninth centuries began the re-education of the continent.

It was, indeed, largely, if not wholly, an ecclesiastical culture, and confined to the monasteries. It was, unlike that of Rome, little concerned with the more material affairs of life. Yet it was eminent in missionary enterprise. Its clergy were notoriously fond of wandering; and their church organization, which was founded on the monastery rather than the diocese as the unit of organization, lent itself to this form of church activity. While Rome was converting the Anglo-Saxons, and long before, emissaries of the Celtic church had found their way to the Continent as well as through Britain, establishing monasteries and monastic schools in France and the Rhineland, in Switzerland, in Italy itself, which had profound and far-reaching influence. From Finnian's famous seminary at Clonard went Columba to found the monastery of Hii or Iona to convert the northern Picts. Thence their activities spread southward, till by Bede's time they had reached Northumbria, where they came in contact with those of the Roman church advancing from the south.

It was not the first time the rival communions had met on British soil. Hardly had Augustine founded his church in Kent when he came into conflict with emissaries from the four Welsh monastery bishoprics, who refused to submit to his jurisdiction. To the British church Gregory the Great and his successors wrote letters adjuring it to conform to the Roman tradition and admit Papal supremacy; and from the Irish church went representatives to Rome to uphold their cause and gain recognition of their contentions. From the beginning to the middle of the seventh century the conflict raged, until at the Synod of Whitby Wilfrid's arguments persuaded King Oswy of Northumbria to adopt the Roman observances. Thereafter the contest resolved itself into a struggle to make the Celts give up their "dissenting" forms; till in the course of centuries the two communions were gradually fused in one.

To the mind of a modern layman there is not much of interest or importance in a controversy over the correct method of calculating the date of Easter, or whether a tonsure should be round or horseshoe-shaped, or what the precise form of baptism ought to be. Yet such issues are still the stuff of much theological argument, and on their acceptance, or rejection, in many minds salvation or damnation hangs by a thread between two definitions of the same Greek word. There is in them some esoteric quality of mystical significance whose importance it is not our province to discuss; and in this case more than theology was involved — ecclesiastical supremacy was at stake.

Moreover, in a worldly sense there is something to be said of this struggle between Roman and Irish Christianity, and for the adoption of the former by the English. The high political sense of the Roman church, its organization by parish and diocese, its centralized control, was in sharp contrast to the loose structure of the Celtic establishment, and in due course of time contributed its share to the political development of its adherents. Its long tradition of government and law, inherited from the old days of the Republic and the Empire; its widespread, closely knit fabric of organization; its active interest in the material welfare of its followers; its rôle of preserver, interpreter, and transmitter of such of the old culture as seemed consistent with its faith, — all these brought the English into the current of the times and made them a part of the European world, in ways which would have been impossible had they been drawn within the orbit of the Celtic church. Viewed merely from this standpoint the victory rested with the communion which deserved to win, and whose triumph, despite the virtues of the Celtic church, seems, on the whole, for their best interests.

How does Bede approach this great contest? In what spirit does he write of his ecclesiastical antagonists? It might well be supposed that the great computator, the author of two chronologies, the eminent champion of the Roman church, would have attacked his opponents with all the vigor of the *odium theologicum* so dear to his profession as a whole. In some measure that is the fact. The last, most learned, editor of Bede, indeed, bewails the injection of the Paschal controversy into the *History*. But the surprising thing would have been its omission; and, considering the usual acrimony of such controversies from that time to our own, it would have been a miracle greater than any the historian records had such a question been omitted from his book. As to his treatment of the great Celtic churchmen, let his own account of Aidan bear witness.

"I have written this much concerning the person and works of the aforesaid Aidan," he says, "in no way commending or approving what he imperfectly understood in relation to the observance of Easter; nay, greatly detesting the same, as I have most manifestly proved in the book I wrote, *De Temporibus*; but, like an impartial historian, relating what was done by or with him, and commending such things as were praiseworthy in his actions and preserving the memory of these for my readers; namely his love of peace and charity, his continence and humility, his mind superior to anger and avarice, and despising pride and vainglory, his industry in keeping the heavenly commandments, his diligence in reading and keeping vigils, his authority, befitting a priest in reproving the arrogant and powerful, his compassion in comforting the afflicted, and in relieving and defending the poor."

Nevertheless, as Bede repeats, he disapproved of Aidan's not observing Easter at the proper time, "Yet this I approve in him — that in the celebration of Easter the object which he had in view in all he said, did, or preached, was the same as ours, that is the redemption of mankind through the passion, resurrection, and ascension into Heaven of the man Jesus Christ, the mediator between God and man." May one not add, let none of us have a worse account of himself from any of his opponents in whatever field?

Not many things reveal men's characters more accurately than their attitude towards those who oppose them. Bede was at the meeting-point of the rival communions; he had taken an active, even an eminent part in the great controversy; he was convinced that his side was right, yet he called no names, he vilified neither the character, nor the motives, nor even the intelligence, of his antagonists. He believed them, however mistaken on this point, like himself and his fellows, servants of Christ and seekers after truth; and he had seen and bore witness to their manifold virtues.

His attitude towards all heresies was the same. He was a zealous champion of orthodoxy; few heresies or none escaped his refutation. But he descended neither to personality nor to vituperation as an argument. Moreover he seems to have cherished a quiet belief that heresies were not, on the whole, an unmixed evil. He observes philosophically that different forms of error have a way of destroying each other; and he implies that the attacks of heretics have often brought out the best qualities of the Church in her defense; that the fairest harmony often results from difference; that truth has nothing to fear from controversy. It is a comforting belief; and it has more truth in it than unity in forcible conformity.

That spirit was typical of the man. His latest, and greatest, editor has brought together some of his opinions on various problems of life, which illuminate his character more than a volume of appreciations. "To attempt literally to pray or fast or labour without ceasing would," he declares, "be foolish obstinacy. . . . It is safer not to possess riches, but it is the loving them, not the having them, that is the sin. . . . Lazarus was not received into Abraham's bosom because he was poor, but because he was humble and innocent; nor was Dives condemned because he was rich but because he was proud and pitiless. . . . Christ Himself did not literally observe the precept to turn the other cheek to the striker, and although we should give to every one that asketh, it does not follow that we should give him what he asks. For there is a weak kind of compassion which amounts to sympathy with crime, and merely encourages wrongdoing. . . . The command 'Judge not' does not mean that we are not to condemn open and flagrant sins; the command against wearing two coats does not forbid the use of extra clothing in cold climates." In brief, to be a Christian, in Bede's eyes does not mean the abdication of one's common sense. It is, indeed, this same sturdy common sense, no less than his broad charity, which commends him to us.

Such was the spirit in which he dealt with the most difficult of the problems of his history. That spirit was characteristic of the whole; and it is apparent that this remote Northumbrian monk had somehow in him that combination of qualities which men recognize as belonging to the office of historian. What are those qualities? They are, first and foremost, a love of truth, and the capacity of perceiving it — that mysterious quality we call judgment. They are, secondly, the industry and ability to secure the facts. They are, thirdly, the capacity to arrange and to present those facts in a truthful and a readable narrative.

Or, if you prefer — as you should — Bede's own statement of the case, here is his preface. "I, Bede, servant of Christ and priest, send greeting to the well-beloved King Ceolwulf. And I send you the history which I lately wrote about the English people, for you to read and to examine at your leisure, and also to copy out and impart to others more at large; and I have confidence in your zeal because you are very diligent and inquisitive as to the sayings and doings of men of old; and above all the famous men among our people. For this book either speaks good of the good, and the hearer imitates that; or it speaks evil of the evil, and the hearer flees and shuns the evil. For it is good to praise the good and blame the bad, that the hearer may profit. If your hearer is reluctant, how else will he gain instruction? I have written this for your profit and for that of your people; as God chose you out to be king, it behooves you to instruct your people. And that there may be the less doubt whether this history is true, I will state the sources of my narrative."

There you have his simple historical faith. If history is to be worth writing it must be of some use to someone; it must be read in high places and spread abroad; and it must teach its lessons. For Bede was of an old-fashioned school which had standards of life and conduct and was not ashamed of them, nor thought that good and evil were relative terms which should not be taken too seriously. Moreover, he believed that the historian should be a judge and not a mere reporter; and, holding to the moralities as he did, he thus expressed a doctrine of much vogue, that history is, or ought to be, philosophy — or, as he would have said, religion — teaching by example.

Where did he get his training and material? That, too, he tells us. "My first assistant and teacher," he goes on to say, "was the venerable abbot Albinus, a man who had traveled and studied much, and was the best scholar in England. He told me chiefly about Theodore of blessed memory, who was bishop in Canterbury, and of the abbot Adrian, under whom he had chiefly studied. All that he ascertained in Kent and the adjoining districts, from written documents and the traditions of the old inhabitants, or from the disciples of the blessed pope, St. Gregory; all that was memorable he transmitted to me through Nothelm, a pious priest of London, either sending him to me in person, or sending me a written statement. From the beginning of these books till the English received the faith of Christ, I have derived what is here written from the traditions of old men; and thenceforward to the present, chiefly from the disciples of the blessed pope, St. Gregory, with the dates according to all the kings' reigns, all recorded through abbot Albinus and the reports and statements of Nothelm."

This is the first clue to the value and importance of his history, and to his enduring reputation. It is not often that an historian has such assistance in his labors as that of the greatest scholar in England, and of a churchman who, like Nothelm, became archbishop of Canterbury: nor does he often have such an opportunity for collecting material as that afforded by Nothelm's visits to Rome in search of documents. Yet even this was the least of the assistance he received. For through Albinus and the West Saxon bishop, Daniel, came material for the history of the conversion of the West and South Saxons and the Isle of Wight; from bishop Cedd the progress of the faith in Mercia; from Chad further material regarding Mercia

and the East Saxons; from the monks of Lastingham, from
the abbot Isse, and from ancient traditions transmitted to
him, the antiquities and conversion of East Anglia; from
bishop Cynebert the conversion of Lindsey; and from a
cloud of witnesses, as well as from his own memory, the
conversion of Northumbria. Finally, from the documents
he found at Lindisfarne and York and his conversations
there he learned much of Cuthbert and Wilfrid. Such
were some of the authorities for his history. "And now,"
he adds, having enumerated them, "I humbly beg and
entreat the reader that if he find or hear anything different he will not blame me."

Two things are evident from his relation of his list of
sources; perhaps three. The first is that seldom if ever has
any historian had such an opportunity as Bede. He was
like Herodotus, save that he did not have to travel to
secure material, for most of it was brought to him. He
was like Thucydides in that he knew many who had
taken part in the events he describes. Fully conscious of
the great historical importance of the movement of
peoples which had transformed Britain into England, and
had begun to bring its new masters into the current of
continental faith and practices, he and his friends determined to commemorate this to posterity, and the whole
strength of the Roman church in Britain, and even in
Rome itself, was lent to its historian. He was more than
an individual, he was the representative of the most
powerful organization in the world. Beside his sources of
information even the richest of modern archives seem
barren. This fact explains, among other things, how this
humble monk in a remote Northumbrian monastery,
apparently far removed from all worldly affairs and connections, came to be in one sense a world figure and remembered until now.

He had this enormous advantage besides — his informants were the men who had done, or who had known the

men who had done, the things of which he wrote. Bede lived almost in the dawn of English history; less than three hundred years after Hengist and Horsa had first landed in Thanet; less than two hundred years after Ida, the "flame-bearer," had founded the kingdom of Bernicia in the Scotch Lowlands; less than a century and a half after St. Augustine had landed in Kent. During Bede's own lifetime king Ine of Wessex gave his people the first code of written Anglo-Saxon laws "after the Roman fashion" of which we have knowledge. While he lived Cædmon was writing his poetry; Willibrord was converting the Frisians, Boniface the Germans. The wars of the Saxons with the Celts of Cornwall and of the Scotch Highlands were still going on and the conquerors were still contending bitterly among themselves for the possession of their great inheritance. Wilfrid, whose eloquence had won Northumbria for Rome at Whitby, was still alive in Bede's time and Archbishop of York, nor is it improbable that he was fond of telling how he got the best of his Celtic opponents in that argument.

One only needs to read the *History* to see that Bede's formal acknowledgments to his collaborators are only half the tale. Continually through his pages he notes his indebtedness to a host of other informants — to Bercthun, deacon of Hexham, who told him of Bishop John; to those who told him of Aidan's life; to the physician Cynefrid, who related the miracle of the uncorrupted body of St. Ethelthrith; to Deda, the priest of Putney, who told him of Paulinus in Lindsey; to Ædgils, a monk of Coldingham, who came to Wearmouth-Jarrow and told him of Adamnan; to Trumberct, who told him of his teacher Chad; to bishop Benedict's friends, who told him of that prelate's activities. The list is almost endless; it reads like a catalogue of the English church.

Nor is this all the help that he received. Much of the information sent him by his correspondents was, without

doubt, transcription in some form of those monastic memoranda or chronicles which, as Bede observes in one place,
"the priest went and consulted" on some disputed point.
Some of it came from existing manuscripts, like that anonymous life of Pope Gregory written by a monk of Whitby
from whom Bede copied it; from Eddius' *Life of Wilfrid*;
from the *Life of Cuthbert* by a monk of Lindisfarne; with
other similar material now wholly or largely lost to us.

Thus was the material assembled for the first English
history; and it is apparent that, though the writing is said
to have taken no more than a twelvemonth, the work is
that of a lifetime. The mere copying and transmission of
the Papal letters it contains, the epitaphs of those distinguished Englishmen who died in Rome, must have taken
years. The transmission of manuscripts from one house
to another, by that curious lending-library system which
the monastic world practised, took as long. The infinite
correspondence which Bede must have carried on, his
lengthy conversations with all sorts of men who brought
him information — all this was not the work of one year
nor of ten. So we must look on this great history not as a
twelvemonth's task of a single individual, but the life interest of a whole generation. And, if nothing else, it serves
to show that the life of a man like Bede was far from being
"remote, unfriended, melancholy, slow." He was, in fact,
though at the extreme corner of the European world, in
constant touch with many of its greatest figures and events.

He was a great reader, and he had a whole library of
mediæval, even ancient, writers from which he drew his
inspiration and material. Orosius, Eutropius, Isidore of
Seville, Pliny, Virgil, Tertullian, Prosper of Aquitaine,
and a score of others; with Gildas and Nennius among
British historians; chronicles, biographies. The books on
all sorts of subjects from poetry to geography which he
mentions prove that he was not only a studious but, what
is a far different thing, a well-read man. Thus, like his

far later successor, Green, he managed to "hide in his study and yet gain a quiet name."

Yet with all this, with all his reading and correspondence, all his informants and all the documents they provided him, there remains the fact that he wrote the history in such fashion that it has lived not as a mere source of information for scholars but a book read by men. This is his great achievement, this is the thing which above others keeps his name alive, this is the real test of his talents and his character; and this is due to two things — to his selection of material and his style. The latter is, indeed, remarkable at any time, but especially when he wrote. Simple and clear, neither Virgilian nor Ciceronian, neither involved like Livy nor blunt like Tacitus, much less has it the turgidity of much mediæval Latin nor the puerility of much more. It is rather like that of the Vulgate, which it often quotes, and thus, in so far as possible, he follows the dictum so often imposed upon us. He could not found his style on the Bible and Shakespeare for reasons of chronology, but he did the best he could. He tells a simple and for the most part a straightforward story in a simple and straightforward style. He never forgets that most important fact, so often neglected by so-called historians — that he is telling a story. Moreover, he is not afraid, as lesser men have always been afraid, to tell it in an interesting way. He did not even disdain at times a certain poetic quality; he lingers over Cædmon; he quotes apposite lines and tags of verse; and he perhaps regarded the whole work as a sort of prose epic.

Yet, in a sense, above all the mass of original material which his book contains; above all the unique information which it gives; above its style, and even its subject; the quality which has made it what it is and has preserved it imperishably in literature, is its store of anecdotes which make it seem alive. They have become a part of our literature and tradition; and in them and in their telling is revealed the human touch which makes him kin to us. His motto might have been *Historicus sum, nihil humanum mihi alienum puto* — I am an historian and I think nothing alien to me; and that sentiment might well be pondered by those who are ambitious to shine in the same field.

These, then, are the chief qualities which made his book and his name immortal, — his information and his style, his judgment and his stories. In them you have embodied in his book the man himself, learned yet not pedantic, orthodox but not bigoted, firm in the faith but not intolerant, devout but not fanatical, good but not content with mere passive goodness, a monk but not an intellectual recluse, gifted but modest, a controversialist but not a defamer, a great historian but a greater man. To him may be applied two quotations, old and now shopworn, but none the less appropriate. The first is from a yet more famous pen — Chaucer's familiar lines, "And gladly wolde he lerne and gladly teche." The second is the brief Anglo-Saxon epitaph: "He did his work before he went his way."

For such a man the immortality of worldly remembrance was a simple problem, however little he may have dreamed of it. He was, in the first period of his memory, revered by the members of the great organization to which he belonged; and in the second by scholars; while at all times he had the support of those neither churchmen nor scholars who read books. Thus buttressed, few reputations could be more secure. His book was not merely a great epic of the church; it had that human interest which must have made it doubly welcome to the reading public of the Middle Ages. One may, indeed, reconstruct some of the eager anticipation of that public to secure copies of this best-seller of the eighth century from the extraordinary number of manuscripts which

have been preserved to us. Of these there are still in
existence more than a hundred and thirty copies of this
"father of history," who yields in this respect only to
Geoffrey of Monmouth, the "father of romance." It is
probable that there was no library of any consequence in
western Europe which did not have at least one copy of
the *History*. It was seized on by the copyists and from
the moment of its "publication" it would seem that the
activities of every monastic scriptorium must at some time
have been employed in re-producing it. It spread with
great rapidity; it was continually copied, down to, and
perhaps even after, the invention of printing, both in its
original Latin and in King Alfred's translation, which
had a vogue of its own.

With printing it advanced another stage. It was
among the first of printed books, those rare incunabula
of the "cradle-stage" of typography. The first edition
came from the press of Heinrich Eggestein of Strassburg,
about 1475, who re-printed it some twenty-five years
later, with Eusebius. There are said to have been six editions in the fifteenth century, eleven in the sixteenth, six
in the seventeenth, one — but a definitive one — in the
eighteenth, seven in the nineteenth, and already one in
the twentieth. And besides the Anglo-Saxon version,
which had its own history, every century since the sixteenth has seen a new translation, and the nineteenth
had three. So Bede's "popularity" is no mere dream of
an historian. A book which lives twelve hundred years,
with steadily recurrent resurrections, and runs through
thirty editions, deserves serious consideration, even as a
means of perpetuating a reputation.

The reasons for that reputation and that popularity
are, in a sense, obvious enough; but it is rather by comparison than by absolute standards that we can arrive at
the true value of Bede's historical work. Apart from the
fact that it described a great episode in church history in

an entertaining style, and so became a mediæval classic, as well as a mine of material for modern scholarship, it forms, with the Anglo-Saxon Chronicle, the most notable record of the beginnings of any European people. And it is probably, all things considered, the greatest piece of historical writing produced during the Middle Ages, that is to say, between the Romans and the Renaissance. It is not merely the greatest book of a generation in its field; it is the greatest historical work in near a thousand years — and that is some distinction.

Moreover, Bede's reputation has not lessened through the years. Run through monastic chronicles where you will and you will find among the notes of great events, of great disasters and the deaths of kings, "Master Bede died "; "Redbat king of the Frisians; the priest Bede dies"; "Bede the renowned doctor died "; "Phocas was emperor; Boniface Pope; Bede flourished; Bede died "; "Bede wrote his book; Bede died "; "Bede the noble and renowned doctor died."

That is to be expected in such a society as that of the mediæval church when one of its heroes passes away. Yet who would have reckoned this remote Northumbrian monk a leader of the church? He held no offices; he was neither an abbot nor a bishop, much less an archbishop. To the end he was a private in the ranks, a simple priest; and it is a reflection on human greatness that we can so seldom recall who was the head of any such institution, whether monastery or university, at the time it sheltered a great man. Nor did Bede's fame cease with the Middle Ages. Its circle has widened far beyond even the confines of the church, till there are few educated persons who have not heard it; not, indeed, as that of the famous computator, commentator or controversalist, hymn writer or grammarian, but as the author of the *History*.

So he lives to-day, the man of a book. He is among the Fathers; but it took more than a thousand years for him to be numbered among the saints of the great church to which he still belongs, for he wrought no miracles — except the crowning miracle of his history. He converted none — save those who read it. He held no office — save that of the first great English, if not the first great modern, historian. He was not canonized for more than a millennium — save by the men of his own craft. And, seeking to immortalize the achievements of others, he somehow managed to immortalize himself.

COLONEL JOHN SCOTT
OF LONG ISLAND
1634(?)–1696

COLONEL JOHN SCOTT
OF LONG ISLAND
1634(?)–1696

TO BE a rascal is bad; to be a great rascal, despite the finespun distinctions of the philosophers, is doubtless worse. But to be embalmed in biographical dictionaries for pure rascality unadorned with the gilding of politics, of high finance, of romance, a rascality not even made respectable by success — of all failures in the conflict between man and oblivion this is perhaps the worst. To match one's wit against the world; to gain place and competence; to share in affairs which might almost be reckoned great; and, on the very threshold of achievement which would have drowned the memory of misdeeds and perpetuated one's name as soldier, savant, adventurer, empire-builder, or what not, to find the way barred by duller and more honest men, or by more accomplished scoundrels — this is a hard case. It is not lightened by the sight of luckier or more eminent associates going on to wealth and power and a certain measure of immortality while one is himself thrust back into the old nothingness again. Is not this the crowning tragedy of rascality?

Such is the tragedy of John Scott, sometime colonist and soldier, sometime royal geographer and the agent if not the confidant of the great; always adventurer, and, save for circumstances beyond his wit and skill, and, we may add, perhaps beyond his character, lord of Long

Island, and the founder of a fourteenth original colony
in North America; now but the shadow of a shade of a
dead rascal, whose life serves to while away an hour or
two; perhaps at best to point a moral and adorn a tale.

If this were all, it would, perhaps, not be enough to
justify any of that long and wearying research which, in
such a case as his, resembles nothing so much as historical
detective work. But it is not. The story of Scott did not
end with his departure from the scene of his earthly
activities. However numerous those activities while he
was alive, they pale to insignificance before his achievements once he was in his grave; and it is in these no less,
perhaps even more, than in the extraordinary circumstances of his life, that there lies whatever contribution
to ultimate truth this study contains.

That contribution is, on its face, not great. It may, in
a sense, seem trivial; for it is, after all, only a story, and
in many ways not even a pleasant story. It is a story
without a hero, unless you may call its subject, who was
far from heroic, by the more agreeable title. It is equally
devoid of a moral; indeed its principal character is peculiarly notable for a conspicuous lack of morals. Finally,
to complete the depressing catalogue of its unpleasant
characteristics and so get them out of the way once for
all, it has no particular bearing on the great problems
which present themselves to us urgently day by day —
unless it be that of the most fundamental of all problems,
human nature itself. And, it is only fair to say, a good
many persons have at one time or another, in various
fashions and from the most diverse motives, told parts
of it. No one hitherto has related it in its entirety, and
that is, perhaps, after all, the principal value of this tale;
for it happens to be one of those not uncommon things
whose whole is greater than the sum of its parts.

Thus having in so far as possible dispelled any agreeable, if mistaken, anticipations with which anyone may

have provided himself as an antidote for spending time in reading mere history, and having offered such reassurance as is possible that the story contains little which will either instruct or elevate the mind, it may be proper to add, by way of introduction, that this is a study of what is, so to speak, a cross-section not only of English and colonial, but of general seventeenth-century, history, seen chiefly, as it were, from the under side.

I

THE story begins, as it should, at the beginning, for two reasons. The first is because its earliest scenes are laid in that region and in that period which long conditioned the fortunes and misfortunes of its principal character — Long Island in the middle of the seventeenth century. The second is because the beginning of the tale is in a sense the type of the whole. For it begins in a Long Island jail.

Sometime in March of the year of our Lord 1654 there came to the attention of the authorities of New Amsterdam, then presided over by the redoubtable Director-General, Peter Stuyvesant, news of the activities of a certain young Englishman, known even then, it would appear, by the style or title of John Scott of Long Island. The Dutch, it seems, had for some time been annoyed by nocturnal raids on their property. And Scott's presence in the district from which he took his appellation, his character, his activities, a suspicion that he was concerned in these matters, or something about him, commended him so little to the Dutch colonists in that land then debatable between New England and New Netherland, that he was seized and clapped into jail as an undesirable citizen, together with four or five of his neighbors, including a certain Mr. Baxter who was to be associated with him in later years and in far different circumstances.

Under such conditions John Scott made his somewhat inauspicious entry into history.

Who he was, no one then or thereafter seems rightly to have known; and though during a long and busy life he took great pains at many times to explain to a considerable number of people his precise origin and ancestry, the matter was not thereby much illuminated, partly for the reason that it did not always happen that any two of his explanations quite agreed with each other, and more largely for the still better reason that none of them agreed with the facts which other persons adduced from their knowledge of him. For the moment we may ignore his own story, therefore, and confine ourselves to what his acquaintances and the official records declared of him.

From these it would seem that, about six years before his appearance in Long Island, Scott had been sentenced by the General Court of Massachusetts Bay to serve his master after his term of service thirty-five shillings' worth, "or otherwise satisfy him." That master was one Lawrence Southwick, a Quaker, later banished from Massachusetts for his religion; and, in the person of his wife, Cassandra, commemorated to posterity in one of Whittier's poems. How Scott came into Southwick's hands does not clearly appear; but there is evidence that, with other youths, he had been carried to Massachusetts as a bound-boy in the care of a certain Emmanuel Downing, father of that greater adventurer, Sir George Downing, about the year 1643, and was by him bound over to Southwick. It appears further that in 1647 Southwick received permission to "put forth said Scott for three years to any honest man" — but found no takers; and that two years later the promising youth was brought once more to the attention of the court, this time to be admonished for "profane swearing." This story of his origin is partly confirmed, partly modified, by the fact that some years after he became a noteworthy figure

in the colonies, a certain Captain Richard Nicolls, then
secretary to the first English governor of New York, his
kinsman, Colonel Richard Nicolls, testified that Scott
"was born at Ashford, Kent, of very meane parentage,
was bro't by his mother to New England, who lived mis-
erable poore in this gov't, a poor bankrupt miller's wife
till very lately next to want and beggary."

The testimony is not identical but, despite the assertion of the compiler of the American Scott genealogy
that the young adventurer was "connected" with the
Scotts of Scott's (or Scots) Hall, it is probable that this
relationship was as shadowy as many of his other claims
to lands and titles. It seems at least possible that some
of the American genealogies based upon descent from
him might better be associated with those more genuine connections of the Scots Hall family, whose arrival
in America antedated John Scott's by some ten years.
The English family in later years denied with great bit-
terness his claim of kinship and his right to bear the arms
of the family. Much less is it probable that he was the
son of "the Hon. John Scott, Surveyor General to
Charles I," and grandson of "Sir William, Ambassador
to Turkey and to Florence, who married Mary Howard,
daughter of Charles, Earl of Nottingham." For it is
perhaps not without significance, in this connection, that,
when he became established in his new home, he tried to
change the name of Setauket in Long Island, not to
Mornamont, after the Kentish Scott family estate, but
to Ashford, which somehow seems to echo the English town
with which he was most familiar before his emigration.

But if he lacked authentic proof of lineage and arms,
he did possess talents, perhaps almost if not quite as
useful as birth. For some time after his arrival on Long
Island he seems to have lived a good deal among the
Indians and traded on his own account. And, "having a
nimble genius, tho' otherwise illiterate, with the help of

a little reading, having a good memory and greater confidence, he became somewhat above the common people," indulging in somewhat various and devious activities whose immediate end we have seen in what may be called, in the language of Sir Conan Doyle, "The Adventure of the Long Island Jail."

It is scarcely surprising that the Dutch showed so little appreciation of Scott's peculiar talents at such a time and under such circumstances as those which he selected to make his entry into politics. However that era was adapted to his gifts, it was not one which commended restless and intriguing Englishmen like him to the inhabitants of the New Netherlands. It was a trying period for Hollanders everywhere, but most especially to those on Long Island. England had just transformed her Commonwealth into a Protectorate, with Oliver Cromwell at its head. She was, moreover, just emerging from a war with Holland, in which she had been successful enough to break the hold of the Dutch carrying monopoly which they had enjoyed for nearly a generation. She was on her way to war with Spain; and, with the triumphs of her great admirals over the old masters of the sea, it seemed not improbable that she would presently come to dominate the element on which Holland depended for its living, almost for its life.

But if the situation was bad for the Dutch in Europe, it was worse for the Dutch in America. A generation earlier their traders had begun to plant their posts along the Hudson at the same moment that the English had begun to settle on Massachusetts Bay. From those two points each side had made it way along the coast and into the interior. Moreover, the Swedes had begun a settlement on the Delaware, and New Netherland found itself, in consequence, hemmed in by New England on the one side and New Sweden on the other. The latter was easily disposed of; and in the very days that Scott found his way to jail, the Dutch conquered and absorbed the Swedish settlements. But the English were tougher antagonists. In the thirty-five years since the foundation of Plymouth, they had spread northward to the Kennebec and south and west to Rhode Island and Connecticut. They had settled at Saybrook and so secured the mouth of the Connecticut River; they had built a town at Hartford, and planted a colony at New Haven. They had spread into Long Island and were now in fairly secure possession of the Connecticut Valley, which had been disputed between them and the Dutch, together with the eastern end of the island opposite. Thence they had pushed westward until, at the very door of Manhattan, their pioneers had begun to colonize the Westchester district. With the rise of England and the decline of Holland on the sea, it was thus becoming evident that, short of some miraculous reversal of fortune, the days of the ascendancy of New Netherland were numbered. Under such circumstances English agitators were naturally peculiarly distasteful to the Dutch, and especially to such men as the Director-General, Stuyvesant. Scott was carried to New Amsterdam, there examined, and ultimately released, doubtless with stern admonitions to go, and sin no more.

He seems to have passed the next few years in the pursuit of a more or less honest livelihood. It would appear from some later statements that he divided his time between the exercise of his profession as a blacksmith and the raising of cattle, or as it was less elegantly expressed by his contemporaries, "keeping cowes." But these pursuits by no means exhausted his energies. He had already turned his attention to the chief source of wealth in a new country — land; and even before his entry into international affairs, he had found opportunity to exercise his gifts in that direction. For that the time and place were peculiarly favorable. When he had been released

from his obligations to Massachusetts justice he seems
to have made his way to Connecticut, thence to the oldest
settlement on Long Island — the oldest English settlement, indeed, within the present boundaries of New
York, the town of Southampton, which thenceforth for
some years became the center of his activities. Thither
he seems to have taken his mother, "ould Mrs. Scott,"
but later settled at Setauket.

He chose well. As towns went in those days Southampton was already well established. It had been
founded about 1639 or 1640 by emigrants chiefly from
Lynn, under the lead of Edward Howell, Edward
Cooper, and the minister, Abraham Pierson, the father
of the first president of Yale College. This party of some
forty families had, according to the custom of the time,
formed a company, and secured a concession from one
Farrett, the agent of that Sir William Alexander, Earl
of Stirling, to whom James I had granted and Charles I
confirmed rights over nearly all the best portions of
northern North America, but whose chief source of revenue had thus far been the sale of Nova Scotian baronet-
cies and the rights of colonizing Long Island. For this
land there were already two claimants besides — the
Dutch of New Amsterdam and the settlers of the recently
planted colonies of Connecticut and especially New
Haven opposite; and these, as well as the new colonists
from Lynn, were to play no small part in the fortunes
of Scott.

Those colonists almost at once came into collision with
the Dutch, and, driven from their first landing-place at
Schout's Bay by a force from New Amsterdam, they had
sought out the Earl's agents at New Haven and from
them secured a deed by which, in consideration of £400,
they were permitted to make terms with the Indians for
the eastern end of Long Island, where by June, 1640,
they seem to have established themselves. The colony

had flourished from the beginning. Not only was the
climate peculiarly agreeable, the tillable land, once it
was cleared, sufficiently fertile, but the sea was full of
whales, "crampasses," and seals, from which oil could
be extracted, and teeming with fish and oysters. By the
time of Scott's arrival the settlement was already out-
growing its boundaries; and a year before his arrest he
had signalized his advent into the real-estate field by
selling to its directors the adjoining district of Quogue,
which he had bought from one Ogden, who had acquired
it from the Indians.

The passion for land speculation never left him; and
his stay in Long Island was filled with his activities in
that field. The records of the settlement in the years between 1660 and 1664 abound in the accounts of his land
transfers. For some of the tracts which he conveyed he
had titles from other settlers, for others he claimed to
have — and probably did have — deeds from the Indian
sachem Wayandanck and his son Weacham. Such titles
seem often to have resided principally in his own too
exuberant optimism, and the peculiar psychology of the
savage chieftains. They long remained to vex the colony,
and, however sacred the ceremony of transfer "by turf
and twig" which gave them into his hands, there is at
least one instance which sheds some light upon the doubtful character of such transfers and the titles resulting
therefrom. For in 1664 when the people of Setauket purchased land of the "Sachem of Uncachage, Tobacus,"
they insisted on that noble savage adding to the instrument these words: "Further saith that he sold no land
John Scott" — refraining diplomatically from indicating
against which party the imputation rested. Moreover, he
seems to have wandered much abroad in those years.
Besides buying a "certen little sloop" from two Dutch-
men, he arranged for "one halfe part" of a ketch for a
voyage to Newfoundland in 1660, paying half the amount

of the hire, while he later posed as an authority on that island on the strength of it. He appears to have visited Narragansett Bay and he was almost certainly in Boston.

Besides his canny forehandedness he seems to have shown other traits. A month after his arrrest he was defendant in a suit for defamation in New Haven. Three years later he was made a freeman of Southampton, was granted a house-lot there, was appointed one of the tax commissioners; was suing and being sued by his neighbors, chiefly about land; married Deborah, daughter of one Thurston Raynor of that place; acted as attorney — among other things for a "whale company"; and still later to determine the town boundaries. He appears also in a complaint of having a vessel stolen from him. But through it all ran the *motif* of land, and the continual suspicion that his titles and transfers were more or less questionable. In short he appears to have been one of the first — in view of later happenings one hesitates to say the worst — of that company of plausible individuals who have seen in Long Island real estate the Eldorado so earnestly and so vainly sought by Spanish explorers in South America. Meanwhile, too, he rose in the world. For whereas he had been formerly described as "John Scott, Smith," he now appears as "Captain John Scott."

II

THUS ended the first period of his long and active career. Whether he was moved by the suggestions of those whom he involved in his real-estate transactions, or whether he sought a wider field for his rapidly developing talents, about the end of the year 1660 he set sail for England. To that next scene of his activities he seems to have carried three things, each of some significance in its way. The first and most important was himself, his

COLONEL JOHN SCOTT   269

abilities and his ambitions; the second was a collection of curiosities, not otherwise identified; the third was
a copy of a book printed two years before in Cambridge,
Abraham Pierson's volume entitled, *Some Helps for the
Indians, Shewing them how to improve their Natural Reason
to know the true God and the Christian Religion.*

This last seems, on the whole, a peculiar piece of
property for him to cherish, nor one calculated to advance the fortunes of a Long Island real-estate dealer
at the court of his gracious Majesty, King Charles the
Second, of somewhat less than blessed memory. Just how
the book in question may have helped the Indians one
extract may reveal. "How," says this admirable work,
"do you prove that there is but one true God?" "Because," it answers itself, "singular things of the same
kind when they are multiplied are differenced among
themselves by their peculiar properties; but there cannot be found another God differentiated from this by
any such like properties." This, and much more to the
same purpose, was set forth in the no doubt pleasing but
comparatively rudimentary vocabulary of the Quiripi
dialect, in which it seems, if possible, less comprehensible
than in its original tongue. It may be hoped that it was
more so; but it was never translated, as was originally
planned, into Narragansett, and the natives of Rhode
Island were, in consequence, deprived of the privilege
of possessing a volume which would doubtless have been
of incalculable importance to their intellectual as well
as to their spiritual development.

Yet however little it may have helped the Indians, it
may seem still more surprising that Scott imagined that
this pearl of missionary literature could have helped him.
The explanation is simple enough, though it might not
occur at once to the ordinary mind. But Scott's was no
ordinary mind. The book bore on its original title-page
a statement that it had been "examined and approved

by Thomas Stanton, Interpreter General to the United Colonies." The copy which Scott exhibited with just pride to his new English acquaintances was precisely like the original with one slight exception. Its title-page announced to the reader that the volume had been "examined and approved by that Experienced Gentleman (in the *Indian* Language) Captain John Scot." And it has been perhaps not unnaturally supposed by the learned antiquarians who nearly two hundred years later interested themselves in this earliest product of Scott's literary skill, that the ingenious gentleman had found an obliging printer in London who was good enough to print the title-page thus simply but effectively altered to suit the new circumstances and company in which the book found itself, and so further the natural ambition of a rising young man by commending him to his new friends as a useful agent of his native land in its North American possessions, perhaps in some lucrative official capacity.

If there were any doubt that Scott had a genius for the exercise of certain arts by which men rise in the world it would be at once dissipated by the mere fact that he came to England when he did. The situation might have been made to his hand. The King had just been restored. The court was full of needy adventurers and still needier Royalists, of whom King Charles himself was chief. The country was, for the moment, in a ferment of loyalty; and what was more to the purpose, the unsettled situation of affairs left over from the civil wars and the interregnum, the difficulty of distinguishing true claims from false, and more especially honest men from rogues, offered an unparalleled opportunity to men not overscrupulous in advancing their fortunes. This Scott could scarcely have known in its entirety when he made his exit from Long Island, but that he grasped its significance so quickly and so immediately set himself to take advantage of the blessings fortune had put in his way argues again the adaptable and resourceful qualities which the man possessed, to an even greater degree than his happy inspiration in regard to the title-page of the missionary volume. It argues still more, for it reveals that imaginative quality which was so eminent a feature of his intellectual equipment.

Moreover, there is one other circumstance to be taken into account in connection with Scott's advent in England in the year of the Restoration. Whatever the importance of the reign of Charles II in other fields, in that of colonial development it was one of the principal epochs in English history. In the preceding forty years there had been established in North America a series of settlements which extended from Virginia and Maryland on the south through New Sweden, New Netherland, New Haven, Connecticut, Rhode Island, Massachusetts, Plymouth, New Hampshire, and the Kennebec region to New France along the lower St. Lawrence. The greater part of these colonies were English, and the troubles of the reign of Charles I had poured into them a population which made them the largest European society outside of Europe. The various colonies had found their legal status a matter of considerable concern in the face of the civil disturbances in England; and when the Restoration of Charles seemed to promise settled government, they hastened to have their various privileges confirmed or enlarged by royal charter. In consequence every colony deputed representatives to protect its interests, and among the strange faces with which London was filled in the early days of the new reign, those of the colonial agents were conspicuous. From Boston came Samuel Maverick to represent the interests of Massachusetts; from Rhode Island came George Baxter to second the efforts of Clarke and urge the cause of the English in territories claimed by the Dutch; from Virginia came Governor Berkeley; from

Connecticut came Governor John Winthrop — and from Long Island came Captain John Scott.

In addition to this there was another element involved. The Royalists had come back for the most part stripped of their old inheritance by the catastrophe which had overtaken their party in the preceding twenty years. The number of places and pensions which England itself afforded fell far short of the number of those who pressed their claims on the new administration. The needy Royalists were not long in perceiving that the rapid development of the colonies, and the possibility of forming new colonies, offered opportunities for increase in their fortunes. In consequence, amid the manifold activities which the court and council of Charles II revealed in these early years, colonial projects were conspicuous. From the Lord Chancellor, Clarendon, down, the courtiers bestirred themselves in colonial, and presently commercial, projects, as their predecessors of Elizabethan times had busied themselves with privateering schemes to spoil the Spaniard.

These were supplemented by the issue of new grants and charters which, in effect, reorganized the British colonial empire. A year before Charles II returned to England the Virginians had proclaimed him King of England, Scotland, Ireland, and Virginia, and restored the royal governor, Sir William Berkeley, who made his way to England on the Restoration to plead in vain for the amelioration of the Navigation Act and a guarantee for her constitution. And scarcely had the Restoration been accomplished when Lord Colepeper, one of the members of the Plantations Committee, began those plans to acquire a hold over this loyal colony which bore fruition a dozen years later in a grant to him and to Arlington of its rights for a generation, and perhaps contributed to the so-called Bacon's Rebellion.

Among the earliest acts of the new government had

been the appointment of Clarendon and seven others to act as a council for the colonies, and through that body came a reorganization of the plantations in America. In 1662 the charter of Connecticut was granted by the king at the solicitation of the Connecticut agent, John Winthrop, who for fourteen years thereafter was annually chosen its governor. By that charter, much against its will, New Haven was annexed to Connecticut, whose boundaries were extended from the Narragansett River to the Pacific Ocean. At the same time the government of Maryland was confirmed to Lord Baltimore, and in the following year Baxter brought to Rhode Island the charter which had been obtained through the exertions of Clarke. At the same time, too, the lands south of Virginia were erected into the province of Carolina and granted to Clarendon and his associate, Berkeley. Finally, to make the story complete, when, a few years later, England seized New Netherland, the king granted to his brother, the Duke of York, the lands between the Connecticut and the Delaware; and James, in turn, gave to his followers, Berkeley and Carteret, the land between the Hudson and the Delaware. Thus, within five years after the Restoration, all the colonies of North America, save Massachusetts, had been given new charters or new masters. And it is perhaps no wonder that Scott, surrounded by this atmosphere, conceived that he too might profit by the general distribution of lands and offices. He thereupon bestirred himself to share in this windfall.

The methods which he adopted were characteristic of the man and the situation in which he found himself. Under the circumstances it seemed fairly apparent to many men of his sort and of even meaner intelligence that whether or not Charles II was the fountain of honor and justice, he was certainly the fountain of pensions and patronage. In common, therefore, with a horde of other adventurers, Scott cast about for the best way to

approach this potential source of benefits. After the
manner of his kind, he took what seemed to be the most
direct path to the royal presence — by way of the back
stairs. He made friends with one Thomas Chiffinch,
custodian of the royal jewels, "keeper of rarities," page
of the closet, and, above all, brother of that William
Chiffinch of unsavory memory who was the chief pan-
derer to the royal pleasures. He scraped acquaintance
with a certain Joseph Williamson, then secretary to that
Henry Bennet who was even then on his way to place
and fortune and the title of Earl of Arlington. Under
such auspices Scott went to court, met Bennet himself, and
gained interest with a "potent gentleman," by present-
ing him with a parcel of curiosities valued at £60. And
whither his ambitions tended may be judged by the fact
that in May, 1661, it was reported through Long Island
that the King had bestowed upon him that entire region.

The report was not true, but it was not Scott's fault
that it was false. There was some ground for the rumor.
He had, indeed, petitioned for such a grant; and it even
seemed for a time that he might achieve his purpose. But
among the many characteristics which make Scott's
career so interesting, one is conspicuous. It is what he
and men like him usually call ill-luck. For while his petition was still pending in this winter of 1661–1662, there
arrived in London no less a person than John Winthrop
the younger, chief magistrate of Connecticut, seeking a
new charter for his colony. As events were to prove there
were few men in the world whose presence at this moment Scott should have feared more than that of Winthrop. Connecticut was not only anxious to have its charter rights secured; the colony, or some of its members,
was exceedingly anxious to obtain title to Long Island,
or at least that precise part from which Scott came.
Thus not only were Winthrop's ambitions certain to
clash with those of Scott, but it is not improbable that

Winthrop knew of Scott's past. As between the governor of a commonwealth and a needy adventurer, there could be small doubt which way the authorities would incline. But Scott made the best of it. He promptly sought out and endeavored to attach himself to Winthrop, though at first, naturally, with small success; and his petition was denied in the following spring for reasons which may well be imagined and which presently appeared.

This was, of course, a blow. But your true adventurer is not a man to be daunted by a single reverse, nor is he accustomed to carry all his eggs in one basket. While Scott had been playing his part before court and council, he had been notably busy in other and less public capacities. The story may be briefly told. Somewhere in those busy days of 1661, he met in London a certain Daniel Gotherson, Quaker, sometime an officer in the Cromwellian army, more recently a tradesman in London, and a spy for the government among his old associates, some of whom were more than suspected of treasonable practices. Moreover, by some curious and unfortunate chance, for him, this worthy gentleman was possessed of some lands on Long Island which he had acquired many years before. His wife was a lady of some reputation as an exhorter among the sect to which she and her husband belonged. Her maiden name was Dorothea Scott, of Scots Hall in Kent. Upon the ground of similarity of name Captain Scott, with that ready wit and that openness to opportunity in whatever form it presented itself to him, promptly claimed relationship with Mrs. Gotherson, and had that claim admitted, chiefly, it would appear, on the ground of his real or fancied resemblance to certain family portraits preserved in Scots Hall. We believed his claim, wrote Mrs. Gotherson, in later years, because "some of our Anchesters' pictures were very like him." It is, moreover, not improbable that here, as at a later period, he was aided in his ingratiating design by his early Quaker connection with Southwick, from whom, and from Mrs. Gotherson, he derived a certain fluency in the peculiar dialect affected by that sect which was of much use to him both then and thereafter.

At all events the new acquaintance, cemented by a common interest in Long Island real estate, which has always been famous for bringing together the most diverse characters by its peculiar charm, prospered so rapidly and so completely that from these slender premises Scott presently drew a great and characteristic conclusion. He sold Gotherson sixteen hundred acres of Long Island land for the nominal sum of five shillings, to which he added later another deed for a hundred and fifteen acres "in consideration of a sum of lawful money," amount unstated; and furnished a bond and covenant to bind the bargain. By the middle of 1662 he had devised one of the most remarkable instruments of a career peculiarly notable for remarkable documents. It runs as follows: " I, John Scott, of Ashford, on Long Island, in the south part of New England, Esquire, doe authorize my trusty and well-beloved friend and kinsman, Daniell Gotherson, Esquire, of Egerton in Kent, my true and lawfull attorney for me, and in my name and for my use to treat for 20,000 acres of land lying and being on the South side of Long Island, and between Acombamook and ye land of the aforesaid Daneill Gotherson, lying by Uncochuag on the south side of ye marsh land of ye said John Scott, on which it butts South, and thereupon to conclude for such sum or summes of money as he in his prudence shall thinke a fitt consideration for ye whole or any part of ye said 20,000 acres so soulled, I hereby promise to ratify and confirme under my hand and seale, if ther be any deficiency in ye grants granted by ye said Daniell Gotherson, and to ye performance of premises I bind myselfe, heirs, Executors, and assigns," &c.

To this Scott added an agreement to protect Gotherson's property against the sachems Wackcombwin and Wyandanchchase, together with certain other documents of like import and equal value. These he sealed with his newly acquired signet bearing his coat of arms — which seems to have been the property of Mrs. Gotherson! It is not easy to comprehend how the human mind works, especially in the presence of a superior intelligence; but it is certainly a tribute to Scott's undoubted charm that the Gothersons were under the impression that they had purchased land from Scott; for when, some three years later, Daniel Gotherson died, he bequeathed these mythical Long Island estates to his surviving heirs. It is perhaps not unimportant to observe that, whether or not Scott ever owned the land, or whether it ever existed, Mrs. Gotherson never became possessed of it. It is perhaps even more to the point to observe that, as a tangible result of these documents, Scott came into possession of some £2,000 of Gotherson's money.

Having thus provided himself with the sinews of war, he turned again with fresh confidence to public life. He consorted with the colonial representatives in London, especially with Hooke of Massachusetts and Winthrop of Connecticut; and, in particular, he put himself in touch with the affairs of the so-called Atherton Company. With this we come upon another and peculiarly characteristic example of seventeenth-century colonial enterprise. For this association, which played no small part in the affairs of New England, was a typical product of the period in which it flourished, and its history throws much light upon the methods by which certain phases of early colonial development were conditioned.

The facts are briefly these. The Rhode Island Plantation, as is generally known, was founded between 1636 and 1640 by Roger Williams and others, among whom was a certain John Clarke, who fled or were driven out by persecution from Massachusetts. The four original settlements were united in 1647 under the authority of a patent issued three years earlier by the Parliamentary board of Commissioners for the Plantations; though the two divisions of Providence and Rhode Island were separated for a time in 1654. Thus far all seems clear enough. But in those days of unsettled politics and still more unsettled boundaries, certain ambitious gentlemen of Massachusetts, known, from their moving spirit, one Colonel or Major Atherton, as the Atherton Company, conceived the idea of acquiring from the Indians west of the Narragansett a tract of land, and there establishing a new colony despite the fact that the territory in question was included in the Rhode Island grant. They were somewhat aided in this philanthropic design by the fact that there was in existence a patent for those lands, professing to have been issued in 1643, but which, it seems, was not signed by the proper persons and therefore presumably not valid.

Upon these somewhat slender premises they applied to the government of Charles II for a patent for their claim, endeavoring to have it removed from the jurisdiction of the Rhode Island and Providence plantations and annexed either to Massachusetts or Connecticut. In this case they were more or less abetted by the authorities of the latter colonies, by John Winthrop in particular; and to this end they employed also the talents of Scott, owing, apparently, to the fact that he appeared to have some knowledge of the Narragansett region, which he claimed to have explored, and possibly did visit, on one of his cruises. For a time it seemed that they might put their scheme through. But, unfortunately for them, John Clarke, the able and honest representative of the original proprietors, was still in England, and he now used his best endeavors to block the progress of this promising land deal. On the side of the Atherton Company, Scott

engaged the interest of Chiffinch, who was taken into
the society; and a petition was preferred against Clarke
and his associates as "enimys to the peace and well-
being of his Majesty's good subjects."

This project was, for the time being, successful. A
letter was secured from the King, and countersigned
by Bennet, commending the Atherton associates to
the "neighborly kindness and protection" of the four
New England colonies, Massachusetts, Plymouth, New
Haven, and Connecticut, and urging that the proprietors
be permitted "peaceably to improve their colony and
plantation in New England," the King, "having been
given to understand that his good subjects, Thomas
Chiffinch, John Scott, John Winthrop and others were
daily disturbed and unjustly molested in their possessions by certain unreasonable and turbulent spirits of
Providence Colony." These latter conceived themselves
to be, and probably were, the rightful owners of the land
in question, so that their unreasonableness and turbu-
lence were perhaps not unnatural under the circumstances, nor were they much soothed by the royal admonition, nor, indeed, much terrified by royal authority.

Such were the proceedings to which the authorities of
Massachusetts and Connecticut lent themselves with such
excellent results. There was only one flaw in the scheme.
While the Atherton Company had been busy with its
back-stairs influence, Clarke had gone on the straight
and narrow path which led, as it proved in this case, to
success. The extraordinary letter which the conspirators had extracted from an easy-going king, obtained,
as it were, by stealth, was not a document which stood
the light of day. It was either not known to or not recognized by the Council of which the minister, Clarendon,
the enemy of Bennet, was the head. For, seventeen days
after the letter came into being, the Council passed,
under the Great Seal, a royal charter to Rhode Island,

which nullified the provisions of the letter and, after a long period of dispute, finally brought the machinations of the Atherton Company to naught.

Meanwhile Scott had evolved another scheme. At the very moment that he was thus being endorsed by Charles, he was petitioning that monarch for office; and the petition is worthy of notice, if only on biographical grounds. Scott's father, it recited, had been an ardent royalist during the late disturbances. He had not merely given his life to the royal cause; what was more to the present purpose, he had sold an estate of £200 per annum and advanced to Charles I no less than £14,300. Scott himself had been transported to New England, he averred, for his attachment to the crown; his "small expression of loyalty" having been made, as he phrased it, "by cutting the bridles and girts of some of the then Parliament's horses at Turnham Green." He went on to say that he had been brought before a Parliament committee, by whom, in spite of his giving them £500, he was sent to New England, in the care of one Downing, and abused. He had bought near a third of Long Island; and in consequence of these facts he begged Charles to make him governor of that province and the adjacent islands, or at least allow the inhabitants to choose their own governor and assistants yearly. The petition was favorably received by the King, who was "most graciously inclined to encourage it." It was referred to the committee on Foreign Plantations, and there for a time the matter rested.

While it was being considered, Scott took another step, the first, as it was to prove, though he did not guess it, in a great and unscrupulous design of far-reaching consequence. Upon his complaint that the Dutch had intruded on the New England mainland and islands, especially on Manhattan and Long Island, an order in Council directed Captain Scott, Mr. Maverick and Mr.

Baxter, formerly of New Netherland, to draw up a
narrative of the English king's title to that district,
the Dutch intrusion, their "deportment, management,
strength, trade and government, and means to make
them acknowledge His Majesty's sovereignty." And
it is not too much to suppose that they drew it strong,
for each of them, in his peculiar way, wanted something
which the transfer of Dutch territories to English hands
would or might have given him.

How deep the design was which now enlisted them in
its toils they could not well have known; for it was as yet
probably no more than a suggestion, susceptible of a
variety of interpretations and a still larger number of
possible courses of action. But, as events were soon to
demonstrate, Scott was at the beginning of a policy,
which he seems to have done much to suggest, of the
utmost importance not only to his adopted home in
America but to England and the British Empire generally. This even more than his other activities gives him
a certain historical importance.

Meanwhile he had not neglected his interests in
America. In these same busy days he had several letters
from one Captain John Leverett, then titular "governor
of Boston," in regard to the Scott claims — one dare not
say estates — on Long Island. From these it would appear that Leverett, who seems to have been induced to
act as Scott's agent, had been to Long Island to see
about the payment of bills drawn by Scott upon his old
neighbors, or the occupiers of the lands he professed to
own in that region. Leverett's visit was unfruitful, for
he writes that these stubborn people had not only taken
time to consider whether they should pay, but that they
had sent a certain Captain Young, as their representative, to Boston, to ask for the original writing by which
Scott was entitled to payment — Leverett having only a
copy. Upon the latter's failure to produce the original

patent, Young departed; and, Leverett wrote, the con-
tumacious party which sent him showed "very unbecoming jealousyes about your actings respecting the writing,
and also some affirmations about the deed of purchase
you have for the tract of land." There was, it appeared
from Captain Young, "no expectation of payment to be
had" from them. Moreover, Captain Scott's lady had
requisitioned from the confiding Leverett divers things
which he had supplied, including some thousands of feet
of lumber, for which he desired payment to one Francis
Smith, then on the way to England, together with various sums advanced by Leverett on Scott's account to
several persons whom he enumerates. It is possible that
the Bostonian might even have added his prayers to those
of Scott's neighbor, Giles Sylvester of Shelter Island,
who, having lent him money, found out too late of his
rascalities and wrote home that "if the gallows hath him
not he will rot whilse he liveth." More than a year later,
so deeply was Sylvester moved, when he heard Scott had
fallen foul of the Connecticut authorities, that he wrote
Governor Winthrop how Scott had not only got goods
of him in England, but persuaded Gotherson to go bond
for his obligations, £104 — and Gotherson was now
bankrupt and in King's Bench!

One would like to think that Leverett got his money
back. Perhaps he did, though it seems at this distance
somewhat improbable. But if he did not, it was certainly
not because Scott was in want of funds. By the time
Leverett's letter advising him of the approach of Smith
had been despatched, he had received the decision of the
Plantations Committee on his petition for the governorship of Long Island. Despite his moving account of his
father's sufferings and his own, his request was politely
but firmly denied for a variety of reasons, some of which,
at least, appeared in the sequel. And upon this, having
exhausted his not inconsiderable ingenuity for the time,

he set sail for America in the fall of 1663. He did not go empty-handed; for though he had been disappointed in his dearest hopes of land grants and office, he had substantial consolation. He carried with him certainly some part of Gotherson's £2,000, and, incidentally, Gotherson's man, Matthew Prior, to manage the Long Island estates. He was accompanied by Gotherson's son, whom, with some other youths, he had induced to accompany him to America, by hope of preferment there; and these, on his arrival, he promptly sold into service for sums which probably recompensed him for the expense of the voyage He would seem, moreover, to have taken the precaution before his departure to secure Mrs. Gotherson's jewels to the value of some £200, which also accompanied him to America. Besides this, he had been commissioned, apparently, to bring over the Privy Council's instructions regarding the Navigation Act and was thus enabled to return in a quasi-official capacity. So, taking all these items into consideration, with all his disappointments, he had concluded a not unprofitable venture. And with it there ended another stage of his active career.

III

IT IS apparent in the mere statement of the case that his second appearance on Long Island was of a very different character from his first. He was now more experienced in the ways of the great world. He was a man of substance if not of much real property; he had been at court and talked with the king; he had even been received into royal favor. He had money to spend; and it was not his fault that he did not bear his Majesty's commission beside. No one as yet knew, in fact, that he did not. With that thought a new and brilliant idea took form in his fertile brain and presently produced consequences of no small importance to him and to others.

Why should they know? Why should they not remain in that agreeable state of ignorance?

He was, in a sense, a representative of the English government; he had done something at least to direct their minds to a new policy; it may well be that he had received a hint of what that policy might be, and of possible rewards which might accrue to him were it successful and his actions agreeable to its promoters. All this was soon reflected in his activities. Before Christmas, 1663, Colonel Scott, for so he now aspired to be called, was reported as buying lands of the Indians. He did actually begin to buy property, thirty acres of "lands and meddowe both at home and in the old fields and the little neck about the town of Ashford," with its houses, "smith's tools and Indian harness" from Robert Blumer or Bloomer. He sat as a magistrate in the Ashford court which fined one man for cursing and two for "liing." He divided with one Richard Smith a tract of land which he professed — falsely it would appear — to have bought from Lyon Gardiner.

He was appealed to by intending purchasers of land from the Indians near the Raritan River to advise them from his "expert knowledge in all affairs of this kind." He seems to have exercised himself in requiring the enforcement of the Navigation Act against English goods being carried in Dutch ships. He got himself appointed, apparently on the strength of this, one of three commissioners empowered by Connecticut to settle the differences with the Dutch of Long Island; and he wrote to his friend Williamson, prematurely, that the English on the west end of Long Island, long enslaved by the Dutch, had rebelled, with the assistance of Connecticut, and desired that Williamson prevent any trouble with the Dutch ambassador until New England could be heard.

By the fourth of January, 1664, on the strength of

his assertion that the King had granted Long Island to the Duke of York, Flushing, Hastings, Oyster Bay, and other towns had formed a confederation. He had had himself made "president" of the English towns of Long Island and "gave oaths" to men who swore they would execute laws irrespective of Connecticut. He called on the men of these towns to "declare whether they were a free people"; asserted that the island had been granted to the Duke of York; proclaimed Charles II; persuaded them to elect him president. This they did, chose deputies to meet and treat with him, and agreed to accompany him "with horse and foot" against the Dutch. Shortly thereafter, followed by one hundred and seventy men, he invaded Breuckelen and the neighboring towns "with sounding trumpet, beaten drum, flying colors, great noise and uproar," declaring England owned the land and that he himself would run Governor Stuyvesant through. To demonstrate his valor he even struck a little Dutch boy who refused to take off his hat to the English flag, harangued the people at Midwout "like a quacksalver," but failed to shake their allegiance, and so proceeded to Amersfoort and New Utrecht, where his men seized the blockhouse and fired a royal salute.

He was now at the climax of his American reputation. New Haven instructed a committee to treat with him about a patent for Delaware; Connecticut made him a magistrate on Long Island. In this capacity he met the Dutch commissioners, and exhibited to them a patent from Charles II granting to him the whole of Long Island — which only lacked that monarch's signature to make it valid! The Dutch bent to the storm. They made an arrangement with him, as "President of the English on Long Island," that the English at "Gravesend, Hasting, Foketone, Caffard, Newark and Hemstead" should remain according to the new settlement under the King of England without interference from New Amsterdam.

They extracted from him an agreement that he would leave their towns unmolested for a month, though Scott declared that he would return in the spring with the Duke of York and secure not only Long Island but all New Netherland for the English crown. In the face of this declaration, however, the Dutch authorities induced him, some six weeks later, to extend immunity for a year — and meanwhile they prepared for war.

Never was a demonstration better timed. But whether Scott was actually an agent of Charles II's government, or whether he merely guessed at the design then being formulated from the gossip he had heard about the court, and thought to anticipate it to his own advantage, it is possible he might not have lent himself so readily to this course of action had he known just what was in the minds of the English court. For, consciously or unconsciously, he played a part in that unscrupulous design of the party about the Duke of York to seize New Amsterdam, to which the King, as usual, lent himself. The accusations against the Dutch drawn up by Scott, Maverick, and Baxter served as its foundation. But there were other stones in the edifice. For a variety of reasons the court had decided on war with Holland; but it was impossible for the court of Charles II to follow a straight and honorable course. The war was desired partly for reasons of state, but more largely for reasons of profit to the court. A sum was subscribed among the war party, two expeditions were projected, and for them the King's authority to provide a fleet was secured. Sir Robert Holmes was despatched to attack the Dutch posts in Africa; another expedition under the command of Colonel Richard Nicolls was prepared to act against New Netherland. That province was, as Scott had prophesied, granted by Charles to his brother, the Duke of York ; and in May, 1664, Nicolls sailed to secure the territory already disposed of. Thus, in the very days that

Scott engineered his demonstration against the Dutch —
perhaps with the connivance of his English associates —
and so made a pretext for hostilities, the stake for which
he played was given to another. And, had Scott no other
claim to the attention of history, the fact that he was one
of the prime movers in that disreputable design which
brought New Netherland into English hands, would entitle him to a place, however dishonorable, in its pages.

Meanwhile, what of his career after his warlike efforts
against New Netherland while this project was being
set on foot? The record of the General Assembly of Connecticut, held at Hartford in March, 1664, while Scott
was resting from his patriotic exertions and Nicolls was
preparing his expedition, tells the story clearly and effectively. Under the presidency of John Winthrop, the
court ordered that the letter, with "the warrant and instructions to the marshal, that have been read in this
court," be attended to. That warrant is an illuminating
document. It is to the effect that "John Scott, inhabitant
in the liberties of Ashford, alias Setawkit, on Long
Island, stands charged in the court at Connecticut for
sundry heinous crimes, to wit, for speaking words tending to the defamation of the King, for seditious practices
and tumultuous carriages in several plantations, for
abetting and encouraging the natives in hostile practices
towards each other; for usurping the authority of the
King in tending to pardon treason; for threatening His
Majesty's subjects with hanging and banishment; for
gross and notorious prophanation of God's holy day;
for forgery and violation of his solemn oath; for acting
treacherously towards Connecticut colony; for usurping
authority on pretence of a commission; for calumniating
a commission officer in this corporation; together with a
general charge of villainous and felonious practices."

Even from the briefest summary of this dry and formal legal document it will appear to the most casual

reader that Scott had somehow not commended himself
to the authorities of Connecticut. The officials of New
Haven, Milford, Branford, Stratford, the coast towns,
and presently those of the islands adjacent, were ordered
to deliver him to the marshal, Jonathan Gilbert, to be
taken to Hartford for trial. His property was seques-
tered and commissioners ordered to invoice it and keep
it from embezzlement; and Scott himself was presently
arrested and carried to Hartford.

The report of the committee appointed to seize him
is not without interest. (1) "When we came in sight of
the house of John Scott," it relates, "we saw him draw
forth those men which came from New Haven to aid
him, with some others into a body." When they came
nearer, he ordered the committee to stand on its peril.
(2) He ordered them off his land. (3) He asked their
business, and Nathaniel Seeley asked a parley, which
was agreed to. (4) Scott demanded Seeley's commission,
which Seeley read and demanded Scott's surrender.
(5) Scott said he would "sacrifice his heart's blood on the
ground" before he would yield to Connecticut jurisdiction. The New Haven men said, "So will we." (6) Scott
brought a letter from Winthrop and read it, saying "if
you will return to your body I will bring a letter under
His Majesty's seal." He dared them "with a flourish" to
lay hands on him, saying, "let them take me if they dare,
let the proudest of them try to take me if they dare."
(7) Then Nathaniel Seeley arrested him in his Majesty's name and demanded that he release the four officials he had arrested. Such is the laconic ending of the
epic of the encounter between John Scott and Nathaniel
Seeley as reported by the committee from Hartford in
their carefully itemized statement.

All this seems a curious return for his military services
in behalf of the English government; and, on its face, a
great injustice. Yet the explanation is comparatively

simple. It lies in the peculiar situation of colonial affairs in this transition period. On his return from England, bearing the Council's instructions in regard to the Navigation Acts, he had been received with favor, especially by the New Haven authorities, and he had, it may be remembered, been appointed a magistrate on Long Island by the Connecticut officials of Hartford. It was the earnest desire of the latter to bring Long Island under their jurisdiction, now that its eastern part had been liberated from the Dutch by the Treaty of Hartford. But on that proposition the Long Islanders were divided. The Baptists, Quakers, and Mennonites who had found refuge there from New England persecution dreaded Puritan government; even many who favored annexation to relieve them from the fear of the Dutch declared they had received little but "if so-be's and doubtings" from Connecticut. In this situation they had welcomed, if they had not invited, Scott to help them; with what result we have seen. But the opportunity had appeared to him too good to be lost; and he had promptly taken advantage of his momentary ascendancy to attempt to free Long Island from the dominance of Connecticut and make it a more or less independent province under his own presidency. It was not very surprising that its inhabitants were inclined to follow the lead thus given, for independence was a very dear thing to them; but it is equally natural that the Connecticut authorities were infuriated by his ambitions.

Yet — possibly in view of their connection with the Atherton Company — Winthrop and his associates considered the question of sufficient importance to summon a council of the four New England colonies, among other reasons because they feared, from Scott's assertions, that he was possessed of some secret authority from the English Crown for his actions, which might make proceedings against him inadvisable if not positively dangerous.

Accordingly they wrote to the officials of the other colonies, especially to Major-General Leverett of Boston, Scott's old correspondent, inviting them to a conference, Scott's trial meanwhile being set for May 8. The invitation was promptly accepted. Massachusetts sent down Leverett and Captain Davis; Plymouth sent William Bradford and Thomas Southworth, and these, with other representatives, held deep speech on the case.

Scott was not without friends. A hundred and forty-four inhabitants of Flushing petitioned for his release. A letter from Newark in his favor was signed by thirty-eight men — all the signatures being, apparently, in the same hand. His wife, Deborah, wrote from New Haven. The New Haven delegates favored him; and the Plymouth delegates inclined to his cause, though the Massachusetts General Council authorized its representatives to tell the Governor of "Kenectecut" of the "severe proceedings" they had taken against Scott and offer their aid in keeping the peace. But Winthrop and his followers were firm. Scott was not released, his trial was duly held, he was convicted, and sentenced to pay a fine of £250, to be imprisoned at the pleasure of the court, and to give bond in the sum of £500 for his future good behavior. At first Scott blustered and threatened his accusers with charges of treason, relying, apparently, on his connection with Chiffinch and Williamson and whatever understandings he may have had with those who promoted the seizure of New York; but he ended by humble submission, repentance, and the retraction of the charges he had made against one person in Connecticut, probably the governor. Winthrop was not slow in following up his advantage. First the secretary and then the governor himself visited Long Island; conferred with the delegates of the English towns there; placed them under the authority of Connecticut; took steps to acquire the land between Westchester and the Hudson; met Stuyvesant, who urged the Dutch title, which Winthrop incontinently rejected, claiming all for England; replaced all the officials appointed by Scott with his own nominees; and so returned triumphantly to Hartford, in whose archives are still preserved those numerous documents which commemorate the activities of this adventurer.

Scott's cause was now wholly lost; and before Winthrop had returned he broke jail and escaped, taking refuge with his friends on Long Island. Winthrop and his Hartford party had won. But their triumph was of few days and full of trouble. On the twenty-sixth of August the first vessel of Nicolls' squadron anchored in Gravesend Bay. It was soon joined by others, bearing the levies from the New England colonies, as well as English troops. The Connecticut contingent appeared under the command of Winthrop. The Long Islanders gathered in force, conspicuous among them Colonel John Scott at the head of his company. Winthrop with his followers brought from Nicolls a demand for surrender; and on September 8, hopeless of defending the town in the face of threatened bombardment, Stuyvesant ratified the articles of surrender, which had been drawn up by commissioners appointed from each side, and New Amsterdam passed under the authority of the English Crown. For Connecticut it was a barren victory. Four days earlier, Nicolls had made public the Duke of York's patent, and Winthrop had resigned, on behalf of Connecticut, her claim to Long Island; and with that the disputed province came finally under the authority neither of Scott nor Winthrop, who had striven for it so strenuously, but of the Duke of York, who never saw it.

To this historic event there are two corollaries relating to Scott. The first is a pass from Nicolls three days after the surrender, empowering him to return to his house at Ashford, without hindrance from the Connecticut authorities; and this, at least, he gained by his share in the surrender. The second is a bill from his jailer in Hartford for "12 weeks' dyat and other expenses," Mr. John Scott, as the petition relates, having escaped. There is a certain grim humor in the court's reply. It grants to the said Dan'l Garrad (Garret) the sum of £10 out of Mr. John Scott's estate, "if he can come at it." That, as one might surmise, did not prove possible, and two years later it was added to the general levy on the county and so, presumably, ultimately paid by those in whose behalf as well as his own the Colonel had contended so valiantly.

The controversy thus determined on the principle of entire injustice to all parties concerned, Scott appears to have taken up his old life and practices, little altered by the passage of years and the changed circumstances in which he found himself. Again, as a decade earlier, he is reported as buying and selling land, and again his name appears in records of lawsuits on Long Island. One man he sues for £100 for slander, the fault is acknowledged, and Scott "forgives" him. Another he sues for trespass, and with another he divides land bought from a third. He appears in New Amsterdam to testify before the "Schout and Schepens" of the Court regarding the articles stolen from him by his employee, Thomas Fais, or Fahey; persuades Thomas to plead guilty, pays the costs of the suit, and gives his unfaithful servant another job. The "Sunk squa Quashawam" desires and empowers her "ancient and great friend John Scott" to sue for all lands bought and paid for on Long Island by the English and the Dutch, to receive satisfaction for them, and to sell all lands not already sold. There is a dispute over the Quaquantanock lands, in the course of which Scott was appointed to go to Hartford to clear up the town's title with respect to the Earl of Stirling's claims, and he seems to have been there in December, 1663, desiring to have his agreements and contracts made with people at Ashford entered on the records. Besides these items we may note that Southold and Southampton unite to sue Scott for costs and damage incurred in connection with land titles.

Moreover he is accused of fomenting disturbances according to his wonted course among the people of Setauket. Against him the Governor and Council of Connecticut protest to Nicolls that Setauket men say their plantation will be destroyed if the claims of ownership advanced by him on the ground of purchase from the Indians are allowed; and, still further, if the principle of engrossing land from the Indians for private uses is permitted, it will ruin the whole township. Therefore they pray for an order that no land be bought from the Indians without consent of the General Court. And from this two things appear which throw a light upon the times and the position of Scott. He thought he was merely endeavoring to secure his share of this world's goods; and perhaps no one would have been more surprised to learn that he was rather a type than an individual, the representative of a principle rather than a mere adventurer in land.

For, in the first place, Scott did not belong to that inner circle, which, in the language of the time, were "those who managed." The underlying spirit of his age was monopoly. Men formed corporations and associations and secured their position by royal patent, which attempted to prevent all competition within their chosen field, whether Indian trade or American lands. Perhaps in each case there was reason in this, but it unquestionably aroused bitter opposition among the outsiders. The records of the East India Company are full of complaints against those "interlopers," as they were called, who ventured to infringe the monopoly of the licensed company. The annals of the colonies are no less full of complaints against those who, like Scott, acted on the principle of a fair field and no favors, of individual enterprise as against chartered privilege. It was his misfortune, throughout his whole career, to find himself in opposition to those on whom the Crown — perhaps, in their view, Providence itself — had conferred that monopoly against whose restrictions his best efforts beat in vain.

Had he been a different sort of man, it would be impossible not to feel a considerable sympathy with him in his endeavors to break through that charmed circle and establish his own fortunes by virtue of his undoubted abilities. But the trouble is in his case, as in so many others of like sort, that his character deprives us of that sympathy which we might otherwise feel. The martyr is so often inferior to the oppressor in the qualities which make him endurable to society in general; and it is his misfortune, if it is not his fault, that he destroys by his own actions that hope of common support on which rests whatever hope of success he may possess. It is not possible to feel the same admiration for the Massachusetts authorities, or even for Winthrop, which historians like Bancroft voice in such fulsome words. Yet, however we may sympathize with the principle for which Scott stood, it is difficult to condone the private character of the man, even though it was, perhaps, no worse than that of some of the more eminently placed rascals who managed to cheat him out of his inheritance and cast him aside as a broken tool.

Still more, it seems probable that the colonial authorities, with all their shrewdness — to give it the mildest name — in defending their monopoly were, on the whole, right. The Indians with whom the colonists dealt had no notion of property or titles; they sold the same land over and over again, as often as they found a new purchaser. The ensuing complication where this took place may be read in every page of colonial history; and had free competition been allowed it would have made an end of all

security, and perhaps in many instances of the settlements themselves. To unscrupulous operators in land
titles this situation has offered at all times an opportunity
of which they have never been slow to avail themselves.
Of these, as well as of the class opposed to monopoly,
Scott seems to have been an eminent representative.

How he managed it is apparent from another order
of the court, this time in New York. In February, 1665,
he was ordered to bring in, at the General Court of the
Assizes following, a certain deed or writing "called by
the said Captain Scott a Perpetuity, with the King's
picture on it and a great yellow wax seal affix't to it
which he very frequently showed to divers persons, and
deceived many therewith" by what another correspondent calls his "cnaveri." That "Perpetuity" was, apparently, a royal grant of twenty miles square in the heart
of Long Island, the township of Brookhaven most probably. At the same time that the authorities of New York
took this step, their colleagues in Connecticut were de-
liberating whether Scott's fine would reimburse the
colony for the damage he had done, and were considering what further measures should be taken in the matter.

In addition to their other grievances, it appears from
their statement of the case against him that he had dis-
pensed justice in his own house and told disgruntled
litigants they could appeal to Connecticut if they did not
like the judgments of their own courts; that Hartford
had no right to levy on Southampton, but ought rather
to pay back the taxes already collected, as Long Island
was not in Connecticut jurisdiction; and more to the
same purpose. In addition, he was charged with having
stolen the instructions to Massachusetts and Mr. Maverick's petition from Lord Arlington's office. These actions
evidently gave the Colonel matter for serious reflection,
and when October came, with an order from the New
York governor for him to appear before the General

Court of Assizes and produce the letters patent which
he claimed to possess; to show his authority for the Long
Island lands then in dispute; and, finally, to account for
his other offenses; together with a warrant for his arrest, it seemed that the time for his departure had arrived.
In point of fact, he had already gone. He gave the sheriff
the slip, took ship for Barbados, and palmed himself off
on Colonel Morris — notable for his later removal to
New York, where he settled in that district known as
Morrisania — as a Quaker escaping from persecution in
the New England colonies. He was received, apparently,
with open arms, and so, like a skilful commander, made
good his retreat to a new position. Thus ended his career
in America, where, as elsewhere, he was described as "a
bird of prey and passage."

IV

BUT before he went he made his mark on history, and
incidentally avenged himself on the courtiers whom he
considered to have cheated him out of his rightful inheritance, especially the Duke of York. Though his plan
could not possibly have brought him any reward, and
thus bears little relation to his career as he or we conceive it, it is noteworthy not only for its ingenuity and
efficacy but for the extraordinary results it produced on
the geography, and even on the history, of the United
States. For it seems that to him more than to any other
man is due the peculiar and unfortunate circumstance
that New York does not control both shores of the harbor
on which it lies. The circumstance finds its first expression in the Duke's division of the lands granted him by the
King, his brother. In June, 1664, before that grant was
confirmed, and while Nicolls' expedition was on its way
to America, the Duke of York conveyed to his followers,
Sir John Berkeley and Sir George Carteret, members

COLONEL JOHN SCOTT   297

of the Committee on Plantations, by whose advice New
Netherland was seized, a territory bounded on the north
by a line running northwest from the Hudson River at
about the location of Yonkers, and on the west and south
by the Delaware River; in short, the district known as
New Cæsarea or New Jersey. The new proprietors
promptly drew up a constitution modeled on that of
Carolina, and sent out a governor, Philip Carteret, a
relative of Sir George, who arrived in the fall of that
year.

Such was the news which greeted Nicolls at the moment he found himself in possession of New Netherland
as governor of the new province. As a faithful servant
of the Duke, he was furious; and, apparently in November of that year, he wrote a scathing letter to his master.
He had, he said, seen the grant which the Duke had made
to Berkeley and Carteret for all lands west of the Hudson River; and he cannot suppose that either the grantor
or the grantees could possibly have known how prejudi-
cial it was to the Duke's interest or that of New York.
He must, he went on, "charge it upon Captain Scott,
who was born to work mischief as far as he is credited
or his parts serve him. This Scott (it seems) aimed at
the same patent which your Royal Highness hath, and
hath since given words out that he had injury done him
by your Royal Highness, whereupon he contrived and
betrayed my Lord Berkeley and Sir G. Carteret into a
design (contrary to their knowledge) of ruining all the
hopes of increase in this your Royal Highness his territory, which he hath fully completed unless your Royal
Highness take farther steps herein."

This was the last account against Scott in the North
American colonies. One of a little previous date may be
added to make the story complete. A month before
Nicolls wrote thus to James, he had written to Morrice,
then Secretary of State, that Mr. Maverick's petition

was "stolen from Lord Arlington's office by Captain
Scott and delivered to the governor and council of Boston — tho' Scott said Williamson had given it to him."
This same Scott, he went on to say, "by a pretended seal
affixed to a writing in which the King's picture drawn
with pen and ink or black lead with His Majesty's
hand C. R. and subsigned Henry Bennet" (probably
the "Perpetuity" of which we have heard before) had
abused his Majesty's honor in these parts and had fled to
Barbados. But Lord Willoughby, then governor of that
island, had sent word he would arrest Scott and send
him prisoner to England.

This would certainly have seemed enough to settle the
case of Scott. Pursued by three colonial governors,
driven from his home by enough counts to keep him in
prison the greater part of his life, and subject to enough
fines to ruin what estate he had left, the fugitive would
seem to have had small chance for any further activities
in the British Empire at least. Moreover, the Gotherson
matter had come up to plague him again. For, before he
fled to Barbados, Dorothea Gotherson had petitioned the
King for an order to Francis Lovelace, deputy-governor
of Long Island, to consider whether she had any claim
to land bought there for her son; alleging that her
husband had paid Scott £2,000 and thereby died in
debt, his lands had been taken, and though she had
brought him an estate of £500 a year she was obliged to
work for bread for herself and her six children. Scott
had gone before this matter could be attended to, but it
remained, as it proved, to vex and finally to wreck his
fortunes in another land. Meanwhile, Governor Nicolls
issued a special warrant to the high sheriff to seize all
lands, goods, or chattels "which Captain Scott hath any
right or pretense to within this government." The goods
he bought of Bloomer were returned by the court. He
was "Cawled according to law, and not appearinge he

was nonscheiuted" in an action for debt and trespass. His suit for £1,000 against one Arthur Smith brought him a judgment of £50. "Mrs. Scott being about to remove," in 1664 a committee was appointed to invoice and store his goods. In February, 1666, it is briefly recorded that "John Scott sold to Zakery Hawkins all his lands." And as late as 1670 there appeared Colonel Lewis Morris in Hempstead to lay claim to the land he had bought of Scott. So ended Scott's connection with Long Island real estate.

But this was not the end of him, even in the colonies. Mrs. Gotherson was a persistent as well as a greatly wronged woman. A year or two later it appears that she agreed with one Thomas Lovelace, kinsman of the deputy, that if he could make any money by the sale of her land which her husband had mortgaged, she would bring a hundred and twenty families into Long Island "to ye g't advantage of ye place." Accordingly, when Governor Lovelace went to New York to succeed Nicolls in 1668, he appointed a commission, of which Thomas was a member, with "Captain Morris of Barbados," to enquire. But they could find nothing. The houses which Scott had built or bought had been taken down and moved to Setauket, and given to Mrs. Scott by Governor Nicolls for her support after her husband had deserted her. It is not without interest, perhaps even significance, to observe that from the Oyster Bay town records it appears that two "Town Shipps" which Major Gotherson had bought from John Richbell had been seized for a debt of Gotherson to Matthew Pryor and were granted to Pryor by Lovelace in settlement of that debt. But there seems to be no record of the sixteen hundred acres sold by Scott to Gotherson, much less of the twenty thousand which Gotherson was to purchase for Scott.

One thing, however, the commission did find — Gotherson's son, who had been sold into service by Scott to an innkeeper in New Haven. That individual was willing to release him from his duties as stable-boy for the sum of £7; and with that, presumably, Mrs. Gotherson had to content herself for the time. And with that, too, as the learned gentleman who wrote an account of Scott's life many years ago for the Massachusetts Historical Society declares, Scott disappears from history. Not quite — for Scott had found the refuge which he sought in the West Indies. There Lord Willoughby, it appears, intended, in pursuance of Nicolls' request, to catch him and send him prisoner to England. But again Scott seems to have exercised his undoubted charm, drawn upon his credit with Williamson, and emerged presently reinstated, and, in so far as possible, rehabilitated; for by the middle of the year 1665 we find him with a commission in Sir Tobias Bridge's regiment stationed there.

It was a fertile field for his talents, for there was much doing in that quarter of the world which might well serve as an opportunity to reinstate himself. England was then at war with Holland and France; and Barbados, where Bridge's regiment was stationed, was a storm-center of affairs. Scott landed there in April. In June he, with Colonel Stapleton, commanded the reserve in an attack upon the French stronghold of St. Kitts, concerning which he wrote a full account, in accordance with Willoughby's letter to Williamson that the latter's friend Scott "had escaped" and would inform him of the fight. Scott was not content with describing his own prowess. He took occasion to condemn his brothers in arms, and contrasted their conduct with his own, — he, according to this account, having been wounded in the arm, breast, and shoulder, and inflicted a loss of twenty wounded in the crews of the four boats that tried to take him. Accordingly we find him a little later petitioning for rewards. That petition is illuminating. It recites that in 1665 and 1666 he was in command of a small fleet and a regiment of foot on an expedition against the Dutch of Tobago and at New Zealand, Dissekeeb or "Deess Cuba" and "Timberan" in Guiana. At the latter place, by the help of the Caribbees, he burnt and destroyed towns, forts, goods, etc., worth £160,000, and spent for his Majesty's service 73,788 pounds of sugar. He therefore asks a reward, which, on the basis of this and another petition in which he values his expenditures at £1,620, and includes the loss of a ketch valued at £500, he requests that £738 at 4½ per cent be charged on the Barbados excise.

Besides these we have another and even more detailed account from his pen of the war, and especially of the part he took in it. According to that veracious chronicle, he declares that in the month of October, 1665, he "having been commissionated Commander-in-chief of a small fleet and a regiment of soldiers, for the attack of the Island Tobago, and several other settlements in the hands of the Netherlanders in Guiama, as Moroco, Wacopow, Bowroome and Dissekeeb, and having touched at Tobago, in less than six months had the good fortune to be in possession of those countries, and left them garrisoned for his majesty of Great Britain, and sailed thence for Barbados, where meeting with the news of the eruption of war between the two crowns of England and France, endeavoured to persuade Francis Lord Willoughby to reduce those several small garrisons into one stronghold, and offered that was the way to make good our post in those parts, having to do with two potent enemies, but his Lordship, that was his majesty's captain-general in those parts, was of another opinion, and embarked on the unfortunate voyage for the reducing of St. Christopher, etc.," in which design he perished by a hurricane.

Besides these, still, we have another and what appears to be a wholly independent narrative of the same events,

under the signature of a certain Major Byam, who adds
this eulogy at the beginning of his story: "In November 1665 there arrived from his Exc^{llce} [Lord Willoughby]
his Serj^t Maj^r Jn° Scott after his victory at Tobago wth a
smal Fleet and a regiment of Foote under the Carrecter
of Major-General of Guiana, Chiefe Commissioner and
Commander-in-Chiefe by Land and Sea in a few months
his great Fortune and gallantry prudent and Industrious
Conduct made him master of all the great province new
Zealand & Desseceub settled a peace with the Arro-
wayes left both Collonys in a Flourishing Condition and
well garrison'd for the King of England," etc.

Nothing could be clearer than such a story, supported
by the testimony of two witnesses, one of whom was the
hero in question. All the story is partly true. Perhaps it
is all true; and perhaps we should not lay too much
stress on the fact that the second, though written ostensibly by Major Byam, is only known to us through what
purports to be a copy — and this copy is in Scott's own
hand! Probably no one who studies the peculiar form
of this manuscript can help feeling that there is something about it which seems to indicate that it is now not
precisely what it was when it left the hands of its reputed
author, the worthy Byam. Taken in connection with
the fact that it forms, so to speak, part of a trilogy,
"Byam's Journall," "Scott's History and Description
of the River of Amazones," and "Colonell Scott's Preface to an Intended History of America," it seems to
give a clue, among other things, to his literary method.
The story, such as it is, has been accepted by historical
scholars of the highest consequence; and in view of this
circumstance, two other pieces of evicence in the case
are not without interest. The first is a communication
from Sir Thomas Bridge which relates that "Major
Scott sent to the governor of St. Kitts with a letter and
money for the English officers there and to get an under-

standing of the French strength returned with little satisfaction and many complaints. The English officers complained of his imprudent carriage in the message and ill deportment in the engagement."

The second is the record of a court-martial held at Nevis by Lord Willoughby's command on January 4, 1667, before Sir Thomas Bridge, Lieutenant-Colonel Stapleton, Major Androsse, and seventeen others, on a charge against "Capt. John Scott, late colonel of Sir Tobias Bridge's regiment of foot." Its findings begin with the observation that "the said Scott is generally knowne to bee a notorious coward, and whenever hee has been employ'd in His Majesty's service has brought great dishonour upon our King and Country." From that premise it goes on to the specific charges that in the attempt on the mainland fort of Moroco "he absented himself at the instant time of stormeing the said Fort"; that when the fort was taken and the men were on the way back to the ships, he acted very badly in the face of the enemy; that when the expedition came to Barohmah Fort as soon as it was within gunshot he "sculked away alone in a Boat," until the place offered to surrender. Thirdly, that at St. Christopher's, where he commanded a foot company, he "left his men and sculked under a rock," ran away and stripped himself and swam out to the ship, pretending he was wounded. Fourthly, to vindicate himself to the Lieutenant-General, he aspersed several officers, especially Captain John Cotter. And, finally, that for his dishonorable actions in the mainland and at St. Christopher's, he had been frequently "basted and cudgelled by soldiers under his command at Barbados." All this and more was sworn to and corroborated by various witnesses cited before the court, some twelve in number, and by the examination of several officers who were not present at the sitting, and on these grounds Scott was unanimously found guilty. Moreover, Captain

Cotter was given leave to go to England and was ex-
onerated from all of Scott's charges by Lord William
Willoughby, who had succeeded Francis.

It seems, therefore, at least possible that Scott was
not the hero that he, and his friend Byam, through the
medium of Scott's pen, painted him, during the entire
war, however he may have distinguished himself on occasion. And to this again there is somewhat to be added.
Later in the same year Willoughby sent a letter to Williamson by Scott, declaring that the latter "had done
his duty well since Portsmouth," and later still, in January, 1668, he writes Williamson again that he will come
home and give as good an account of the Indies as Major
Scott, who he hopes has arrived, and if so has probably
told Williamson "some truth but not all gospel." Which
observation reveals in some sort that Willoughby had
not the greatest confidence in his late lieutenant's veracity. And that is confirmed by the governor's pass to
Cotter, which included the somewhat irrelevant remark
that if Scott had come to trial before the court-martial
"his smooth tongue would not have saved him." To
this, again, may be added the testimony of Mr. Jeremy
Wells, writing in later years to Mr. Samuel Pepys, that
he would like "to add a little to the legend of Col Scott's
life," namely, that he was "an errand coward and a great
Rogue."

V

IN any event, Scott left the service and arrived in England sometime in the latter part of 1667. As appears by
a document still preserved among the Colonial State
Papers, he signalized his coming by informing Williamson that the president of Harvard College was a 'Presbyterian Anabaptist,' and that the earlier disturbances in
New England had been due to Sir Henry Vane, the

younger, who had come out to the colony with two mis-
tresses, Mrs. Dyer and Mrs. Hutchinson! Apart from
that entertaining news, his arrival is in a sense characteristic of his extraordinary quality of reaching a particular spot at the moment when circumstances were favorable to his designs. It had been so in 1660; it was to be
so on at least one other occasion; and it was peculiarly
true in the present instance. In June the Dutch, who
were still at war with England, had made their raid into
the Medway and the Thames. Partly owing to that
exploit, England and Holland had made peace in July.
In August Clarendon, who had been made the scapegoat for the miscarriages of the war, had been driven from
place and fled from England. And at almost the precise
moment that Scott arrived in England, big with the news
and the importance of his heroic exploits in the West
Indies, and the less romantic but perhaps more accurate
information that the Dutch and French had been defeated in that part of the world, a new ministry was just
being inducted into office. That ministry, known as the
Cabal, numbered among its members Scott's old patron,
Bennet, now Earl of Arlington, who, with two of his colleagues, Buckingham and Shaftesbury, played so great a
part in the determination of Scott's fortunes thenceforth.
Here, as in his earlier advent at the court of Charles II,
was a situation made to his hand, and he was not slow
to take advantage of it.

His first experience was, however, unfortunate; for
the year 1668 had hardly dawned when he was arrested
for debt and taken to the Gatehouse prison. He promptly
appealed to Arlington for relief, and reiterated — with
some small additions — his recent eminent services to
the government. In this petition he raises the sum he
spent in behalf of his native land to £3,000; asserts
that he had resettled Antigua and Montserrat, made
peace with the Indians before he had been thirty hours

in Barbados, and had sailed to England on Lord Willoughby's motion, to give the King an account of affairs in the West Indies. Moreover, he had saved the King's ships from a hurricane. He had served a gracious prince, he concludes, yet for £30/10, not yet due, he is in jail without influence on his Majesty for release and must go from jail to jail.

It is a pathetic plea, and Arlington was apparently touched by it, for, through some influence, Scott's petition for £100 was allowed, and apparently by July or August he actually got the money — and how great a feat that was at this precise period of English finance can only be appreciated by a somewhat intimate acquaintance with the circumstances of English administration of the time. He got, indeed, much more; for by the end of August a royal warrant, countersigned by Arlington, conferred upon him a government appointment, the post of royal geographer! For he had approved himself, as Buckingham observed in later years, "a very useful rogue."

And with this we come to another remarkable passage in a remarkable life. For a dozen years or more Scott had played some little part in public affairs. Now, moved by the situation in which he found himself, and mindful of his unusual gifts and experiences, he aspired not to make but to write history. As soon as he was settled in his new post — probably even before — he had begun an attempt to justify his appointment by the execution of a great work on the "Coasts and Islands of America." This included, among other things, a "Discription of Guiana," which was one day to give him standing in the world where even he could scarcely have imagined it.

What, we may well ask, were the qualifications of such a man to undertake this most difficult form of literary composition; what was his training, his purpose, and his hope of success in that field? That question was to be asked again on at least one occasion of great importance;

and as he has given the answer in his own words it is proper that they should be inserted here. For his methods as he described them were so precisely those of Herodotus, the father of history — or, according to his enemies, the father of lies — that they may well be quoted in their entirety.

"In my youth," Scott begins his narrative, "I was a great lover of Geographie and History in Generall, but aboute the Eighteenth yeare of my age I tooke up a resolution to make America the scene of the greatest actions of my life, and there to sett myselfe a worke (if possible) to finde out the Latitudes, the Longitudes, and to know the oridginall discovery with the situations of all places both on the Continent and in the Islands; as also the names of Persons and of what Nations they were who have possessed them, and what fortune each Nation hath had, and (as neare as I could) the fortune of the severall governors successively, and of the respective Collonies, the most remarkable distempers and diseases, the Commodityes abounding and advantages of trade, what places were more or less Tenable of Nature, and what were made strong by fortifications, in what manner, and to what degree; Moreover how these colonies have prospered or declined in Trade, increased or decreased in number of Inhabitants from Europe, and the proper causes thereof; Together with the strength of the severall Indian Nations, their customes, Governments, and Commodities, and what advantages may be made of them in point of Warr or by Trade. I labour'd likewise to discover the Rocks, Sandes Shelves, and Soundings about every Island, and in the Entrance of all Ports, Havens, Rivers, and Creeks, as well on the Terra firma as the Islands, my scope at first being only for my owne particular sattisfaction, but now I am not out of hope these things may be both of some reputacion to myselfe, and a generall advantage to the English Nation, by which especially I shall have my

end and reckon these eighteene yeares past, by running
through all manner of dangers (at seve'll times) to make
Collections and Observations, have been spent to good
purpose for my Country, and thereby put mee in possession of the greatest fellicity that can befall a man in this
life."

"I had once a purpose," he continues, "to have given
you a large discription of all America," but, considering
the Spanish Indies had been fully treated, he decided to
confine his book to "new accounts from observations of
my owne (or such living Testimonies as I could credit)
Touching those places which have not been sufficiently
sett forth by any man before me; Purposely omitting that
part of the Spanish Indies that I have noe knowledge of.
. . . I chose rather to content myselfe with what (in great
part) I know, what my owne eyes have see, and much of
what my feet have trodden, and my sences brought
under an exact inquiry, confineing my selfe with the
River amazon on the South . . . from whence in my
Mappes and History I pass Northward to Newfound
Land.

"More than 1200 miles along the shore, surveying all
the Islands worth notice, comprehended within that vast
part of the Atlantick Ocean one hundred and six of which
Islands I have been Personally upon, have Travelled
most parts of New England and Virginia, and a greate
part of Guiana, and other place of the Maine between
the Tropick of Cancer and the aforementioned grand
River, and with Shipps and Barques have sayled into very
many of the Rivers, Bayes, Ports, and Creeks within the
two boundaries of this discription. As for those places
which have not come under my survey, and the Originall
of many of the Colonies, whether English, Spanish,
French or Dutch, whose plantacions are settled beyond
the Memory of any man that I could meet with, in such
cases I took my measures from the best authors, as Herera

Ovida and Acosta among the Spaniards, Thunis a grave Authour among the French, John Delaet among the Dutch and from many other Authours and sev'll curious manuscripts that came to my hand besides the Carts of which I ever labour to gett the best extant and besides actually to converce with good Artists that had been upon the place, and such persons I ever strove to oblidge and draw to me of what so ever Nation they were; I made it my business likewise to purchase or borrow all the historys and Journalls that I could heare of whether Lattin Ittalian Spanish or Portugais French Dutch or in our Language, wherein I may say I have by reason of a generall generous conversation had luck extraordinary, and herein what paines I have taken what cost I have been att is so Notorious, that over and above the knowledge of a great number of Gentlemen which I have been oblidged too for a communication of printed books, Manuscripts, Patents, Commissions, and papers relating to those parts, the many booksellers of England and Holland will doe me Right to testifie my continuall inquisition."

Concerning this simple and modest narrative of the historian-errant, there is perhaps only one observation necessary. It is that, taken in connection with the extremely active life which Scott led during those same years in which he was engaged upon his historical labors, one can only marvel at his extraordinary industry and concentration and his application to such scholarly ideals when his mind must have often been so busy with other matters than the pursuit of ultimate truth.

Perhaps in this connection, if it is not too wearisome, it may be interesting to compare with this, and with the narrative of his life up to this point, the preface which he composed for this great work. Amid the strenuous activities with which his earlier and later years were filled it may be worth a quiet hour to stop, as he did, and contemplate the eternities and immensities.

"Deare Countrymen," he begins: "Forasmuch as man is not borne for himselfe, or to confine his Aimes within the narrow compass of his owne poor pleasures or advantages, but being a creature of celestiall extract ought ever to be looking upwards from whence he came, Proposing to himselfe an imitation of God, that universall goodness after whose image he is made, and after that Glory and greatness in some measure, which is absolutely and infinitely inherent only in him, but displayed throughout the frame of this wonderfull Globe of Heaven and Earth (which glory consists in the Ample manifestation of that goodness by acts of benevolence towards the whole race of mankinde, doing good through all generations, teaching us thereby what we ought to doe for one another) Therefore Pardon mee (Sirs) if I who, knowing the circumstances of my owne Life have reason enough to consider that having been bred much in warrs, & the world might judge those imployments might neither give mee time, nor inclinations for such a worke do yet nevertheless presume to tell you that I would faine be an humble follower of that great Example of publick good, because we are all commanded to follow it and be like him," he has, in brief, begun this book "because it comes attended with all the affections & dutyes which I owe unto our Native Country." As to the subject matter, he continues, "Peradventure the like may not be seene again, if I perish before the Publication; and this is said (I assure you) not in vanity of mind to prize myselfe above others, but rather to magnifie God's goodness to me who hath by carrying me through innumerable labours and hazards, in various imployments, given me such opportunities as have not been afforded to many in times past & will rarely befall any one man hereafter, in that part of the world which I intend to discribe."

This, among its other revelations, shows that Scott's connection with Southwick and the Gothersons was, after all, not wholly without its effect upon at least his literary style. One part of this entertaining preface is unquestionably true, the like of Scott's narrative, even so far as it went, has not been seen again. It is a loss to literature that he was not permitted to complete this great work and that only a part of what he did write has seen the light of print; and when one considers under what auspices his efforts did finally appear, it goes far to justify his assertions and to increase the regret at its incompleteness. But if it is unfortunate that he never completed this work, it is perhaps a still greater loss to posterity that he was able to enjoy his new dignity so short a time. Three days before Scott was commissioned royal geographer, Colonel Richard Nicolls, having been superseded as Governor of New York by Colonel Francis Lovelace, sailed for England, where he arrived in the latter part of the year 1668. Within six months we find, whether in consequence of his arrival or of other circumstances, two pieces of evidence material to the case of Scott. The first is a series of communications from Dorothea Gotherson to Governor Lovelace and his brother Thomas, reciting the fact that she had appealed to the King to right her wrongs, that Charles had taken pity on her, and that steps had been taken through the Council to communicate with Lovelace, with what result we have already seen, in the discovery of her son and the attempt to recover some of the property lost through Scott.

The second is an intimation that on Nicolls' arrival in England he informed the King of Scott's career in America, and that upon this Scott "vanished from Whitehall." That he did vanish appears from another note from Mrs. Gotherson indicating that she had received letters from him, and expressing the hope that he would return from Holland, whither, it appears, he had gone. To this may be added a communication from Scott to Williamson disavowing all connection with a certain

Andrews whom Scott had recommended and who had committed some unnamed villainy, with the result that, joined to these other circumstances, Scott completely lost Williamson's favor and with it his principal claim to recognition and respectability. It is, perhaps, small wonder that this is accompanied by "a scrap of paper," requesting "prayer for a troubled, sinful, and almost despairing soul." He did not return from Holland for reasons known to himself and to the English government, and probably not wholly unsuspected even by Mrs. Gotherson.

VI

WHAT those reasons were, and in what activities and society he busied himself is shown, among other testimony, by the deposition of a certain John Abbot, an English resident of Harlem. He declared, in later years, that between 1669 and 1672 he had often had at his house "one John Scot, commonly called Major General Scot," who went in company with "an ancient gentleman, Coll. Wogan," William Cole, Dr. Richardson, and a Mr. Ray, alias John Phelps. He deposed further, that Scott had maps and charts of the West Indies, that he was a man evilly spoken of, and that in spite of the fact that he held a commission in the Dutch army, he had on at least one occasion been soundly beaten by Abbot's servant. Taking all these things into account, there can be little doubt that this was the royal geographer.

But who were these new associates, and what was he doing in Holland? The answer is not wholly clear, but there is evidence enough to enable one to arrive at an approximation to the truth. Wogan and Phelps had been members of the high court of justice which had condemned Charles I to death. Dr. Richardson was one of the most active movers in the Nonconformist plot which had led to a rising in the northern counties of England in

1663. All were proclaimed outlaws and traitors. Their chief business was the fomenting of disturbance against the government of Charles II; their chief hope was to overthrow that government; their chief means of support lay in certain contributions taken up among the faithful in England under guise of sending aid to the Waldensians, the persecuted Vaudois, or the "Poles"; and there is evidence that Scott benefited by this "Polish fund." These men were, in short, the center of a widespread intrigue, which had for its purpose the creation of trouble for the English authorities by whatever means that could be accomplished.

They had many friends and correspondents throughout the world, and with Scott's entry into this circle he came in touch with the underground politics which played such a part in the reign of Charles II, and was thenceforth to condition the late royal geographer's career to the end of his life. In this the old Cromwellians had their full share. Upon the Restoration, their party had been broken up. Some leaders, like Vane and Harrison, had been seized and executed. Some, like General Lambert, whose popularity prevented the government from bringing them to the block, were doomed to life imprisonment. Some, like Goffe, Whalley, Dixwell, and Bourne, found refuge in America. Some, like Ludlow, Sidney, and Lisle, fled to Switzerland. A few took service in continental armies. Others, like those with whom Scott now consorted in this "Adventure of the Regicides," remained in the Netherlands. There they were in close touch with the Dutch government on the one side, and on the other with the discontented Nonconformist element in England that had been driven first from the church, then from politics, by the so-called Persecuting Acts of the Anglican party during the Clarendon administration, which had thus endeavored to crush Nonconformity once and for all. They were a distinct menace to the English government, which could take no step without reckoning the possible danger from these men and the aid which they might bring to the enemies of England. Many of them had actually taken part in the recent Anglo-Dutch war. At least one Cromwellian officer had commanded troops on English soil against his countrymen, in an effort to take Harwich fort; while in the famous raid up the Medway and the Thames the Dutch fleet had been partly manned, and probably largely piloted, by English sailors in Dutch service.

It was, therefore, natural enough that a fugitive like Scott should seek and find refuge and a welcome among this group. It was no less natural that he should acquire a commission in the Dutch service; and it was perhaps most natural of all that he should seek to turn his gifts and knowledge to the account of his own advantage in this environment. One need not accept Mrs. Gotherson's theory that he used the information which had come in his way as commander in the West Indies and as royal geographer to further his fortunes with the Dutch authorities; but there was good ground for that hypothesis and it is not easy to believe that he found these any handicap in his new venture.

At any rate he seems to have commanded at least a company in the Dutch army, though it is not probable that he derived his title as Major-General from that circumstance. It is equally certain that he was implicated with a man named Despontyn in various dubious financial transactions relating to that company's pay. He entered into a plan to defraud a Jew of a considerable sum; he cheated his landlady. It is not necessary to accept the story that he defrauded the states of Holland out of £7,000 or £8,000, and that he was driven from the country and hanged in effigy there in consequence; but probably only the amount and the disgrace were exaggerated; the main fact seems clear. There is, moreover, evidence to show that he provided his new employers with maps, soundings, and plans of the defenses of English harbors, and information of English naval strengths and designs, and in so far Mrs. Gotherson's surmises were justified. In addition there is much evidence that this same Scott, "shield-bearer and geographer-royal," as he styled himself, was, during his stay in Holland, at once dishonest and dissolute in a large variety of ways not necessary to enumerate here.

Meanwhile English affairs, during the period of Scott's sojourn in Holland, took a fresh turn in that devious course which they pursued throughout the Restoration period. In so doing they unconsciously helped Scott in determining his own course, in whose direction he was ably assisted by the authorities of the countries in which he successively sought refuge and a livelihood. His stay in Holland coincided almost exactly with the period during which the Cabal remained in power. That period bears a peculiar reputation in English history, and one not wholly favorable. This is not surprising, whether we consider the character of some of its members, or the policies which they pursued in their collective capacity, and, in particular, the fact that their history has been written chiefly by their enemies, the Anglicans. Whatever religion they professed or despised, they were none of them of the latter party, whose overthrow brought them to power, and whose revival drove them in turn from place.

The first act of their administration had been the signature of the Triple Alliance with Holland and Sweden to check Louis XIV's aggressions. Yet they bore no love for the Dutch, who were the chief rivals of that interest to which the Cabal devoted its best talents — the development of English commerce. That feeling was shared, on different grounds, perhaps, by their sovereign, who, in 1670, signed the secret treaty of Dover with his cousin, the French king, in return for a substantial pension. Thereafter events moved toward an Anglo-French alliance and a joint attack on Holland; and, at about the time that Scott found his position in Holland becoming difficult, his government began to take steps to prepare for war with that power. The Nonconformists were conciliated in so far as possible, and many of the exiles were pardoned and permitted to return. A royal Declaration of Indulgence gave virtual toleration to the Dissenters. The stop of the Exechequer provided the government with a sum which, added to a Parliamentary grant, enabled the administration to equip the navy; and hostilities began by an attempt to seize the Dutch Smyrna fleet. Louis XIV poured his armies into the Netherlands and Holland faced one of the most dangerous crises in her troubled history.

And what of Scott in these busy days of broken alliances and international treacheries? The evidence is conflicting, as it well might be. Some of it goes to show that he improved his stay in Holland to inform his own government of the doings of the exiles, and carried on negotiations between them and the English authorities. Some of it seems to suggest that the attack on the Smyrna fleet failed owing to a warning sent the Dutch by Scott. That there is ground for believing that all of this is more or less true appears from certain testimony that he was employed by Arlington to live at Bruges as a spy; that he was seen there by other English agents — notably the first English woman novelist, Aphra Behn — in the exercise of his profession; that he was paid by the English consul there; and that he presently lost his employment for having opened negotiations with the Dutch. And there is nothing incompatible with his own character or that of the times and class which he adorned in the supposition that he took his profit where he found it, and was paid by both sides. In any event, his stay in Bruges seems to have been of few days and full of trouble, for, besides his other misfortunes, he was found sketching the fortifications of the place, was driven out, and compelled to seek refuge in Paris. There he arrived, as usual, at the opportune moment; for England and France, allied again against Holland, found themselves again in accord, and prepared to employ the services of one so recently in Dutch service.

He did not go empty-handed. As in his earlier exodus to and from the court of Charles II, he brought to Paris an interesting collection of curiosities. First among them were the maps and plans upon which he always relied, and not without much reason, to give him standing in a new community. Moreover, he seems to have secured from various persons small sums of money to meet his unavoidable expenses, a "Silver Belt, a Fowling-peece or two, two or three copper-plates of Mapps, one great picture, of great value as he pretended, and two swords, one whereof (to magnify its value) he pretended to have been Cromwell's." Nor was this all, for we find one Sherwin, the inventor of a new method of casting ordnance, writing about this time to the Marquis de Seignelay, French Minister of Marine, begging him to recover two little cannon, stolen by Scott, whose "intrigues have ruined the whole enterprise" of supplying the new guns to the French government.

Thus equipped, he arrived in Paris at a propitious time to dispose of the information he possessed, and he found the French capital a fertile field for the exercise of his peculiar talents. He was nothing if not impartial, and he was as little bound by any weak scruples of patriotism as the most recent of internationalists. His career, indeed, began auspiciously, for as he had earlier informed the English of Dutch designs, and more recently enlightened the Dutch regarding the English plans, he was now in a position to provide the French with information regarding both the English and the Dutch, and in a fair way, if opportunity presented itself, to gain material which could be disposed of, in turn, to England, or even to Holland if circumstances seemed to make it necessary or profitable.

He set up at first apparently as a map-maker and a geographical expert, with what more obscure relations with the French government may be surmised. He had, it would seem, no great skill himself in cartography, but he was fortunate enough to be able to find a man who could draw, and him he supplied with data from his own knowledge, and, on at least one recorded occasion, from his imagination. Meanwhile he strove, not without success, to ingratiate himself with those in place and power. He dabbled in alchemy; he even seems to have dreamed of getting a French ship and turning pirate. He had some obscure connection with a certain Mlle. des Moulins, to whom he wrote letters in French, signed "Jean Scot of Scot's Hall," and from whom he received various sums for expenses in journeys made on her account. And it may be noted here, as perhaps only a peculiar coincidence but possibly a matter of not entirely extraneous interest, that a man of that name, sometime in Dutch service, sometime secretary to the Earl of Arlington, was hanged in England about this time on a charge of treason.

Scott was more fortunate. He appears to have been employed in some capacity by the Prince de Condé, under circumstances of such peculiar character that it seemed necessary to the French authorities a little later to deny categorically that he had ever been in the immediate service of the French government, without, however, committing themselves to the indiscretion of alluding to his connection with Condé. Beyond this there are scattered notices of other and less public activities. He is reported to have stolen a locket from a certain M. Delavall, a hat from one man, a muffler from another. He

managed to make the acquaintance of a Catholic nobleman, the Earl of Berkshire, then resident in Paris — a
connection which was presently to be of some service in
bringing him again into the public eye; and he seems not
to have wholly severed his relations with the less obtrusive
side of English administration, for there is evidence that
at least during the year 1677 he was at times in London,
in close touch with Sir Ellis Leighton, chief agent of the
Duke of Buckingham, upholding the French interest, denouncing William of Orange, and frequenting the purlieus of the court.

VII

THUS he passed some busy years. Meanwhile the situation in European, and more particularly in English, politics altered, and with it came a corresponding change in
Scott's position and his relationships. While he had thus
busied himself England and France had made their joint
attack on Holland. On the Continent the courage of the
Dutch held the Anglo-French attack at bay, and the outbreak of war had been accompanied by a revolution
which brought to the head of affairs a greater spirit,
William III, whose abilities presently drew together an
alliance against Louis XIV. The support of England
became the prize for which the rival groups of allies contended. London was filled with their agents, the French
striving to hold the English to their allegiance, the Dutch,
the Imperialists, and the Spaniards striving to detach
them from the French cause. The Cabal was succeeded
by the Earl of Danby's ministry. The struggle was transferred to the House of Commons, which first summoned
Arlington and Buckingham before it to account for the
miscarriages of the war and their part in the illegal proceedings which had preceded it, and then, under the direction of the leaders of the Country Party, in which

Buckingham and Shaftesbury came to play the principal rôles, turned upon the King and the French policy.

The result was a complete reversal of parts in English and in Continental affairs. The English king was compelled to break with France, to make peace with Holland, and to give his consent to the marriage of his niece with William of Orange. That astute prince made head against his enemy. The Imperialists, having defeated the Turks, were enabled to throw their strength against the western front. The English Parliament voted great supplies, authorized the raising of an army, and pressed forward to war with France on the side of the alliance now formed against Louis XIV. In the face of these events the Grand Monarque was compelled to peace, and in the month of August, 1678, diplomats assembled at Nymwegen to negotiate the great treaty which takes its name from that place.

Meanwhile the situation in England was complicated by the introduction of a religious element. From the beginning of the reign of Charles II the Catholics had bestirred themselves to recover what they might of the position they once held in the British Isles. The King himself was not unfavorable to their cause. His brother, James, Duke of York, with many members of the court, openly embraced the ancient faith; and among the results of the anti-French agitation the passage of a Test Act drove him, with his co-religionists, from civil and military command. The Catholic minority, like the Cromwellians before them, resorted to conspiracy against the government of Charles II. The King took no steps to combat the movement. The people became aroused to the danger, and their alarm was fostered by the leaders of the Country Party. The result was an explosion. At almost precisely the same moment that the diplomats assembled at Nymwegen one of the most extraordinary episodes in English history began its spectacular course, for the King was

warned that there was a Catholic conspiracy, famous as
the so-called Popish Plot, then on foot against his person
and his crown, as well as against English Protestantism.

To that warning, drawn up in the form of an elaborate
memorandum by two men, Titus Oates and Israel Tonge,
he paid little heed. But when, two months later, a London justice of the peace, Sir Edmundberry Godfrey, before whom Oates had sworn out a copy of his information,
was found murdered, the London mob, the English
people, and in particular the Whig party, under the able
leadership of Shaftesbury and Buckingham, were roused
to a frenzy unparalleled in English history. The whole
great mystery was thrown at once into politics. The
Whigs saw in it an opportunity to dispose of their rivals,
especially the Duke of York, whom they hoped to exclude
from the succession to the throne. What designs the Duke
of Buckingham entertained are difficult to determine, but
it seems not improbable that among them was some wild
project of becoming, if not king, at least Lord Protector
of the realm to whose crown he pretended to possess he-
reditary claims.

But this much is certain. Almost, if not quite alone of
all the characters who have played a part in English history the brilliant and erratic Buckingham surrounded
himself with a group of bravos, which comprised some of
the greatest scoundrels left unhung in England. There
was that Christian who became the model for the villain
in Scott's novel of *Peveril of the Peak*. There was Colonel
Blood, who had achieved eminence by his all but successful attempt to steal the crown and scepter from the Tower
some years before. These were fair types of the lower
order. Among those of higher rank was Lord Howard of
Escrick, perhaps the most finished rascal of his time; and,
not to call more names, there was the Duke's representative in Paris and at times elsewhere, Sir Ellis Leighton.
For while Shaftesbury relied on his wits, on the famous

Green Ribbon Club which formed the active principle of the Whig party, and on the "brisk boys" of the London mob, the Duke was not so nice in his taste in supporters.

On the other side was a group perhaps more respectable in its personnel, if not more scrupulous in its designs. About the Duke of York had grown up a Catholic cabal among whose membership were numbered such names as Lord Bellasis and Lord Powis; Lord Petre; the Duke's secretary, Coleman; and a company of lesser agents, among whom a section of the Jesuits were the ablest though not the most conspicuous.

In such a golden age of conspiracy nothing could have been more natural, indeed one might almost say inevitable, than that Scott should have found some part to his liking, and, what was always to his liking, his interest. Just how he came into touch with Buckingham we know, but the means are certainly peculiar. For he seems to have been recommended to Leighton about 1676 by Peter and Richard Talbot, Irish Catholics then resident on the Continent for reasons best known to the English government, and with some obscure relation to the Duke of York. Leighton, in turn, brought Scott to the attention of Buckingham, who found him, as he said, "a very useful rogue." There may be some clue to this mysterious connection between Scott, Leighton, and the Talbots in the fact that Scott had commended himself to the Earl of Berkshire by professing himself, according to the testimony of one of the earl's servants, as belonging to the same communion as that of the exiled nobleman, that of the Catholic church.

At any rate he was soon a member of the company of choice spirits enrolled under the banner of Buckingham. In September, 1678, the Duke seems to have visited France, incognito. There, at Abbeville, he met Scott and "such company as ought to be seen in disguise," and probably at that time made such plans as were soon revealed in Scott's actions. For in November we find Buckingham writing to Louis XIV desiring to be of use to that monarch, especially for "the last favor" from the French king's hands. The bearer, Mr. Scott, he goes on to say, will tell him orally the message he sends. This was accompanied by another letter to M. de Pomponne, in the same tenor and by the same hand. All of which, ostensibly, had to do with a plot to assassinate Louis.

Meanwhile in England the Popish Plot agitation, under skilful manipulation, had assumed the dimensions of a national panic. Oates and Tonge became popular heroes. Every Catholic fell under suspicion, and arrests were made right and left. The Earl of Powis, Lord Petre, Lord Bellasis, Viscount Stafford, and Lord Arundel of Wardour — the principal men named in Oates' information — were taken into custody, and presently impeached. Coleman and six other men — almost certainly the wrong ones — were tried and executed as quickly as the machinery of the law could be set in motion. Many more were accused and hard put to it to defend themselves. Parliament devoted itself almost entirely to the Plot. Danby was impeached, and by March, 1679, the Duke of York was compelled to seek refuge in Brussels.

Thus began that great episode which so greatly disturbed the course of English politics in the years 1678 and 1679 and diverted English attention even from the Peace of Nymwegen, which the French king had meanwhile been compelled to sign with his enemies. It need hardly be said that the Whigs, under the lead of Shaftesbury and Buckingham, embraced the opportunity thus afforded them to press hard their attack upon the Duke of York. Every device of political agitation, every means of furthering the Plot, was relentlessly used by them; every informer encouraged, every "discovery" exploited. In turn, after Oates and Tonge, there came other witnesses on the scene, Bedloe, Prance, Dugdale, and others less notable, a choice collection of criminals, conspirators, and perjurers, to give evidence concerning the Plot and the murder of Godfrey, to be rewarded for their services, and, in general, to save the country from the evils which threatened it.

With such matters stirring in the world, this was no time for a man like Scott to be idle; and we find him, in consequence, going back and forth between England and France, busily engaged, apparently on Buckingham's errands. Here, too, we get finally a glimpse of what sort of man he was in his external appearance. On October 19, 1678, traveling at Gravesend under the name of Godfrey, he is shown in the flesh. "A proper well-sett man in a great light coulered Periwigg, rough-visaged, haveing large haire on his Eyebrows, hollow eyde, a little squintain or a cast with his Eye, full faced about ye cheekes, about 46 yeares of Age with a Black hatt & in a streight boddyed coate cloath colour with silver lace behind." Thus for the moment we have him, held by the order of the Admiralty Secretary, Pepys, who did not then apparently know who or what he was, save that his actions had led to suspicion.

By whatever method, he seems to have got safe away, but a month later (November 8, 1678) a royal warrant addressed to Colonel Strode, the Lieutenant of Dover Castle, directed him to seize Scott as soon as he should land at Dover; for his numerous journeys in the preceding months in various guises and under various names, usually Godfrey or Johnson, had made him suspect to the English government, especially in view of his unbridled tongue. With all his gifts, Scott's volubility made him peculiarly unfitted for the rôle of a conspirator. He had continually boasted himself a friend of Buckingham, continually acted in "violent and overbearing fashion," was often "full of Guinneyes," "without any visible estate to support himself with," not seldom drunk, and known to carry with him maps, plans, and estimates of naval and ordnance matters. Thus wherever he went he was a marked man and one, under the circumstances, to be watched and, if possible, apprehended. Despite all this he was not caught, and it was not until the following spring that he came again into public life.

The circumstances were, like most circumstances in his life, extraordinary. In March, 1679, the Earl of Berkshire died in Paris. Some weeks after that — to be exact, on April 28 or 29, a fortnight after Danby had been committed to the Tower, and at the moment that Parliament had passed a resolution against the Duke of York — there arrived at Folkestone a man who called himself John Johnson. On his way to London, it seems, he was arrested at Dover and there compelled to give an account of himself, which he was, apparently, by no means loath to do. He was, he said, a pensioner of the Prince of Condé. He had formerly commanded the Prince's regiment of horse in the French service and had surveyed the Prince's land in Picardy and Burgundy. His name was Scott, the occasion of his return was to see his native country, his profession that of a soldier, his landing at Folkestone only to see the boatman who had transported him in the preceding October, "whom he understood to be in great trouble for carrying him over." He offered to take the oaths of Supremacy, Allegiance, and the Test.

This was perhaps the more desirable, inasmuch as it appeared from his testimony that he had been most solicitous for news relating to Parliamentary votes of money to raise a fleet and an army, and peculiarly inquisitive regarding naval and ordnance estimates. To gratify that curiosity, it appeared that a certain Captain Newman finally drew up for him in a little book "a collection of the severall estimates from the offices of the navy and ordnance" the charges, the members, the rules, the force and the state of the coast fortifications, especially of Ports-

mouth, Plymouth, and the Isle of Wight. Whereupon the
Colonel disappeared for five or six weeks, returning in
funds and bringing with him a rich wardrobe and some
sort of a paper "under the French King's own hand."
All this was in due time set forth in a deposition by Captain Newman himself, though his testimony was, apparently, not available until too late to be of much use for the
purpose for which it was taken.

Accordingly, Scott was carried to London. There he
told a curious story, and produced a still more curious
document. The Earl of Berkshire, he said, having long
been ill, sent for him in March to advise about a physician. One was procured, but it was too late, and the
Earl, having had Scott brought to him, sent the servants
away and confided to him that there had been "a foolish
and an ill design" carried on in England of which he had
known nothing till Lord Arundel, Mr. Coleman, and
others had told him it could not miscarry, and that he
should be "looked on as an ill man if he did not come in
in time." He had heard nothing about killing the King
or he would have revealed it. Lord Bellasis was an "ill
man"; "he and others were accustomed to speak ill of the
king, indeed very irrevently." He refused to tell Scott
who the others were, made him promise to tell the King,
and so continued: "My Lord Stafford was all along a
moving agent — though not very malicious. . . . My
Lord Powis his covetousness drew him in further than he
would have gone. — My Lord Peeter . . . was ever averse
to all things of intrigue in this matter." And so, Lord
Cardigan being at the door, he dismissed Scott, urging
him not to forget this, "nor the business at Rohan." This,
with some circumlocution and much elaboration, was the
message Scott brought to London.

It is not easy to discover what, if any, benefits or injuries accrued to Scott or anyone else from this curious
episode. The most recent historian of the Popish Plot is

himself somewhat at a loss to account for it, since, as he observes, Scott "ran counter to the testimony of Oates as to the designs against the King's life, he never sought reward as a professional informer would have done, he gave no evidence against those condemned for the Plot, and his name does not appear in the secret-service lists." He concludes that he must have had some knowledge of Berkshire's correspondence with Coleman from the nobleman himself, and that "a scoundrel following in the track of Oates and Bedlow would never have concocted such a story" — hence it is "probably genuine." Moreover, he adds, like the worthy member of the Massachusetts Historical Society who fifty years earlier contributed to the biography of Scott, "Nothing more was known of him." This he qualifies a little in a footnote recording that Scott testified before the House of Commons later that Pepys had given information to the French court regarding the navy "but the affair was never investigated."

What, then, can be made of this? As it has been observed of an earlier episode, all of it is partly true, perhaps part of it is all true. Scott had known the Earl of Berkshire; the Earl of Berkshire was a Catholic; he had had some communication with the Catholic party in England; he was now dead. That much is certain. Oates' testimony, now fairly well known, had implicated Lord Bellasis, Lord Petre, Lord Arundel of Wardour, the Earl of Powis, and Viscount Stafford. They were, as a matter of fact, then prisoners in the Tower. Coleman had been tried and executed for treason, and the five Popish Lords impeached. All of this, and much more, was matter of common knowledge. Thus far we are willing to go with the chronicler of the Plot, or with Scott, or with any man who had read or heard of the events of those busy days between August, 1678, and April, 1679, and there must have been very few men who had not. But it would hardly require any very intimate acquaintance with those

circumstances, any power of divination, or any very profound ability, to draw up such a statement as that which
Scott brought to the attention of the government, for all
of it, save Scott's connection with the Earl of Berkshire,
had ceased to be even news. And while we may admit,
with Mr. Pollock, that the surprising thing about this information is its moderation, we may not, in view of
Scott's history, be willing to agree with him that this is
any necessary proof of its truth or of Scott's importance as
a witness.

In any event, everyone is agreed that nothing came of
it. The Long Island real-estate dealer was not destined
to occupy a niche in that temple of fame presided over by
the pious Dr. Oates — at least for the present. And this
negative conclusion seems justifiable on the ground of
certain other testimony not wholly impertinent to the
case. For a Mrs. Escott, sometime servant to the Earl of
Berkshire, testified presently that Scott showed her master
a map of the places in England which were to be taken
by the French, that he often entertained the Earl with
"stories of ye cheats hee has put upon ye world in several
places," that they both agreed that innocent blood had
been shed over the Plot, that Scott went to mass and
passed as a Roman Catholic, that Benson, "a rogue,"
also came to see the Earl, who a month before he died
"was so deaf that no stranger spoke to him but as shee
went to him and hallowed it in his ears." Which testimony, inasmuch as it was taken in another matter, may
perhaps be not unworthy to set beside — or even against
— Scott's entertaining narrative of Berkshire's last hours,
and may, perhaps, even modify somewhat the importance attached to Scott's testimony by Mr. Pollock.

VIII

HOWEVER that may be, Scott no longer appears as a witness to the Plot proper. None the less he was not idle. For scarcely had he emerged from this exploit when he began to figure in another and scarcely less interesting episode which grew directly out of that frenzy. This was the attack made on Samuel Pepys, Secretary to the Admiralty, and on Sir Anthony Deane, his colleague, for furnishing information to the French government concerning English naval affairs and, incidentally, for Pepys' alleged Catholicism, which, under the Test Act, would have cost his place. Here Scott was cast for a leading part.

The plot developed clearly and rapidly. On the twenty-seventh of October, 1678, ten days after the discovery of Godfrey's body, a certain Captain Charles Atkins laid before Secretary Henry Coventry information against a friend and namesake of his, one Samuel Atkins, clerk to Samuel Pepys, which, however vaguely, seemed to point to some obscure connection between the accused and Godfrey's murder. Three days later he appeared before the Privy Council. On November 1 he swore to his statement before a justice of the peace, and Samuel Atkins was promptly seized, carried before the committee of enquiry of the House of Lords, where, in spite of every inducement to give testimony unfavorable to the Duke of York and his party, he indignantly denied the whole story. Thence he was sent to Newgate. A new informer, Bedloe, was pressed into service against him, other witnesses summoned, and, on February 11, 1679, he was brought to trial. There the case collapsed. The witnesses were vague and unsatisfactory, the prosecution weak, and at the crisis of the trial Atkins produced an alibi so strong that the case was dismissed; an effort to prove the accused a Roman Catholic broke down ignominiously, and he was triumphantly vindicated on every count.

But the men behind this case, Shaftesbury and Buckingham at their head, did not rest here. Scarcely had
Atkins been acquitted on the ground of the alibi, which
had been prepared by his master, when the attack was directed against Pepys himself. It was some time getting
under way, but once it began it assumed formidable proportions. On the twentieth of May, 1679, Mr. William
Harbord, M.P. for Thetford, reported to the House of
Commons from the committee of enquiry into the miscarriages of the navy "some miscarriages of Sir Anthony
Deane and Mr. Pepys relating to Piracy &c." These related ostensibly to the fitting out of a privateer from government stores six years before, securing for her a French
commission, and employing her against the Dutch, with
whom England was then at war. To this, it would appear, he added a charge that Pepys and Deane had suppressed or destroyed a journal of a voyage to St. Helena,
kept by Sir Richard Munden—which the latter promptly
denied ever having written. But it appeared almost
immediately that the matter was far deeper than this.
For the first witness and the first piece of evidence sub-
mitted to the committee and by them to the House was
Colonel Scott and his testimony.

That gentleman, as always, provided an interesting
narrative. "Having been acquainted with several great
men belonging to the navy," he began, "by their death
he was now discharged from privacy, things being set-
tling in England." "M. Pelisary, Treasurer General of
the French King's navy," he deposed, "had shown him
draughts of English ship-models, the government of the
Admiralty, the strength and condition of the English
navy, its methods of fighting, maps and soundings of the
Medway and Kent shores, and of the Isle of Wight, plans
of Sheerness and Tilbury, all signed by Mr. Pepys, who,
it appears, received for them some £40,000. But," he
added, with his wonted caution, "there is a mystery in

this, more than I dare speak of." With that regard for religion and that high sense of patriotism which he showed at all times in his career, Scott testified that hereupon he had said to Pelissary, who was a Protestant, "I hope these rogues that have betrayed their country are not of our 'Religion.'" Pelissary answered, "They are of the Devil's Religion; let us drink off our wine."

Such evidence, despite its clear and convincing presentation, it may well be imagined, did not go wholly unchallenged. There being some efforts "to take off Scott's testimony," Harbord observed that he would like to present two other witnesses. The story of one of them at least could hardly have afforded him much comfort, since the witness merely deposed that five years before he had been refused the command of the frigate *Jersey* by Pepys, and further that a short time before he had heard Scott declare that Pepys was "a great betrayer of his country and in time he would make it appear, and that Pepys was one of the Arch-Traytors of the Kingdom." To this he added that he had "heard Pepys commend the Catholics for their constancy in Religion" — which last was, save at this time, perhaps, no hanging matter.

With that we come to the real root of the matter. Passing by the charge that Pepys had sold his country's secrets to France, Harbord pounced on the charge of Papacy. "There had been," he said truly enough, "reflections upon Pepys formerly as to his Religion, and by collateral proof I shall much convince the House that he is not of our Religion. I am sorry," he added, "I must say it of a man I have lived well withal." That there had been rumors of Pepys' Catholicism — as of that of every man in anyway connected with the Duke of York, who was Lord High Admiral — was true enough. What Harbord omitted to say was that neither on the occasion he mentioned nor on any other had there appeared any ground whatever for such a charge.

That ground now appeared in the evidence of John
James of Glentworth, Lincolnshire, sometime Pepys'
butler, now, for obvious reasons, not in that service. He
deposed that there was one Morello who used to say mass
at the Queen's Chapel, St. James', Somerset House, and
Whitehall. He had heard this man say that he had
studied at Rome. "He had Beads and Pictures, and a
private door to his room. He used to carry a pistol and a
dagger and went often into St. James's Park, and went to
Pepys's house at Chelsea. He was frequently shut up with
Pepys in his closet singing of Psalms often till three o'clock
in the morning. He was a learned man and would dispute with Pepys in Philosophy. When a Proclamation
was out for Papists to go out of Town, Pepys helped him
away with his Papers and Books." When James added to
this the statement that Pepys had said there was no employment in the navy for any man save by favor of the
Duke, the case was complete.

In brief, it was sought to prove that Morello was a dangerous man — as must appear to the most casual reader
of this damning indictment! James' story was true. At
any other time and under any other circumstances the
fact that one had as a friend a man who shared his tastes
in music and learning, or even that he sat up until three
in the morning singing psalms with him, would have been
laughed out of court as proof that he shared that friend's
religious views or that he was a danger to the state. That
men obtained employment in the navy by favor of the
Lord High Admiral was hardly surprising, much less
ground for an accusation of either treason or Popery.
But at this precise moment men were being sent to the
block on evidence no less flimsy. Sir John Hotham rose
promptly to add that he had spoken to Oates in the lobby
and that Oates told him he knew Morello as a Jesuit who
had "importuned to have charge of the English business." Another leader of the Country Party, Garroway,

declared this was "evidently one of the branches of the Plot." "We have a Land-Plot," said he, "this is a Sea-Plot." Sergeant Maynard declared that this was almost as bad as the charges against the Lords in the Tower, and that the papers should be put in the Speaker's charge.

Then Pepys spoke. First he traversed Harbord's whole statement. He had, he said, been a member of Harbord's committee, he had attended its meetings, and he had never heard there any accusation either from Scott or from James. He denied that the Admiralty or he himself had ever known about the alleged privateering scheme detailed by Harbord. "As for the charge of Col. Scott (Lord! Sir.) . . . This Gentleman I know not, nor ever saw: I know neither his name nor quality, where is his abode or dependencies," unless he was the man who under the name of Godfrey was sought by and escaped the officers not long since at Gravesend, Deal, and Dover, but in whose London lodgings the Lord Mayor found "papers of ill importance . . . just such papers as he accuses me of." All charges made by Scott Pepys solemnly and categorically denied. As to James, he turned him away for being in the housekeeper's room at three o'clock Sunday morning. As for Morello, he was sent to Pepys by one Hill; he was a good scholar and a master of music, harmless and moderate in opinions, and he could and would at the desire of the House appear to clear himself. Deane followed in the same strain. To Scott's charges he replied that he had, in fact, built two boats for the French king — to be used on the Grand Canal at Versailles in three feet and a half of water! He declared, moreover, that a member of the House lately in Paris named Scott as one giving intelligence to the French court.

Then followed a sharp debate. Sir Joseph Williamson, Scott's old friend and patron, although he refrained from all mention of Scott, must have had him in mind, for he vigorously seconded Deane. Sacheverell, the Country Party leader, Garroway, and Harbord pressed the charge. Sir Francis Rolle added a touch of Rabelaisian humor. Sir William Coventry observed that he had had James as a butler, that he did not love to do ill offices to one who had served him, but that James' service "was not so direct as to recommend him to a friend." Coventry's brother Henry, then Secretary of State, contributed two interesting pieces of information. The first was that Scott had absconded from London in the preceding October under a misapprehension. The government was not looking for him at all but for Conyers, a Jesuit, but Scott's flight gave ground for suspicion against him. The second was that Scott had been employed by the Prince de Condé to survey his lands. And to this Harbord added two other bits of biography — or romance — that Williamson had told him Scott was the ablest man in England, and that he had a testimonial from De Witt [who was dead] that he had commanded eight regiments of foot for the relief of Flanders. He averred further that a great man had told him that some had tried to corrupt Scott to bear false witness against him, "but Scott detested it."

The upshot of the matter was that Pepys and Deane were committed to the custody of the Sergeant-at-Arms, with the understanding that they be examined two days later. On that occasion Harbord made another attack on them, and they were committed to the Tower. There they remained for ten days. On June 2 they were brought before the King's Bench, where the Attorney-General refused to allow them to be admitted to bail. Somewhat later, in spite of the fact that Scott meanwhile swore to an information on the lines laid down in his testimony before the Commons, the Attorney-General changed his mind. The prisoners were permitted to offer security in the sum of £30,000 — a huge amount for those days — and so regained their liberty. In the following February they were released from that obligation, Scott having refused to recognize the truth of his deposition and James having confessed that he had concocted his story under Harbord's instigation. Nor is it without some small significance in this connection that about this time the Duke of Buckingham recommended to Sir Thomas Leet and Mr. Vaughan one J. James, sometime in his service, for the post of storekeeper at Woolwich — which casts a certain amount of light upon this episode. And so ended the Adventure of the House of Commons.

What induced Scott to bring these charges of treason and Popery against Pepys? The answer is not difficult to guess. The Popish Plot frenzy was at its height. It seemed to Buckingham, Shaftesbury, and their Whig supporters that, with its aid, they might not only be able to displace the Tories in the conduct of affairs, but even exclude the Duke of York from the succession — with all the possibilities that such a victory might entail. But why attack Pepys? To this three answers have been given. The first is that, ten years before, Pepys had been commissioned by the Duke of York to gather evidence in the matter of Mrs. Gotherson's appeal to the King for justice against Scott, that it was on the strength of this testimony that Scott was driven from place and court, and thereafter nourished a grudge against Pepys. The second is the general explanation that Pepys was, in his capacity of Secretary of the Admiralty, very close to the Duke, who, until the passage of the Test Act, had been Lord High Admiral; that a successful attack on Pepys might well involve James, and in any event would have a powerful tendency toward weakening the Duke's position before Parliament and the country.

The third is the answer which, in later years, was given by Scott himself, an answer which is perhaps as good an explanation of his own conduct and of the Plot in general as can be found anywhere. "Their Design," said he, "was to destroy the Government and make themselves Kings, or rather Tyrants, and for that end did all they could to bring an odium and hatred upon his Majesty and Family, and by their fictions delude a Giddy and un- thinking people. Their party was of three sorts. Those that wanted office and were disappointed. Those that were enemys to the Government of Church and State, and Fooles that the other two brought over to be of their side."

And to which of these groups did Scott belong? If we had not his own confession, it would be easy to guess. Despite his manifold protestations it is fairly apparent that he was no zealot for either church or state; and hitherto, save in a larger sense, he had been a knave rather than a fool. In this affair, he admitted, he "ac- knowledged himself a Toole, much used, as well as a Cabinett Counselour." "One that had hoped to be [Pepys'] successor in the Secretarye's Employment," he declared, "had putt him upon contriving [Pepys'] de- struction." The design was to take Pepys' life, "but the said person found he was not likely to succeed in case they had proceeded." Besides, he added, Shaftes- bury had made great promises to him to further this design.

The scheme was not unpromising. Pepys was a de- voted adherent of the Duke of York. Though not himself a Catholic, he was no fanatical Protestant. Holding a lucrative office, and being a highly efficient public serv- ant, he naturally had enemies. He was thus, under the circumstances, a shining mark. But in all the mistakes of a mistaken career, Scott never committed a greater error than when he joined in the attack on the Secretary to the Board of Admiralty. Pepys was what he was because of his qualities. He had risen by his abilities, he had main- tained himself not so much by favor as by his courage and intelligence. He had not dealt with dishonest contractors, surly sailormen, and shifty courtiers, for fifteen years, without acquiring a fairly thorough acquaintance with the world and its wickedness, together with some knowledge of how to meet the exigencies of life. Moreover, he had an extraordinarily wide acquaintance; and, above all, he was, by the accident of fate, set in the precise position, as it chanced, to deal with a man like Scott. He had for many years been in the closest touch with the navy — and he turned at once to his friend, Captain Dyer. He was the intimate friend of the Duke of York, who was the grantee of New York — and he despatched a letter at once to the Duke's appointee, Governor Francis Lovelace, for a record of Scott's activities in that quarter of the world. He wrote Mrs. Gotherson for information; to Savile, the English ambassador in Paris; and just at this time, by chance, Thomas Lovelace turned up in England and agreed to testify for Pepys — or at least against Scott. Pepys had married the daughter of a French Huguenot refugee — and he sent his brother-in-law, Bartholomew in St. Michel, posthaste to France to secure evidence. Thence, after nine months, he returned, not only with depositions but with witnesses. Besides this, Pepys entrusted a Captain Gunman with a similar errand in Holland, and employed, among others, a well-known secret-service agent, Puckle, on the same task. He wrote to a score of individuals himself. He put into action his intimate knowledge of London; he sent to the port towns, where his acquaintance was naturally extensive; and he enlisted the services of his many and intimate friends. As a result, it seemed that everyone Scott had ever injured — and their name was legion — presented himself by letter or in person to contribute to this grand assize. Incredible as it may seem, at least two hundred persons came forward in person, or by letter or affidavit, to contribute information; English, Dutch, French, European, and

American, if united in nothing else, found themselves in
accord on Scott.

The consequence was what might have been foreseen,
and it is perhaps small wonder that by September Scott
was making enquiry into the laws against perjury. In
the Pepys manuscripts in the Bodleian Library and in his
own collection, which he presented to his college in Cambridge, there are two full volumes of manuscripts, marked
the "Mornamont Papers." Probably nowhere in the
world is there so complete a record of the activities of a
private individual in one place as these manuscripts contain of the doings of John Scott. For these documents go
to prove that he had meddled, or tried to meddle, in
every shady transaction and every dark intrigue of his
day, from the conspiracies of the Cromwellian refugees to
the Popish Plot, from the seizure of Long Island from the
Dutch to Louis XIV's designs against the Netherlands.
Witnesses deposed that he boasted of providing the Dutch
with plans of the "River of London" and other information which would "make England dance"; and of the
Dutch towns which would presently — and presently did
— fall into the hands of France. They said that he had
declared he had information to prove that Charles II had
married the Duke of Monmouth's mother, a tale, which,
had it been true, might have altered history. These informations, whatever other value they may have had,
proved one thing beyond all question, that Scott was a
colossal and congenital liar. But it seems certain that he
collected all possible information as to English and French
sea-power, all gossip, and all documents that he could
lay his hands on, and highly probable, perhaps more
than probable, that he sold this information and misin-
formation wherever he could find a market.

Every twist and turn of his dishonest career, every
piece of villainy, every shift and device of his shifty and
devious life, every exhibition of cowardice, dishonesty,

untruthfulness, every scheme he entertained, every rebuff
he suffered, every disgrace and punishment inflicted on
him, is recorded in these documents. His obscure origin
and his poor pretense of gentility, his disreputable actions
in America, his cowardice and court-martial in the West
Indies, his treachery in England and on the Continent,
his discreditable relations with the governments of the
Netherlands, France, and his own country, his thefts, his
plots, his private debts and dishonesty, his efforts at
bigamy (for he seems to have aspired to the hand of Lady
Vane!) — everything, from triple treason to the evasion
of board bills, is there set down. The collection includes a
letter from Henry Savile, then minister to France, with a
comprehensive endorsement of Scott as "a fellow who I
thank God is not of my acquaintance but is of so despicable and vile a reputation in all places wher hee has lived
that a real criminall would be very unfortunate to suffer
by his means"; and another — endorsed on the back of
one of Scott's letters — by Lord Winchelsea to the effect
that Scott was "represented to me by his Majesty about
8 or 9 yeares since for a very bad man." Were it not for
the fact that so many of its statements are corroborated
by independent testimony then unknown to Pepys and his
informants, we might almost doubt its accuracy. It is, one
may say, written by his enemies for his greatest enemy,
and so to be read with caution and allowances. But he
had tried to swear Pepys' place and life away — and no
homest man could possibly have had so many enemies!
It is a damning record; and it reveals, more clearly than
any mere statement can express, one great outstanding
fact. There was no man in the British Empire, no man in
the whole world, probably, that Scott would not have
done better to let alone than Samuel Pepys. Reading its
manifold testimony one is inclined to the belief that of the
three categories into which Scott himself divided those
who entered into the machinations of the Popish Plot,

he belonged to the third; he was not only a knave, he was a colossal fool for ever having had anything to do with this disreputable business. And this no one realized more clearly than he himself.

For, whatever else the Popish Plot accomplished, whatever effect it had upon the Duke of York and Pepys, however it affected the course of English history, it did one other thing. It made an end of John Scott. It is commonly said that the matter was "allowed to drop." As a matter of fact, Scott went into hiding, and probably left England for a time. For Samuel Pepys was not a man to let such an attempt upon his life go wholly unnoticed, once he was clear of the preposterous charges brought against him; nor were the men of the court party likely to err on the side of leniency. For the moment, indeed, they did nothing against those who had engineered this tremendous attempt to alter the course of the English government. The Whigs were still too strong. But when Shaftesbury's last coup had failed; when the eloquence of Halifax had defeated the Exclusion Bill; when another election had put the House of Commons in the hands of the King, and the Whig leader had sought refuge in Holland, they struck. A stringent Test Act was passed against the Presbyterians; the Scotch Covenanters, who had risen in revolt, were cruelly suppressed; and the Duke of Argyle, tried and condemned for treason, saved his life only by flight. The Duke of York was despatched to Scotland to stamp out the remaining embers of opposition, and the King's natural son, the Duke of Monmouth, found his triumphal progress in the north cut short by imprisonment. The Duke of Buckingham retired from public life, and the Whig cause descended from politics to conspiracy.

And, at this precise moment, the Lord delivered Scott into the hands of his enemies. With the fall of his fortunes, he had begun to drown his sorrows more and more in drink. He had always been quarrelsome; he now became what he seems never to have been before either to soldiers or servants — dangerous. One evening, being farther gone than usual, he killed a hackney-coachman named Butler, for refusing to carry him home to his lodgings from the public house where he had been spending the evening. The occasion was too good to be lost. He was arrested. Immediately two powerful influences joined issue over him. On the one side Pepys promptly bestirred himself. He wrote to his clerk and friend, Hewer, concerning Scott, "whome God is pleased to take out of our hands into his own for justice. For should he prevail with the widow for forgiveness (which in some respects I could wish might be prevented) there is the King's pardon behind, which I am confident he is able to make relating to the state as well as us, that it might well enough atone for this his last vilany. Nor do I doubt but to save his owne life he will forget his trade and tell the truth, tho' to the hazard of the best Friends he has, which pray let Sir Anthony Deane think of, and of putting in a caveat against his getting any pardon from the court (if he should attempt it) till we are first heard."

IX

PEPYS was right. Scott escaped, leaving this time even his famous charts and papers behind him. These were promptly appropriated by Pepys and added to the collection already secured by the Lord Mayor on the occasion of Scott's earlier flight. Together they formed a notable body of literary and cartographical remains. Included among them were accounts of proceedings in Parliament, lists of the map-makers in London, lists of ships, both French and English, much miscellaneous information relating to the army and navy, notes on al-

chemy, even some poetry, all bad and almost all amatory.
Of this five lines will evidence the quality.

> "Your welcome, Dearest Madame
> From place of greatest Joy,
> It's not to say how glad I am
> And goes my little Troy
> Like Hermetissis all alone."

There was the unique copy of the *Helps for the Indians*,
which by this almost miraculous chance was thus preserved to puzzle bibliographers and blacken Scott's reputation among them. There was the beginning of his
history and description of America; and it is probable
that through Pepys these came into the hands of his friend
Sir Hans Sloane and so ultimately into the British Museum collections, where they still remain.

And among them there were two exhibits which might
have given a clue to those bibliographers who racked their
brains over the *Helps for the Indians*, since one of them at
least was of a precise piece with that ingenious help to
Scott. The first was a map of the Strait of "Mageline,"
nominally by Scott, but in fact made by Sir John Nar-
borough. The second was a map of England, "A perfect
direction to travell all England by Post, seven miles an
hour in the summer and five in the winter," with an inscription in French, English, Dutch, and Latin "for the
use and benefit of all such as shall occasionally travel into
England, whether my Country-men or others." It is ostensibly by "Johannem Scot Nobilem Anglum," and was
published, apparently, about 1670. But, unfortunately,
one Richard Carr had, in 1668, published a map which,
with a few trifling differences, was precisely that of Scott,
even to the name of the engraver. Among those differences was the inscription: "Drawn and perfected by J.
Scot, Esquire, Geographer to his Majesty of England," in
place of the original inscription: "by Richard Carr."

But this was the end at least of Scott's adventures in geography. He took refuge in Norway, supported, it was declared, by those who feared his return to England. There he was seen in the summer of 1683 by a certain Captain Gelson, who promptly wrote of his meeting to Pepys, and of his account of the Popish Plot which we have read. It is small wonder that Pepys consulted with Deane as to how they might bring him back and so manage affairs that, to save his own skin, he would tell what he knew and so ruin "the other party, notably Herbert and other rogues," especially since Scott seems to have admitted the object and the falsity of his charge against Pepys. That purpose they were not able to accomplish. He remained safely on the Continent, pensioned, it was supposed, by these same "rogues," for many years. He did not even dare to return in 1688, when the Glorious Revolution brightened the lives of so many patriots. Not until 1695 did he show his face in England again, and even then he promptly met with arrest and imprisonment in Newgate, and condemnation at Old Bailey, for coming from France without leave. But he was now a harmless, broken man, against whom even Pepys was not willing to move. Moreover, his friends were now in power. His old sponsor, Harbord, had been made a privy councillor after the Revolution, vice-treasurer for Ireland, and finally ambassador to Turkey. He was now dead, but there were enough men left of the party which Scott had served to heed his appeal, backed, no doubt, by his threats. In the summer of 1696 he was pardoned and, in the words of another of his biographers, we are again informed, "we hear no more of him." This, as it was to prove, was very far indeed from the fact, but at any rate he seems to have passed shortly thereafter from the scene of his earthly activities. And so, for the third time, it would appear that was the end of John Scott.

What of the family whom he deserted? Concerning

them there are many references. His wife, as we have seen, was given certain of his possessions to keep her from starving after his flight. Not to enquire too closely into her character and career, she ultimately married a resident of Southampton. There were two sons, the elder, John, and a younger who rejoiced in the name of Jeckomiah, apparently a perversion of a name rare even in Biblical nomenclature, Jeconiah. The elder, about the time of the Popish Plot, came to England, like Japhet, in search of his father, whom, however, he did not find. And there he seems to have remained until his death in 1692, his will of that year bequeathing sundry Long Island lands to his kinsfolk in Southampton. In this document he describes himself as a "mariner," and died, apparently, a bachelor. The younger son became, in turn, a "Captain," and his somewhat extravagant conduct still forms a picturesque page in the annals of Southampton. It is probably to him that this edifying letter was addressed.

LONDON, May the 6th, 1681.

My deare child,

I have sent to thy Brother a hatt, a Suite of Cloaths, a pair of stockings, some Gloves, Cravats, Paper, a grammar, to send to you by Capt. Bound in a portmantle, and have writ to Capt. Howell to take you Into his famely. I charge you yield to him exact Obedience and be verry Diligent in wrighting and such other Rudiments as your Skoolmastor is capable of Instructing you in, and lett me find by a letter by Capt. Bound what Profisiency you make in Wrighting and Casting accompts. Mr. Laughton is very able to Instruct you, and I am sure will do Itt to the utmost. If you give me Incuragement I shall be very kind to you and take great care for your Preferment, and shall send for you as sone as your Brother had made one voige to gett the Practicall Part of Navigation, that at his Returne to Southampton he may be able to give such account of himselfe that Render him usefull and acceptable to his friends, and if God preserve him, come master and merchant, of a shipp and cargo, but I Designe you for annother sort of Life, thearefore do not through want of an Industrious address Injure your selfe by Destroying my hoapes and Expectations, and had your Brother com over when I sent for him he would have learned that which I find he is now uncapable of in a great measure, and might have bin back againe before this time, and soe has in effect lost to or three years which I hope he will with great Industrey Retrieve. I have sent you a hod and Skarfe, and three Paire of Gloves, for you to make a present on to your mother to shew your Dutifull Respect to her, for what ever Differance, she and I have had Remember shee is your mother, and you ow her a Dutty of the Greatest tendernes. I charge you keep close to your Book; the first good accompt you give me I will send you anything that you signifie to me you have occation for, by a Letter firmly wrighte by yourselfe as sone as you can. Capt. Howell must be an evidence for you, as also of your sivell Gentle behavior, I trust God in his mersey will dispose you to have an Ey to his service and not to think It labour lost, for it is the Interest of Every Private Parson to make a search Into ye Nature and Quallity of the Relligion by which aloane he can hoape to be Etternally happy. Present my humble service to Capt. Howell and Give him this Incloased Paper, my service to your unckle Joseph and all my friends, wright upon Mr. John Topping and present my service to him and Pray his Excuse for not wrighting att this time, I shall sudenly God willing Doe him the trouble of a Letter, I am your very Affectionate

Loveing ffather

JOHN SCOTT.

Such is the story of the life of this extraordinary character during those years when he played an active part in the affairs of this world for good or ill. It may be there was something good in it; but, if so, it is not easy to discover; for though he lived long and touched many sides of life it seemed always to be the wrong side. Yet to it, as to so many other tales, there is an epilogue. From the days when he first met the Gothersons and conceived the idea of linking his obscure and anonymous origin to that of a family of place and consequence in the world as he knew it, to his last endeavors at respectability, he never lost sight of this self-imposed gentility. He continually described himself as John Scott of Scot's Hall in Kent, in the face of all the facts, and of the bitter opposition of that family, which sought by every means to disavow the relationship. He invented a name for his imaginary English domains, Mornamont, and it was under the sarcastic title of the Mornamont Papers that Pepys bound up the collections he made of Scott's activities when he was defending himself against Scott's charges. In accordance with his favorite technique, which makes his touch unmistakable wherever we find him, he took the trouble to have a new and garbled page inserted into a history of Kent to bolster up his claim. But it was never allowed — until it was too late. Among the little ironies of his ironical history it is worthy of note that when Scott was at last pardoned by the government of William III at the solicitation of those who had used him for their purposes, he finally achieved his ambition. For that paper describes him as "John Scott, Esquire, late of Scot's Hall in the county of Kent, *Gentleman*." Of all his pretensions, this alone was left to him. Almost at once he died; and if he departed not wholly in the odor of sanctity, he bore with him at least a distinct aroma of gentility to comfort him in his last moments.

X

Nor is this all, or even the most entertaining part of the epilogue. Much the most important chapter remains — the chapter which relates the adventures of his posthumous reputation. If, from whatever limbo he entered on his departure from this world, he could have beheld the fortunes of his memory, he would have been filled with exceedingly mixed emotions. For two hundred years his name occurs nowhere without some reference to his dubious character and his undoubted rascalities in America, in the West Indies, and in those European countries which witnessed or suffered from his activities. As late as

1882 a certain G. D. Scull issued an account of what he calls "the troubled life" of Dorothea Gotherson, for circulation among her descendants in America, and this in the following year was expanded into a volume which included her writings. That volume contains a full if not very accurate account of John Scott and his practices toward the Gothersons. So long does the smart of a land-swindle endure. Some fifteen years later Scott was included in the *Dictionary of National Biography*, purely, it would seem from reading its brief and somewhat inaccurate narrative of his life, on account of his various villanies, and perhaps as a horrible example. So far he had fared as badly at the hands of the historical muse as he had at the hands of his outraged contemporaries. But his revenge was ultimate and complete. For, as he finally made good his claims to the recognition of his gentility by his government, so he seems finally to have vindicated his veracity before the bar of history in a manner so surprising and unexpected as to deserve more than a passing mention.

It will be remembered that in the month of April, 1895, the Venezuelan authorities brought to a head the long-standing dispute over the boundary between British Guiana and Venezuela by the arrest of two members of the British Guiana police for trespassing upon Venezuelan territory. The men were released and made their report to their government; and Venezuela applied to the United States for aid in the controversy which they foresaw would ensue with the British authorities. Under these circumstances President Cleveland undertook to reopen a controversy of long standing over this matter. In December of that year he sent to Congress his famous message declaring that in case the commission which he asked permission from Congress to appoint to investigate the matter should find after careful enquiry that Great Britain was taking territory to which she had no right, the

United States would resist such appropriation by every means in its power. Congress supported the attitude of the President, and, in pursuance of the determination of both sides, a commission was promptly appointed by the United States to investigate the whole question. The commission engaged the assistance of expert historians, employing on that work the talents of Professor George L. Burr, of Cornell University, and Professor J. Franklin Jameson, then of Brown University, the editor of the *American Historical Review*, and more recently director of the historical division of the Carnegie Institution. The English goverment later appointed a similar body, under the direction of Sir Frederick Pollock and including Mr. Edmundson, and Mr., later Sir, C. A. Harris of the Colonial Office. The earliest settlements of the Dutch upon the Essequibo and the adjacent lands were investigated, the earliest maps collected and compared, and an amount of light shed upon the beginnings of European occupation in that quarter of the world which was of the utmost value and interest to historians.

And conspicuous among the witnesses thus summoned to the bar of history was Colonel John Scott! For it will be remembered that he not only wrote the beginnings of a projected *Discription of America*, but a *Relation* of his own valiant achievements and adventures in precisely that obscure corner of the world now suddenly made the test of good faith and friendship between the two great Anglo-Saxon nations which had earlier had the privilege of sharing the blessings of Scott's residence among them. That was printed in the British Bluebook, identified as Scott's work by Professor Jameson, and further investigated in manuscript by Professor Burr.

His testimony did not, indeed, finally determine the question at issue, though he was a material witness. But the result was curious in the extreme so far as Scott's fortunes were concerned. Each side found in his statements

some confirmation of its contention. The Americans who
discovered, or at least identified, the manuscript as Scott's
— and it may be noticed that he was not so favorable to
their views — were somewhat prone to rake up the old
colonial scores against him. The English were rather
more inclined to admit his testimony without troubling
much about searching the records for evidence of his character. Each side seems to have more or less tacitly assumed that whatever his deeds or misdeeds elsewhere, his
account of what he saw in the West Indies was, on the
whole, tolerably credible. And though the Dutch historian Netscher was inclined to doubt Scott's geography
as well as his history, and was confirmed in this by the
later researches of Mr. Oppenheim, his views did not
seriously influence Scott's evidence in the Venezuelan
case. In consequence, Scott cuts a better figure before
this court than before any of the numerous tribunals
which summoned him as defendant or witness during his
lifetime.

More was to follow. Some six years after the Venezuelan controversy, a relative of Sir Frederick Pollock's,
John Pollock, published the most elaborate account of the
Popish Plot which has yet appeared, a work marked, on
the whole, by admirable spirit, much knowledge, and
remarkable ingenuity. In that narrative Scott plays, if
not a leading, at least a conspicuous part in building up
the argument to which Mr. Pollock addresses himself.
The author does, not, indeed, commit himself irrevocably
to the contention that the Colonel was an unimpeachable
witness. But, as we have seen, he lays great stress on the
fact that Scott did have genuine knowledge of the Earl of
Berkshire's correspondence, that "the simplicity and
directness of his relation points to its substantial truth";
and that the moderation of his narrative is a further proof
of its genuineness. He goes farther still. No one looking
for the rewards of a professional informer, he says, would

have acted as did Colonel Scott; no scoundrel following
on the track of Oates and Bedloe would ever have concocted such a story; and, in brief, "His information may
be accepted as genuine." Here, then, we have a clean bill
of health.

Nor is this all the tale of his long-belated vindication.
Some years after the Venezuelan controversy was determined, an English historical scholar, the Rev. George
Edmundson, contributed an article to the *English Historical Review* entitled "The Dutch in Western Guiana." In
the forefront of his contribution he sets out that the American scholars who gathered the evidence in the Venezuelan case had endeavored, not without a considerable
measure of success, to throw discredit on Scott's testimony
in its bearing upon the history of Dutch colonization in
western Guiana. He continues: "A careful examination
of all available evidence has led me to form an entirely
different opinion upon the trustworthiness of Scott." For,
he declares, "The credibility of a writer relating otherwise unknown historical facts depends upon (1) his near-
ness to the events narrated, (2) his personal access to sure
sources of information, (3) his motives in writing, (4) his
proved accuracy in cases where his statements can be verified." All these tests, he concludes, are "absolutely satis-
factory in the instance of Major Scott." He was in fact the
commander of the English expedition of 1665–1666; and,
as Mr. Edmundson says, "he tells us in his preface that he
had always been a great lover of geography and history,
and that from an early age he had purposed to write a
large description of all America, also that he had personally been upon no less than one hundred and twenty-six
[*sic*] islands in the Atlantic Ocean, and had travelled over
(among other places) a great part of Guiana." Whereupon Mr. Edmundson quotes Scott's description of his
Herodotean method of research and concludes: "It is
clear then in the narrative given by Scott of the early his-

tory of the Dutch colonies in Western Guiana that we are dealing with the narrative of a contemporary, familiar with the localities about which he was writing, conversant with all the literature upon the subject, including documents and journals in manuscript, and having exceptional opportunities for personal commune with men intimately acquainted for a long period with the country and its history. It is further important to note that the work, which was never published, and of which only a fragment was committed to paper, was a long-cherished design, the preparation for which was scientifically thorough, and carried on for years; and that it is impossible to attribute to the writer any motives of political partisanship, or any other aim than that put forth by himself 'of giving new accounts from observations of my owne.' More than this, his claim is fully borne out by the accuracy which is shown by him in those parts of the narrative which can be historically verified."

Some years later, again, Sir C. A. Harris, chief clerk of the Colonial Office, and Mr. J. A. J. Villiers of the British Museum, in their edition of the despatches of one Storm van's Gravesende, sometime Governor of British Guiana, took a hand in the matter. Backed by the authority of an "acute critic," Sir J. A. Swettenham, they opposed the opinion of General Netscher, endorsing wholly the "clever and convincing argument of Mr. Edmundson."

Finally, since this essay first appeared, Mr. J. A. Williamson, in 1923, published a volume on "English Colonies in Guiana and on the Amazon," in which he expresses his indebtedness to this "shrewd seventeenth century historian," "usually well informed on Guiana history." "Scott's character and the incidents of his career," he admits, "have been shown to be entirely discreditable. Nevertheless," he declares, "this condemnation must not lightly be extended to cover his work as a historian. His circumstantial narratives allow of two interpretations; either he possessed a critical mind and an extraordinary memory, exercising these faculties in the cause of historical truth; or he had a fertile imagination and the wide reading of a Defoe, and deliberately used them to concoct false history. . . . For a highly detailed narrative it possesses a self-consistency which is hardly compatible with romancing, and especially notable when contrasted with the looseness of the English style. . . . The just conclusion would seem to be that his writings are a real authority on the events they describe, and fill a gap in the record caused by the disappearance of the original documents with which he was familiar, and the absence of the written memoirs of pioneers from whom he received oral narratives." For Scott, as Mr. Williamson observes, "had also a talent for extracting sound information from the talk of veterans with whom he came in contact in the course of his wandering career."

Moreover, he adds, "Dr. G. Edmundson . . . vindicates Scott's accuracy concerning the Dutch colonies in western Guiana." He is rather inclined to accept Scott's version of his military exploits, from his own account, "corroborated by Byam's Journal," observes that "there are reasons for thinking that the evidence [of the report of the court-martial] is not so conclusive as it appears on the surface, and some circumstances telling in Scott's favour need a good deal of explaining away."

Here, then, is the last word in our hero's behalf. And it is the more generous since so many instances which Mr. Williamson adduces — despite his declaration that documents obviously unknown to Scott confirm some of his statements — show the Colonel unreliable as to the events, especially in Surinam, which he should have known best, on the basis of Mr. Williamson's own researches as recorded in his footnotes.

What, then, is the explanation? Surely, if one considers

the long career of Scott, at least one answer suggests itself. Laying aside the possible revelation of his character as appears in the incident of his arrest by Nathaniel Seeley, and the not dissimilar report of the court-martial as to his behavior under fire, let us turn to the root of the matter — his *History*, which has provided him with such whole-hearted English championship. Is there not another possible solution besides the inconclusive dilemma which his latest advocate propounds, which is contained in his own pages? For there he notes that Scott's *History* was "compiled from contemporary authorities still available to us, and also from a quantity of maps, charts and journals purchased by him from Mathias Matteson, a Fleming, who had been long in the Portuguese service on the Amazon and other rivers."

The explanation seems obvious — perhaps it is too obvious. Yet as one reflects upon his literary and cartographical career, on the *Helps to the Indians*, on the *Perfect Direction to Travell all England by Post*, and on other similar episodes of his life, what conclusion can he come to about the *History*? That Scott used "contemporary authorities still known to us," he admits. That he had a "looseness" of English style, we know from many examples. But where did he get the "highly detailed" narrative possessing such "self-consistency"? Was it his at all in any greater sense than that it is in his handwriting and adorned with his own touches? For, with all due deference to the undoubted ability, industry, and honesty of his advocates, their defense seems, in the light of Scott's methods, to lack something of conviction. Is it too much to ask where Scott got his *History and Discription*? What became of the Matteson papers; where are those "sev'll curious manuscripts" that came to his hand? In brief, apart from his own literary touches, who wrote the book which has given him such high position among posterity? For upon that depends, in the last resort, his historical reputation; and to that problem the attention of scholars might well be directed.

Thus history, like time, whose chronicler it is, brings its revenges. At the hands of these learned gentlemen, Scott has finally come into his own, even though it has taken more than two centuries for him to find anyone to believe him so whole-heartedly. Perhaps Edmundson is right; perhaps Scott did tell the truth — however and from whatever source he obtained it. "Some truth but not all gospel" is what Willoughby wrote of him, and that judgment may possibly still hold after two centuries. It is impossible not to feel a certain regret that such talents as he unquestionably possessed should not have somehow worked to better ends. Had he only succeeded some-where, had he secured the grant of Long Island, had he been able to retain his post of geographer-royal — but the conjectures are futile. He broke on the rock of the Gotherson affair, and that not only deprived him of the sympathy of his own generation and of its successors, it revealed qualities which would at almost any time have made his permanent success impossible.

None the less he is worth knowing — now that he is dead. That he should have done so much to determine the fate of Long Island and New York, that he should have contributed to the settlement of the boundary be-tween New York and New Jersey while he was alive is re-markable enough. But that two centuries after his death he should take such an active part in the adjustment of the boundary between Venezuela and British Guiana and cut such a respectable figure in the history of the two nations with which his life was so intimately and so scan-dalously bound up, passes the limits of what we usually regard as probability. What his tongue but partially accomplished for him while he was alive, his pen did for him among posterity. If he failed in all else it ensured for him a safe corner in a great controversy, from whose records he may henceforth look out with some of his old confidence upon a world which, with all his wit, he was unable to quite deceive while he was still a part of it. Viewing all this, it again becomes apparent why so many men appeal from the harsh judgments of their contemporaries to the serene tribunal of history.

INDEX

INDEX

Quakers, 110, 113, 262, 276, 289, 296
Quashawam, Sunk squa, 292
Quripi dialect, 269

Raleigh, Sir Walter, 68, 88, 92
Randolph, John, 186
Ranke, Leopold von, 176
Rapin de Thoyras, 12, 167
Raritan River and region, 284
Rawlinson, 9
Raynor, Deborah (wife of Col. John Scott), 268
Raynor, Thurston, 268
Redwald, King of East Anglia, 235, 238
Reform Bill of 1832, 41
Reform Bill of 1867, 41, 43, 49
Regalia, Royal, 131 ff.
Republicans, 113, 156, 163, 167, 172, 178
Reresby, Sir John, 157
Restoration, The, 12, 29, 135, 272–273, 313
Revere, Paul, 211, 213
Revolution, American, 169. Cf. also essay on John Wentworth, passim
Revolution, French, 168–169
Revolution of 1688, 7, 78, 343
Revolution of 1848, 49
Rhode Island, 207, 211, 265, 269, 271, 273, 278–279
Richardson, Dr., 312
Richbell, John, 299
Richelieu, 34
Rindge, Daniel, 189, 204
Rindge, Jotham, 204
Rindge family, N. H., 188
Robespierre, 169
Robinson, Sir John, 133, 135
Robinson Crusoe, 11
Rochester, Henry Wilmot, 1st Earl of, 75; John Wilmot, 2d Earl of, 17, 143
Rockingham, Marquis of, 185, 206, 216
Rolle, Sir Francis, 334

Roman Catholic Church, 223–256, passim
Romans in Britain, 232 ff.
Romford, Surrey, 129
Roncevaux, 88
Rosebery, Earl of, 17, 178
Roumelia, Eastern, 63
Royal Society, 4
Royalists, 157, 163, 175, 178–179, 272
Rupert, Prince, 24, 106, 137
Russell, Lord, 47
Russell, Lord John, 173
Russia, 46, 62
Ruyter, de, Admiral, 119, 121, 122

Sacheverell, William, 334
St. Alban, 233
Saint Just, 169
St. Kitts (St. Christopher's), W. I., 301
St. Lawrence River and region, 271
St. Michel, Bartholomew, 337
St. Valentine, The, 71
Salem, Massachusetts, 110
Salisbury, Lord, 45
Sanford, 174
Saracens, 224
Sarney, Ireland, 105
Savile, Henry, 337
Savoy Conference, 111
Saxons, 233; East, 233; South, 247; West, 247
Saybrook, Conn., 265
Scarborough, The, 215
Scots, 233
Scot's (Scott's) Hall, Kent, 262, 275, 345
Scott, Jeckomiah, 344
Scott, Colonel John, ESSAY, 259–355
Scott, John, the Younger, 344–345
Scott, Hon. John, 263
Scott, Mrs. (Deborah Raynor, wife of Col. John Scott), 268, 290, 299, 344
Scott, Mrs. (Col. John Scott's mother), 263, 266